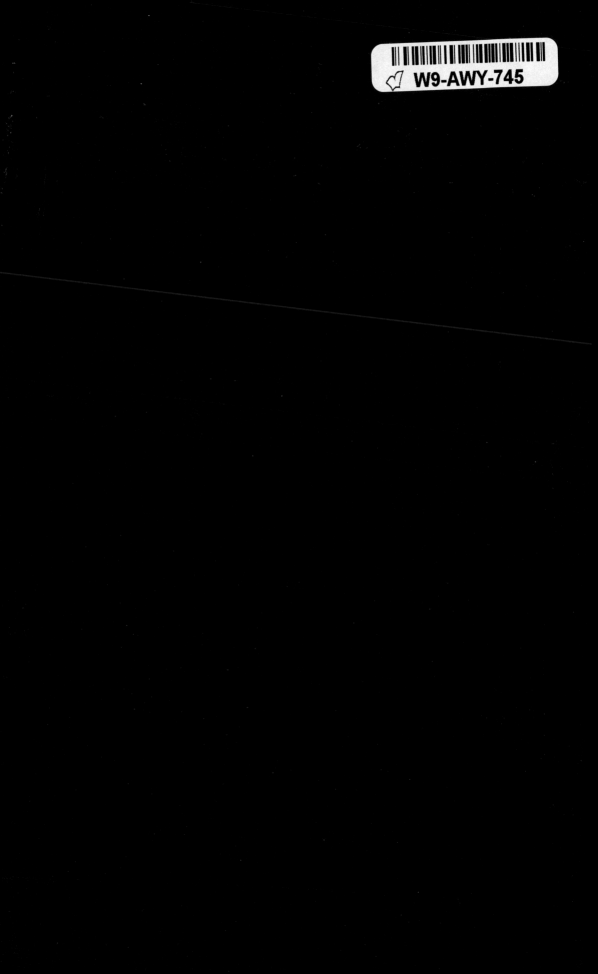

W9-AWY-745

2: THE SECRET ORIGIN OF TONY STARK BOOK 1. Contains material originally published in magazine form as IRON MAN #6-11. First printing 2013. ISBN# 978-0-7851-6834-
ARVEL WORLDWIDE, INC., a subsidiary of MARVEL ENTERTAINMENT, LLC. OFFICE OF PUBLICATION: 135 West 50th Street, New York, NY 10020. Copyright © 2013 Marvel Characters,
ved. All characters featured in this issue and the distinctive names and likenesses thereof, and all related indicia are trademarks of Marvel Characters, Inc. No similarity between any
acters, persons, and/or institutions in this magazine with those of any living or dead person or institution is intended, and any such similarity which may exist is purely coincidental.
, ALAN FINE, EVP - Office of the President, Marvel Worldwide, Inc. and EVP & CMO Marvel Characters B.V.; DAN BUCKLEY, Publisher & President - Print, Animation & Digital Divisions;
Creative Officer; TOM BREVOORT, SVP of Publishing; DAVID BOGART, SVP of Operations & Procurement, Publishing; C.B. CEBULSKI, SVP of Creator & Content Development; DAVID
t & Digital Publishing Sales; JIM O'KEEFE, VP of Operations & Logistics; DAN CARR, Executive Director of Publishing Technology; SUSAN CRESPI, Editorial Operations Manager;
ishing Operations Manager; STAN LEE, Chairman Emeritus. For information regarding advertising in Marvel Comics or on Marvel.com, please contact Niza Disla, Director of Marvel
@marvel.com. For Marvel subscription inquiries, please call 800-217-9158. **Manufactured between 6/7/2013 and 7/22/2013 by R.R. DONNELLEY, INC., SALEM, VA, USA.**

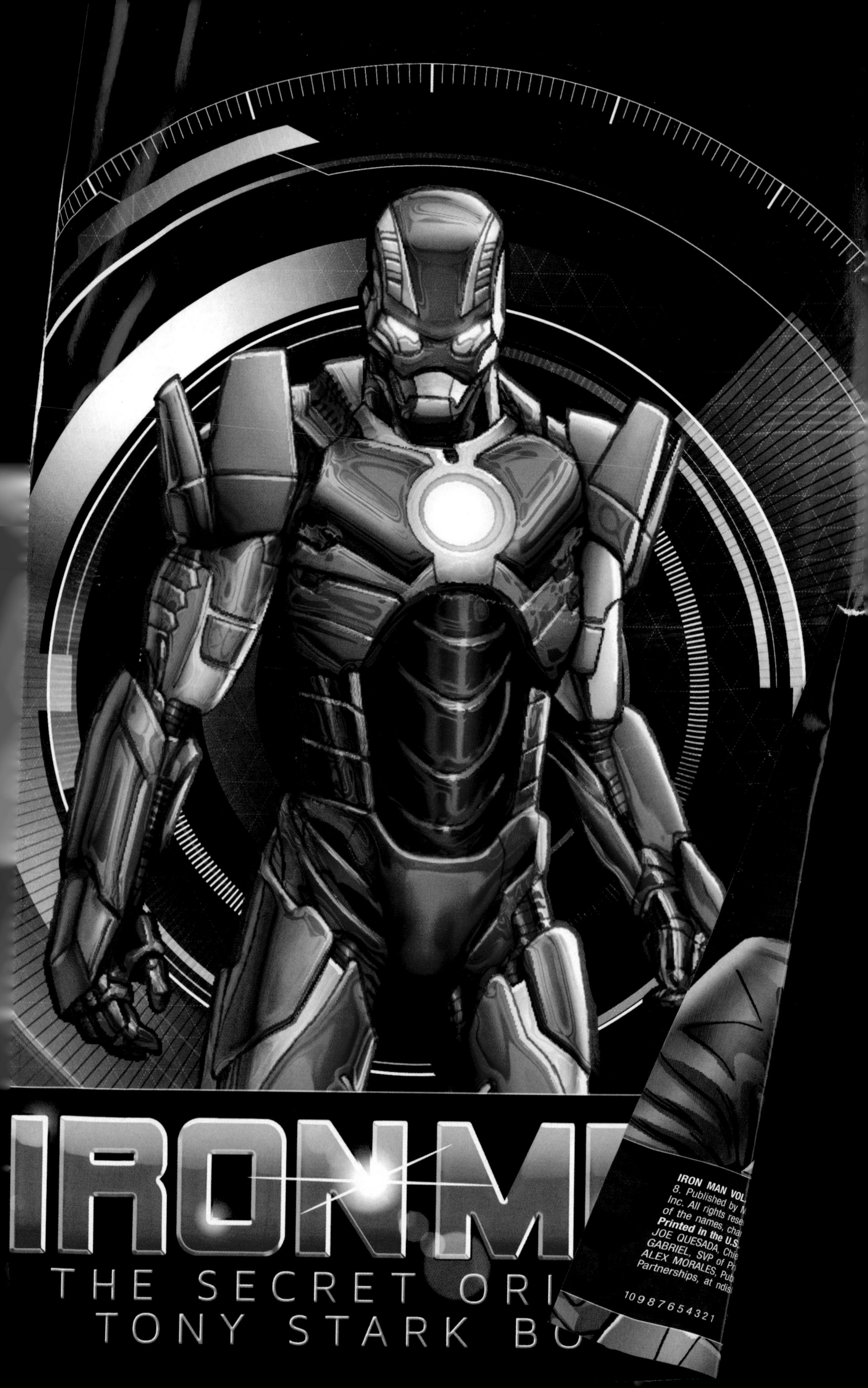
IRON M
THE SECRET ORI
TONY STARK BO
IRON MAN VOL.
8. Published by M
Inc. All rights rese
of the names, char
Printed in the U.S.
JOE QUESADA, Chie
GABRIEL, SVP of Pr
ALEX MORALES, Pub
Partnerships, at ndis
10 9 8 7 6 5 4 3 2 1

To meet the threats of an ever-changing world, Tony Stark (A.K.A. Iron Man) developed a new modular suit of armor that can be modified on demand. With it he was able to defeat four different deadly threats caused by the DNA-modifying techno-virus known as Extremis. Each conflict exposed him to the bold and limitless potential that mankind can hold, challenging his sense of accomplishment. Something had to change.

With an even newer suit of armor, a new AI and a desire to expand his horizons, Tony has ventured into deep space on a hero's journey throughout the stars. But is Iron Man truly ready for the Final Frontier?

IRON MAN

KIERON GILLEN
WRITER

GREG LAND
PENCILER, #6-8

DALE EAGLESHAM
ARTIST, #9-11
WITH GREG LAND (#11, P. 12-13)

JAY LEISTEN
INKER, #6-8

GURU-eFX
COLORIST

VC'S JOE CARAMAGNA
LETTERER

GREG LAND & **GURU-eFX**
COVER ART

JON MOISAN
ASSISTANT EDITOR

MARK PANICCIA
EDITOR

COLLECTION EDITOR: **JENNIFER GRÜNWALD**
ASSISTANT EDITORS: **ALEX STARBUCK** & **NELSON RIBEIRO**
EDITOR, SPECIAL PROJECTS: **MARK D. BEAZLEY**
SENIOR EDITOR, SPECIAL PROJECTS: **JEFF YOUNGQUIST**
SVP OF PRINT & DIGITAL PUBLISHING SALES: **DAVID GABRIEL**
BOOK DESIGNER: **RODOLFO MURAGUCHI**

EDITOR IN CHIEF: **AXEL ALONSO**
CHIEF CREATIVE OFFICER: **JOE QUESADA**
PUBLISHER: **DAN BUCKLEY**
EXECUTIVE PRODUCER: **ALAN FINE**

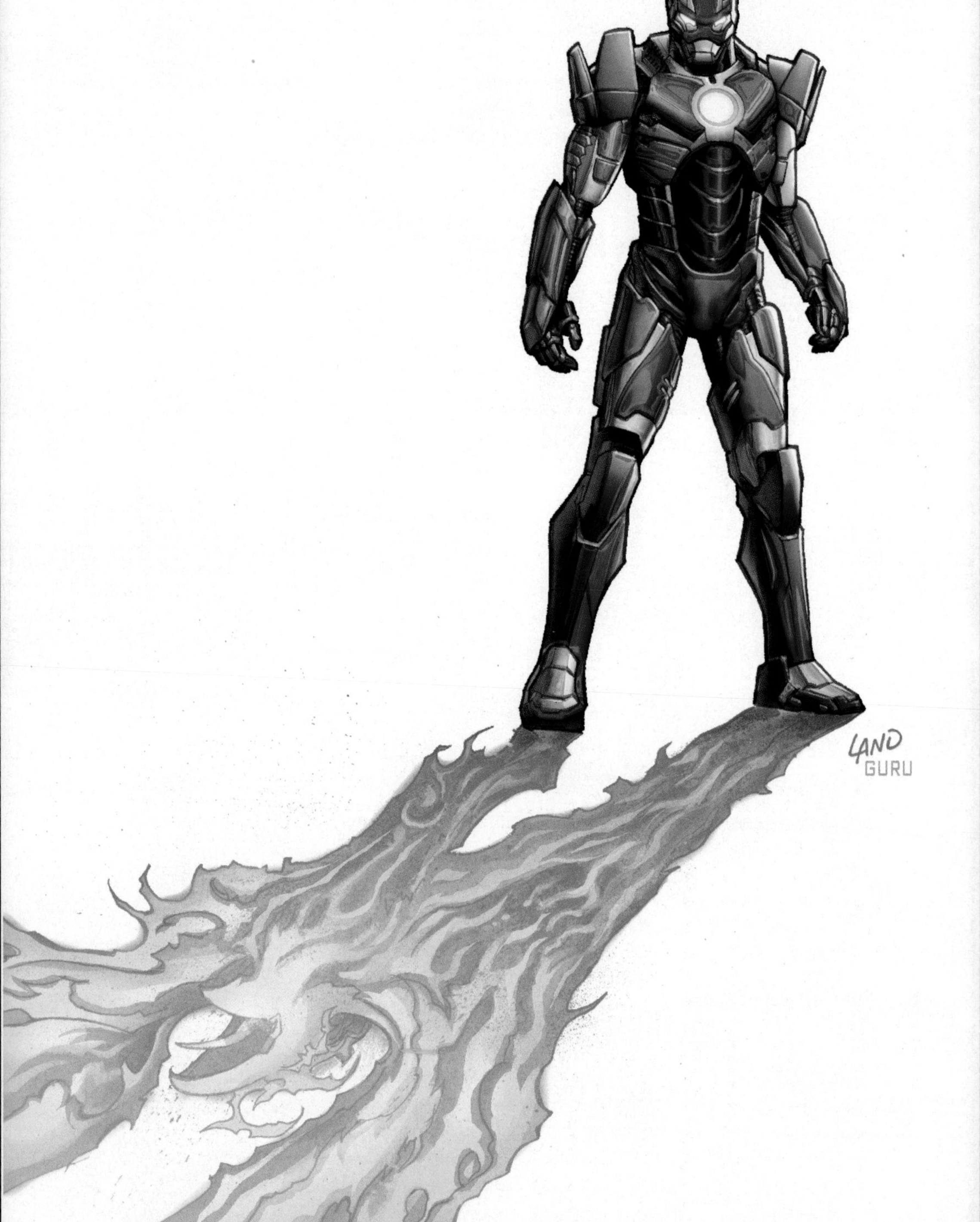
LAND
GURU

06 THE GODKILLER PART 1

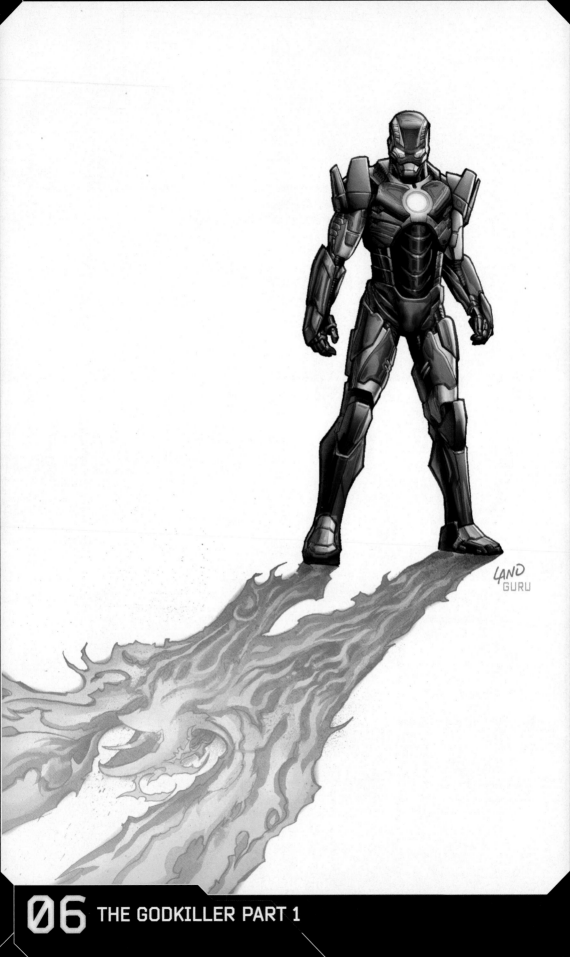

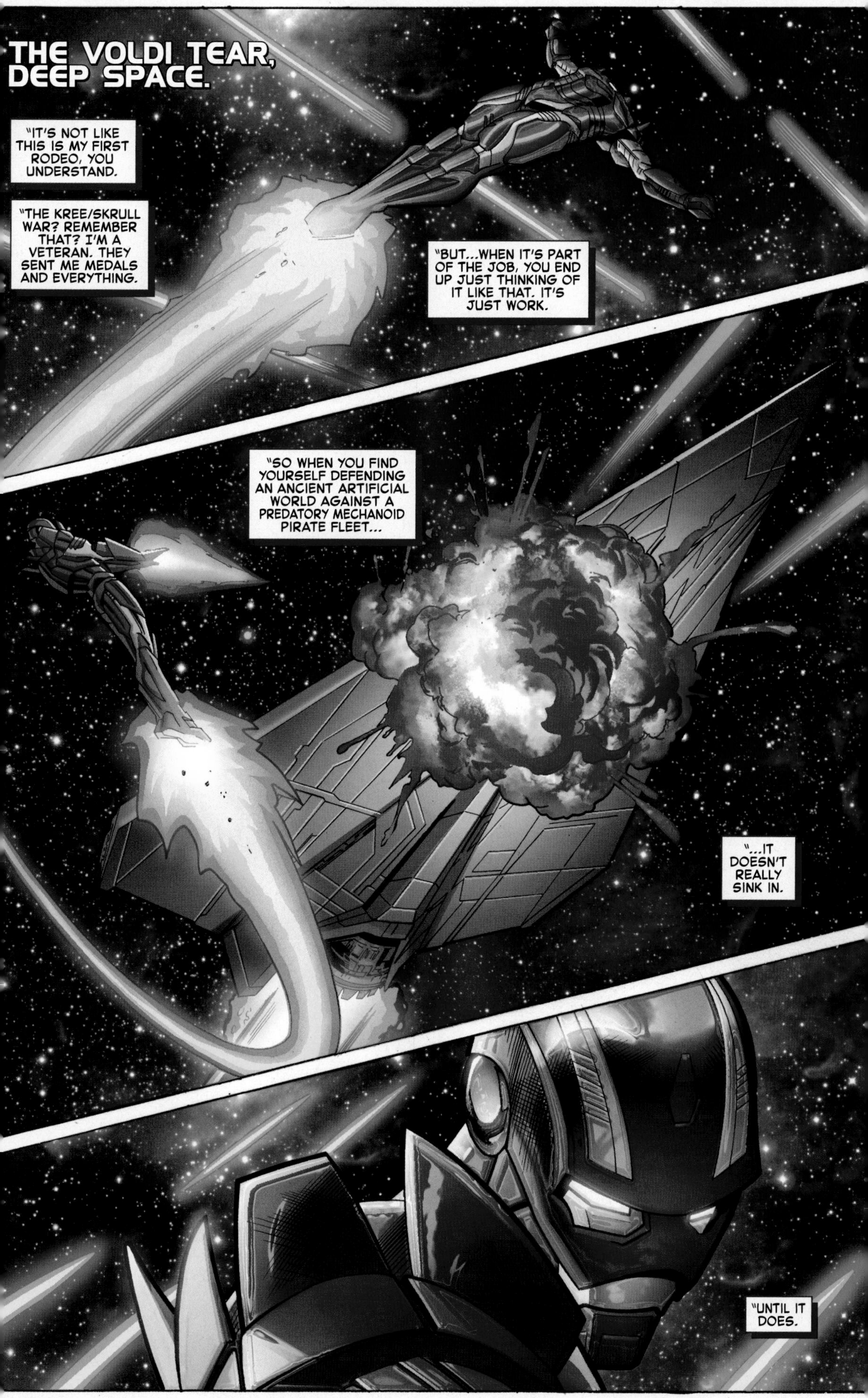
THE VOLDI TEAR, DEEP SPACE.
"IT'S NOT LIKE THIS IS MY FIRST RODEO, YOU UNDERSTAND.
"THE KREE/SKRULL WAR? REMEMBER THAT? I'M A VETERAN. THEY SENT ME MEDALS AND EVERYTHING.
"BUT...WHEN IT'S PART OF THE JOB, YOU END UP JUST THINKING OF IT LIKE THAT. IT'S JUST WORK.
"SO WHEN YOU FIND YOURSELF DEFENDING AN ANCIENT ARTIFICIAL WORLD AGAINST A PREDATORY MECHANOID PIRATE FLEET...
"...IT DOESN'T REALLY SINK IN.
"UNTIL IT DOES.

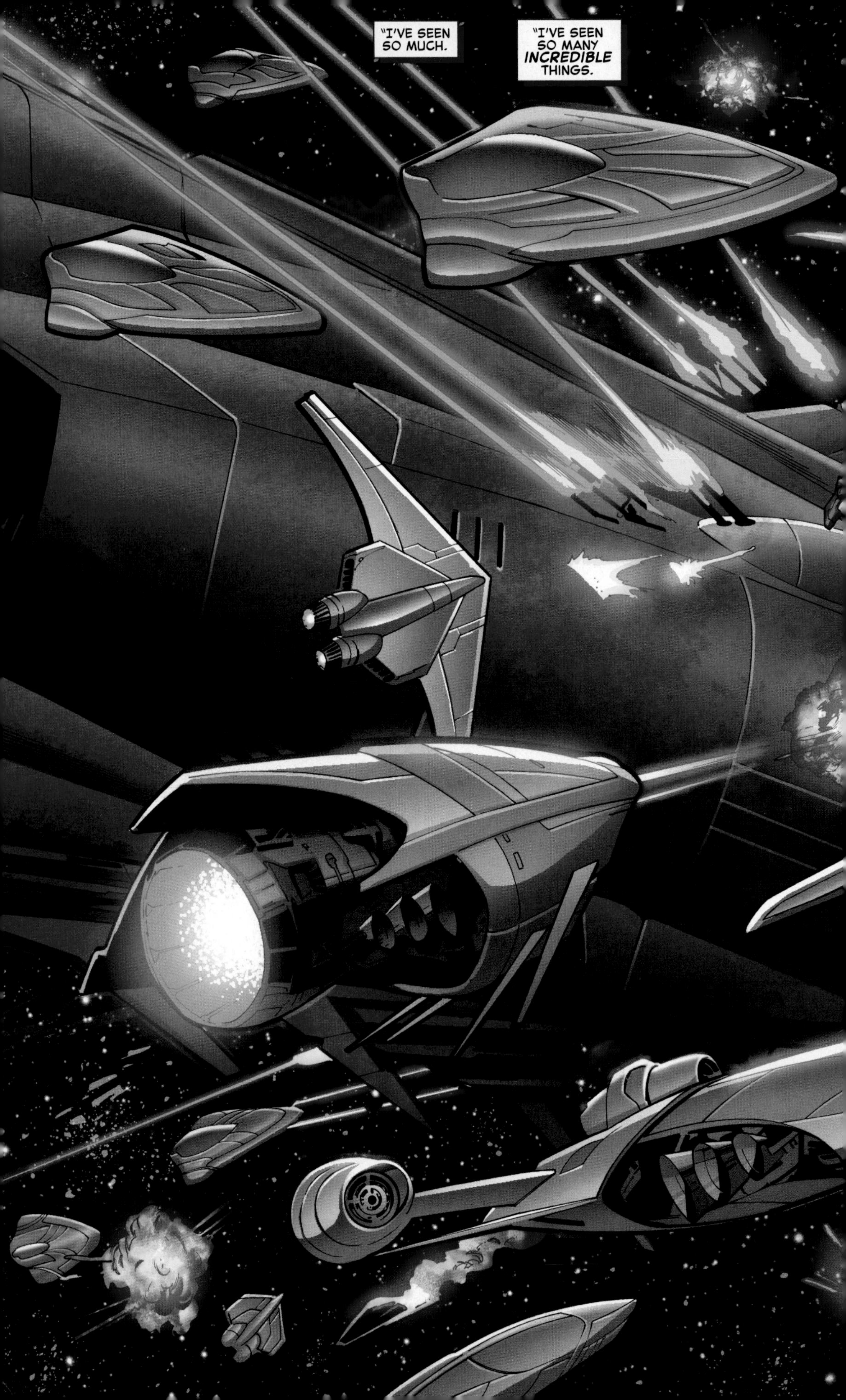
"I'VE SEEN SO MUCH.
"I'VE SEEN SO MANY *INCREDIBLE* THINGS.

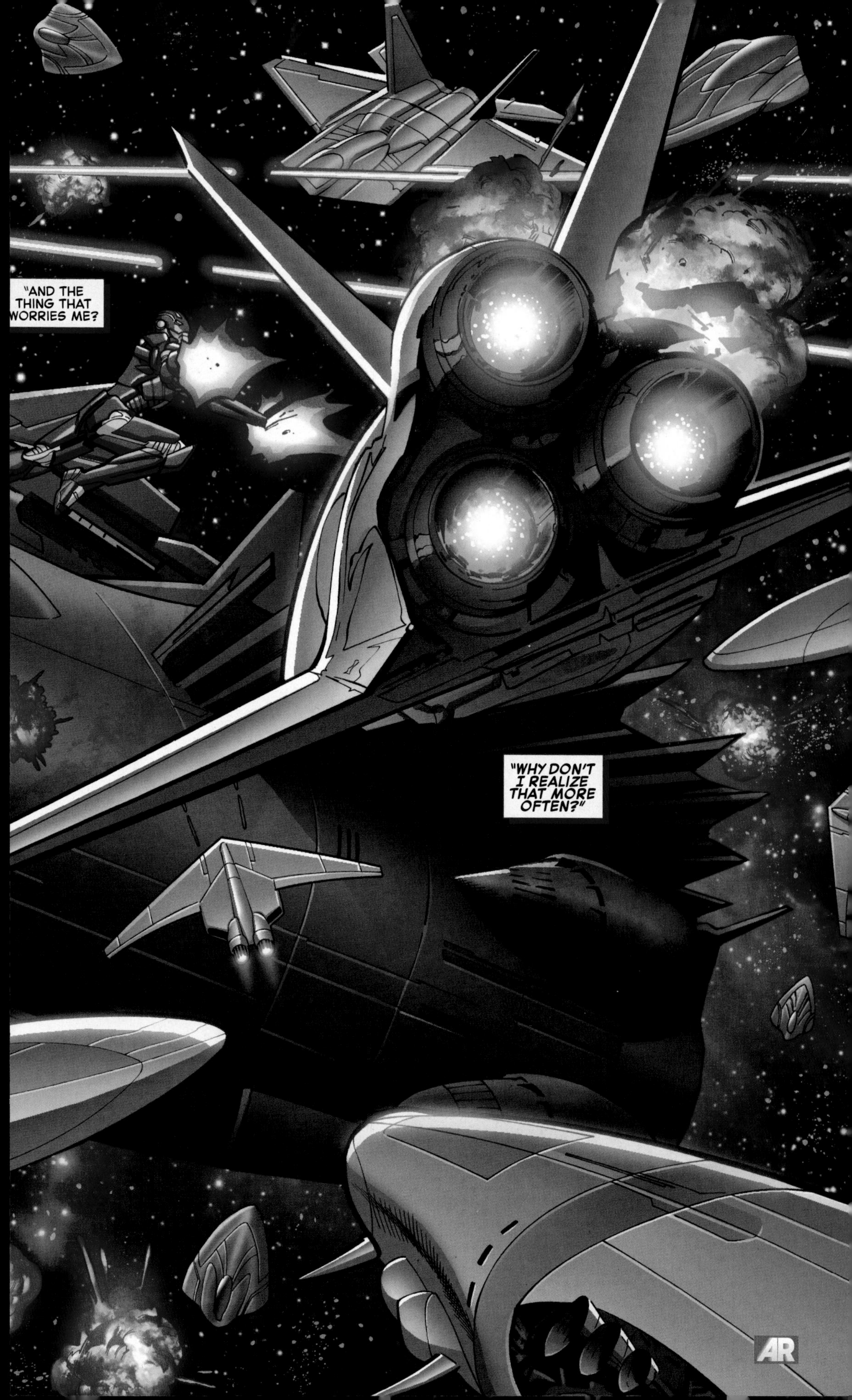
"AND THE THING THAT WORRIES ME?
"WHY DON'T I REALIZE THAT MORE OFTEN?"

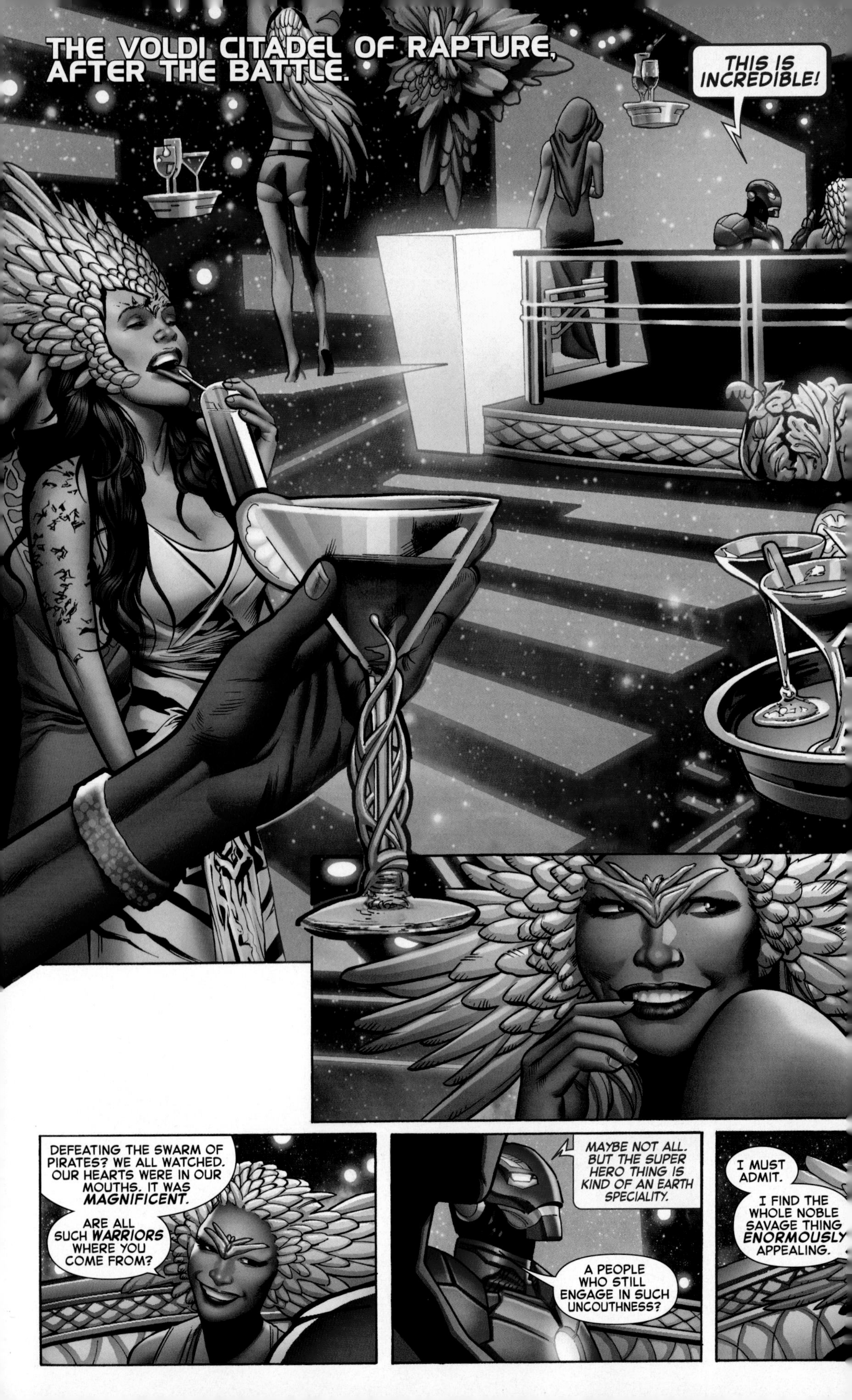
THE VOLDI CITADEL OF RAPTURE, AFTER THE BATTLE.
THIS IS INCREDIBLE!
DEFEATING THE SWARM OF PIRATES? WE ALL WATCHED. OUR HEARTS WERE IN OUR MOUTHS. IT WAS MAGNIFICENT.
ARE ALL SUCH WARRIORS WHERE YOU COME FROM?
MAYBE NOT ALL. BUT THE SUPER HERO THING IS KIND OF AN EARTH SPECIALITY.
A PEOPLE WHO STILL ENGAGE IN SUCH UNCOUTHNESS?
I MUST ADMIT.
I FIND THE WHOLE NOBLE SAVAGE THING ENORMOUSLY APPEALING.

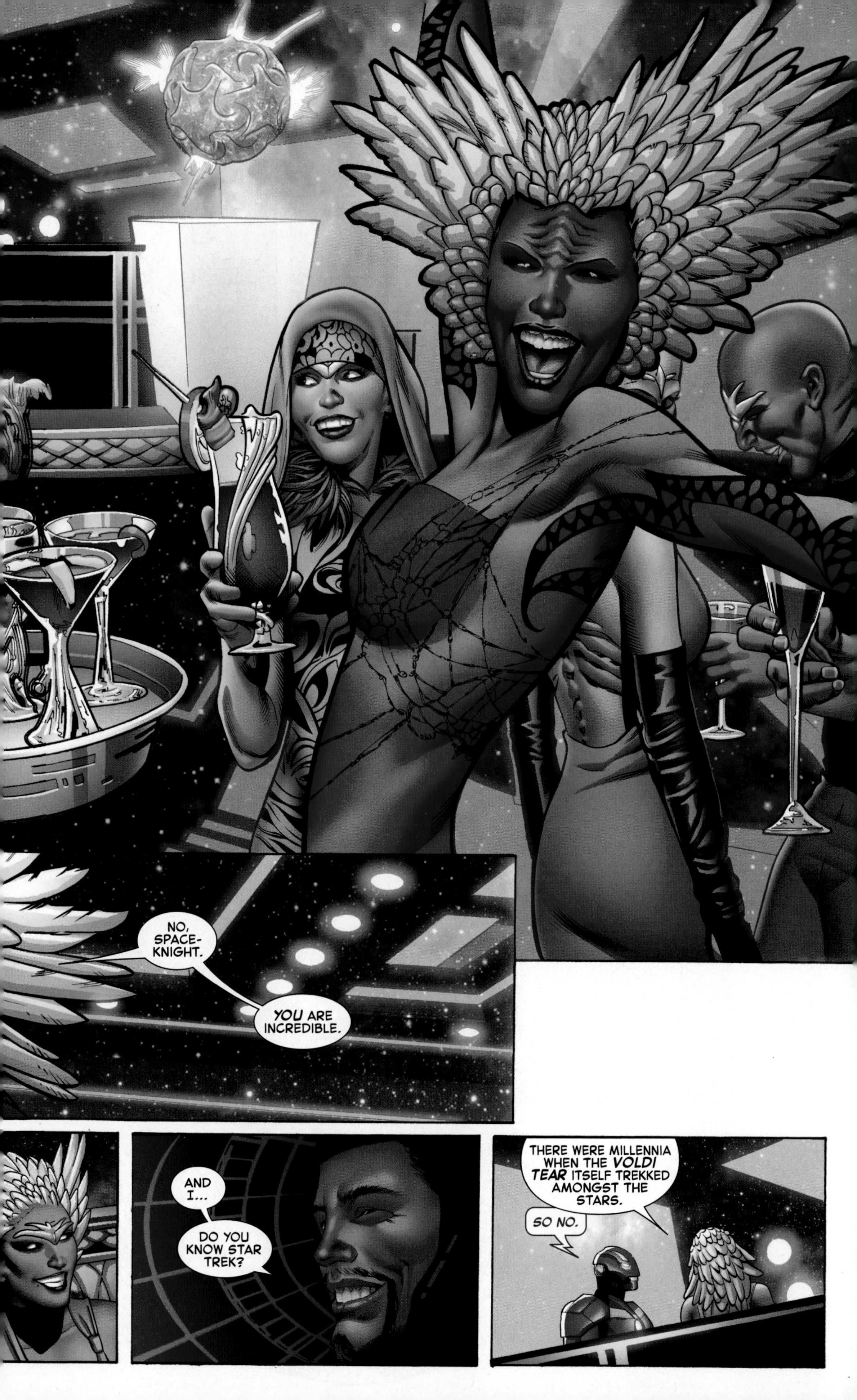
NO, SPACE-KNIGHT.
YOU ARE INCREDIBLE.
AND I...
DO YOU KNOW STAR TREK?
THERE WERE MILLENNIA WHEN THE VOLDI TEAR ITSELF TREKKED AMONGST THE STARS.
SO NO.

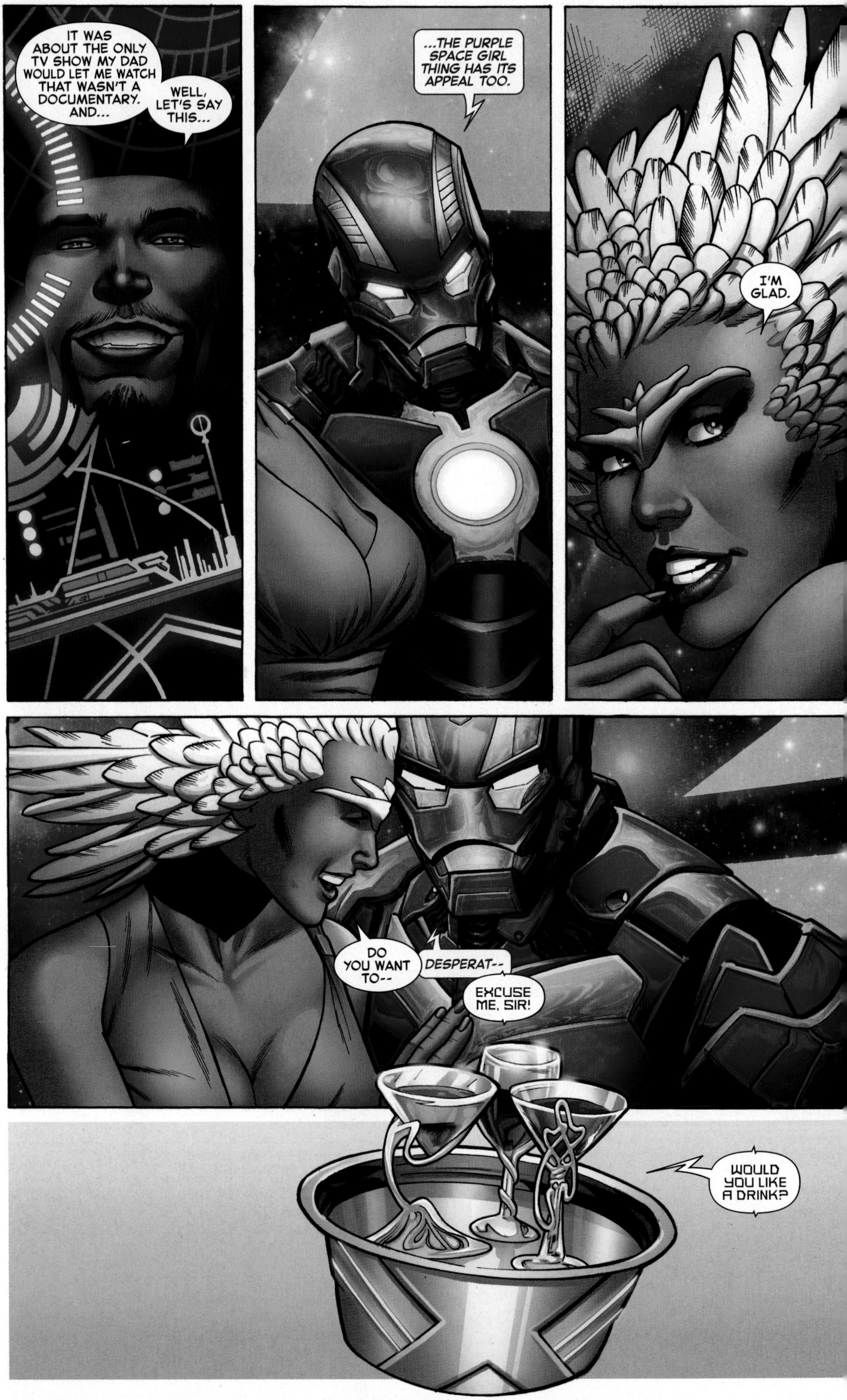
IT WAS ABOUT THE ONLY TV SHOW MY DAD WOULD LET ME WATCH THAT WASN'T A DOCUMENTARY. AND...
WELL, LET'S SAY THIS...
...THE PURPLE SPACE GIRL THING HAS ITS APPEAL TOO.
I'M GLAD.
DO YOU WANT TO--
DESPERAT--
EXCUSE ME, SIR!
WOULD YOU LIKE A DRINK?

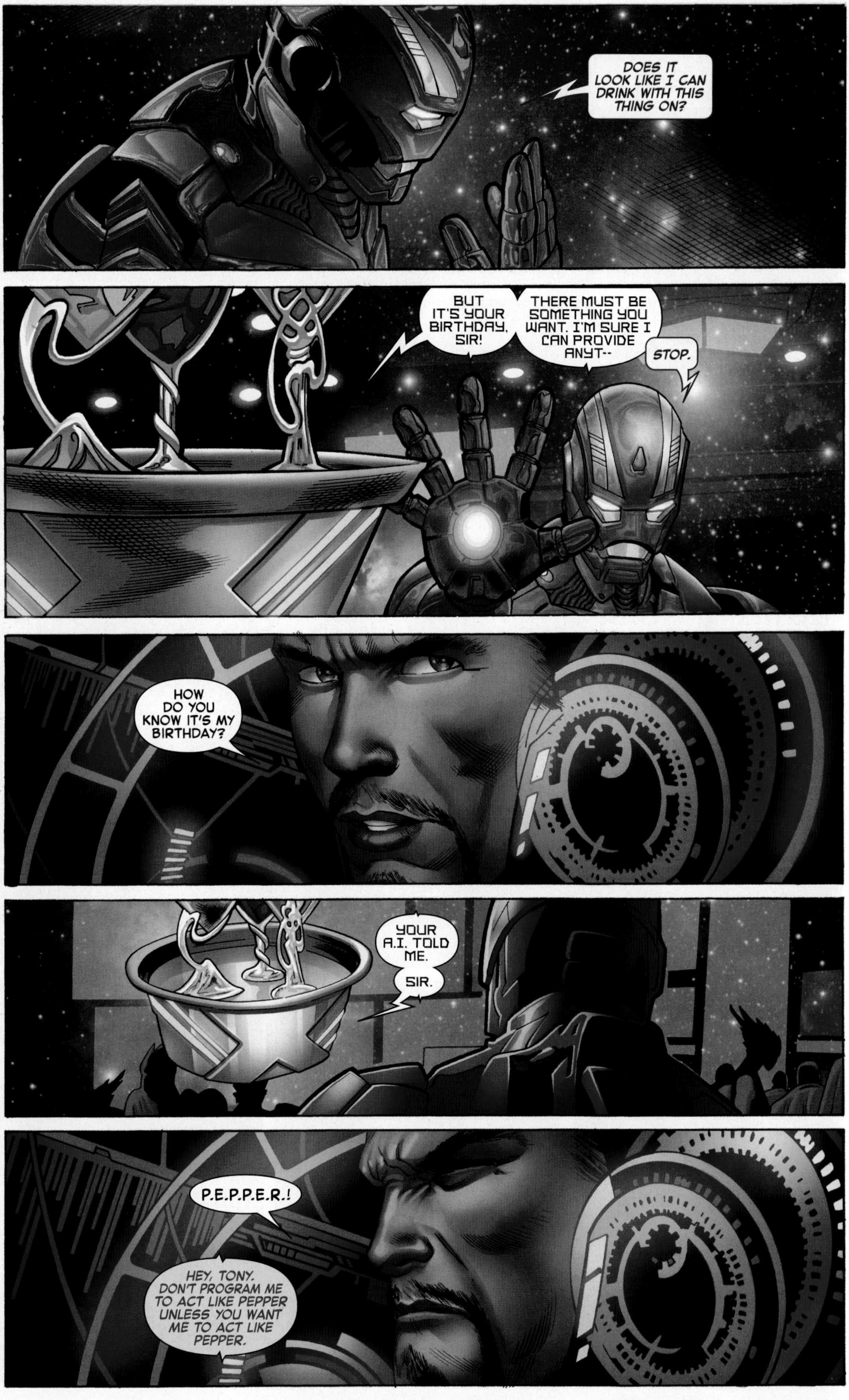
DOES IT LOOK LIKE I CAN DRINK WITH THIS THING ON?
BUT IT'S YOUR BIRTHDAY, SIR!
THERE MUST BE SOMETHING YOU WANT. I'M SURE I CAN PROVIDE ANYT--
STOP.
HOW DO YOU KNOW IT'S MY BIRTHDAY?
YOUR A.I. TOLD ME.
SIR.
P.E.P.P.E.R.!
HEY, TONY. DON'T PROGRAM ME TO ACT LIKE PEPPER UNLESS YOU WANT ME TO ACT LIKE PEPPER.

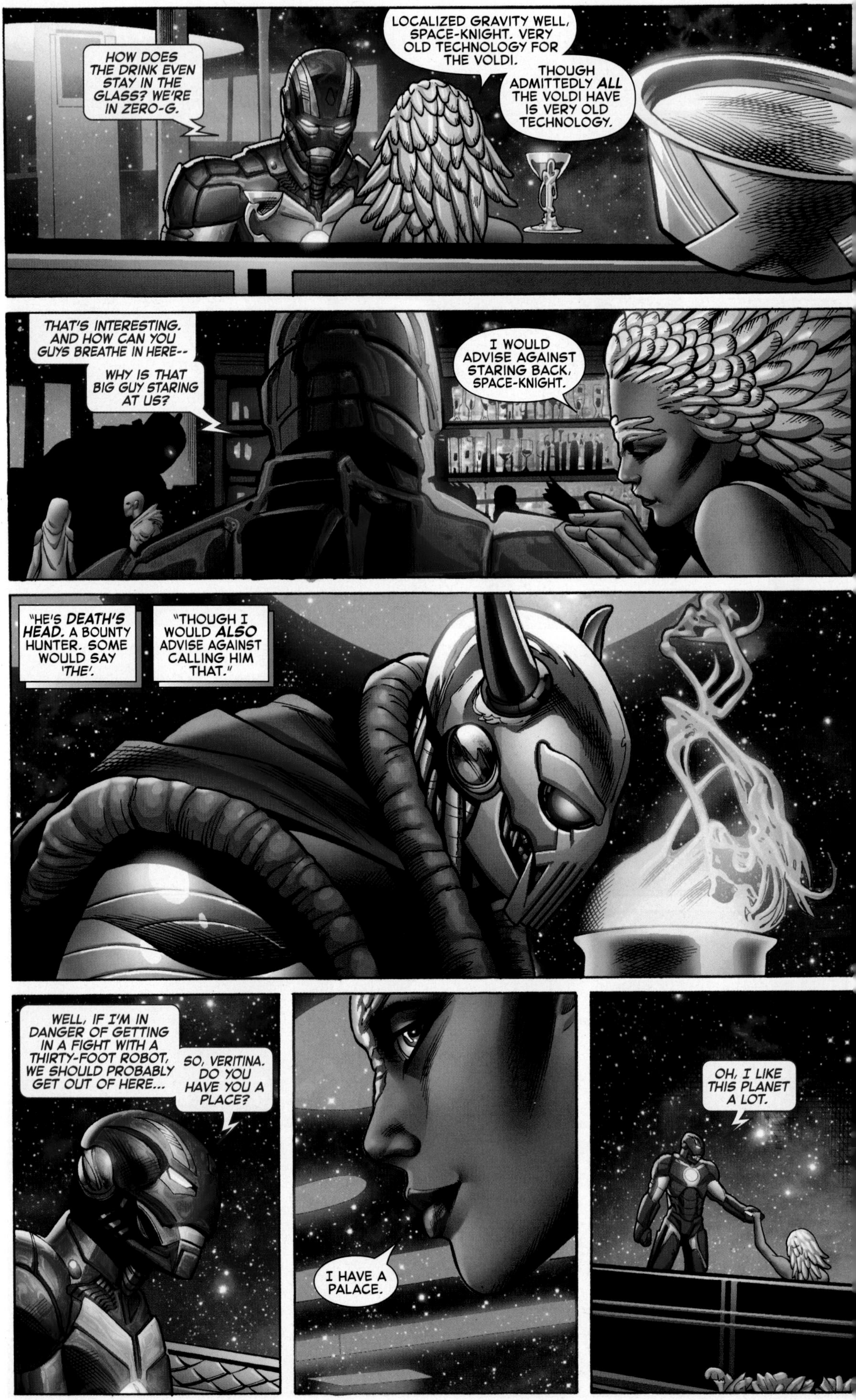
HOW DOES THE DRINK EVEN STAY IN THE GLASS? WE'RE IN ZERO-G.
LOCALIZED GRAVITY WELL, SPACE-KNIGHT. VERY OLD TECHNOLOGY FOR THE VOLDI.
THOUGH ADMITTEDLY ALL THE VOLDI HAVE IS VERY OLD TECHNOLOGY.
THAT'S INTERESTING. AND HOW CAN YOU GUYS BREATHE IN HERE--
WHY IS THAT BIG GUY STARING AT US?
I WOULD ADVISE AGAINST STARING BACK, SPACE-KNIGHT.
"HE'S DEATH'S HEAD. A BOUNTY HUNTER. SOME WOULD SAY 'THE'.
"THOUGH I WOULD ALSO ADVISE AGAINST CALLING HIM THAT."
WELL, IF I'M IN DANGER OF GETTING IN A FIGHT WITH A THIRTY-FOOT ROBOT, WE SHOULD PROBABLY GET OUT OF HERE...
SO, VERITINA. DO YOU HAVE YOU A PLACE?
I HAVE A PALACE.
OH, I LIKE THIS PLANET A LOT.

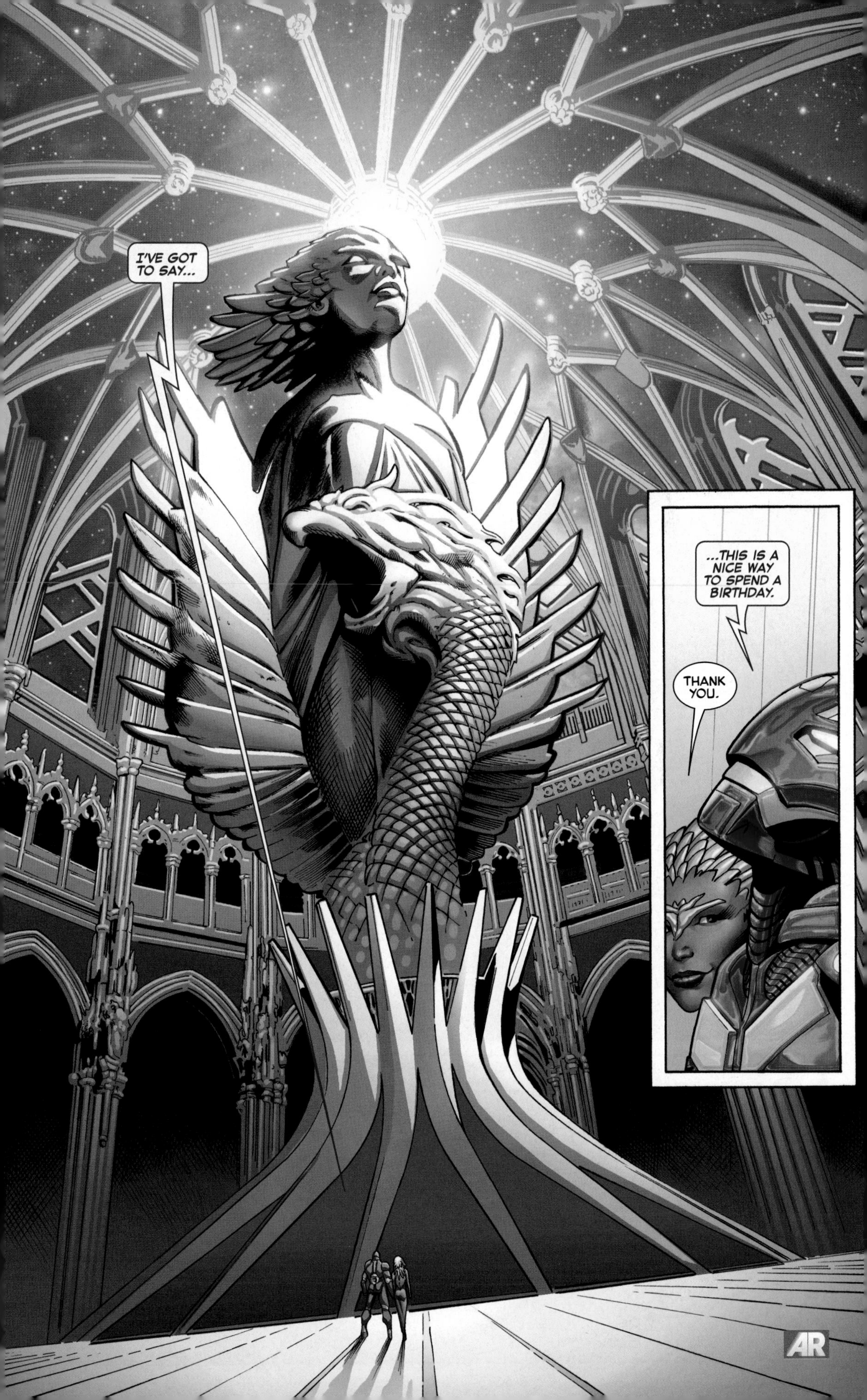
I'VE GOT TO SAY...
...THIS IS A NICE WAY TO SPEND A BIRTHDAY.
THANK YOU.
AR

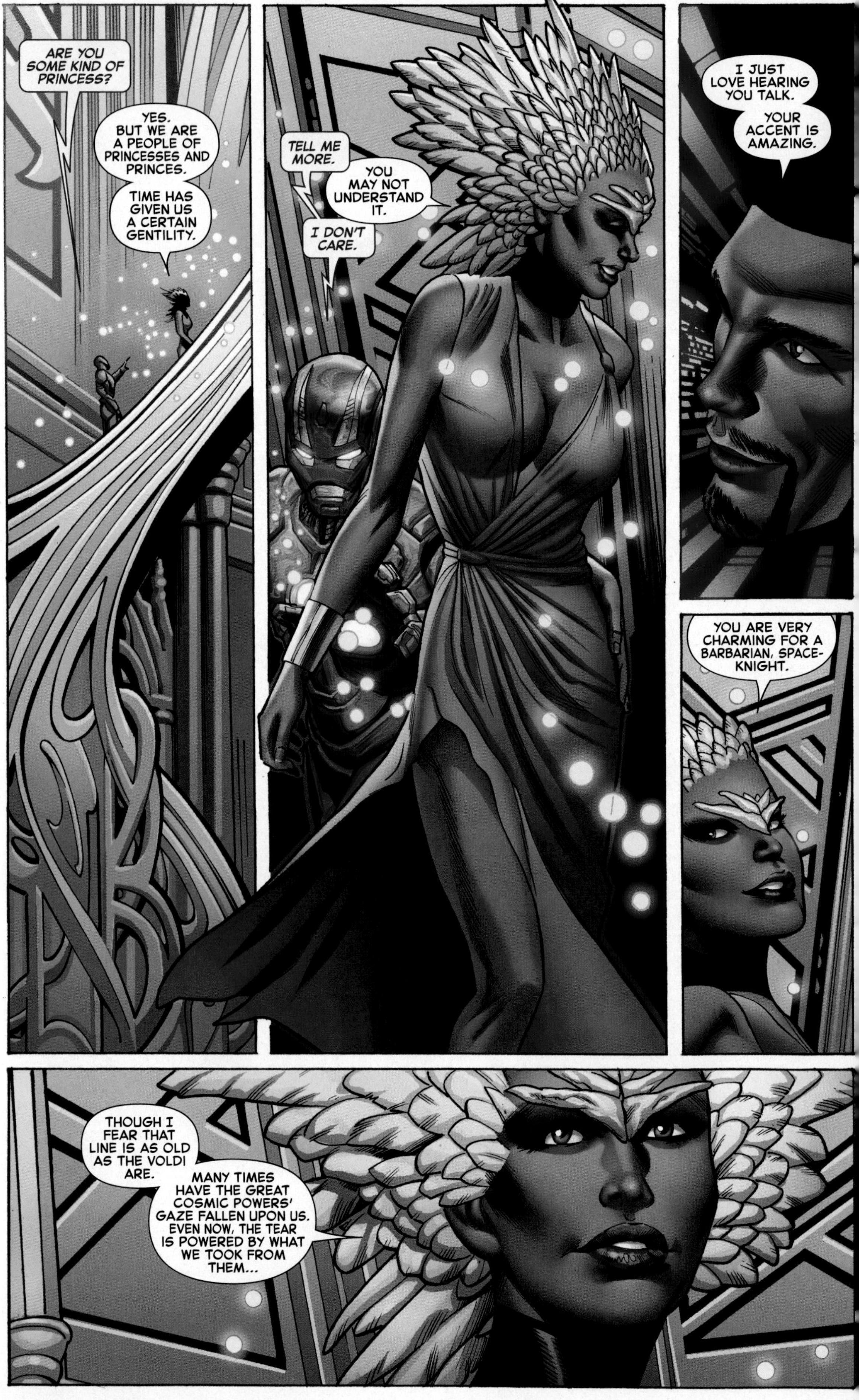
ARE YOU SOME KIND OF PRINCESS?
YES. BUT WE ARE A PEOPLE OF PRINCESSES AND PRINCES.
TIME HAS GIVEN US A CERTAIN GENTILITY.
TELL ME MORE.
YOU MAY NOT UNDERSTAND IT.
I DON'T CARE.
I JUST LOVE HEARING YOU TALK.
YOUR ACCENT IS AMAZING.
YOU ARE VERY CHARMING FOR A BARBARIAN, SPACE-KNIGHT.
THOUGH I FEAR THAT LINE IS AS OLD AS THE VOLDI ARE.
MANY TIMES HAVE THE GREAT COSMIC POWERS' GAZE FALLEN UPON US. EVEN NOW, THE TEAR IS POWERED BY WHAT WE TOOK FROM THEM...

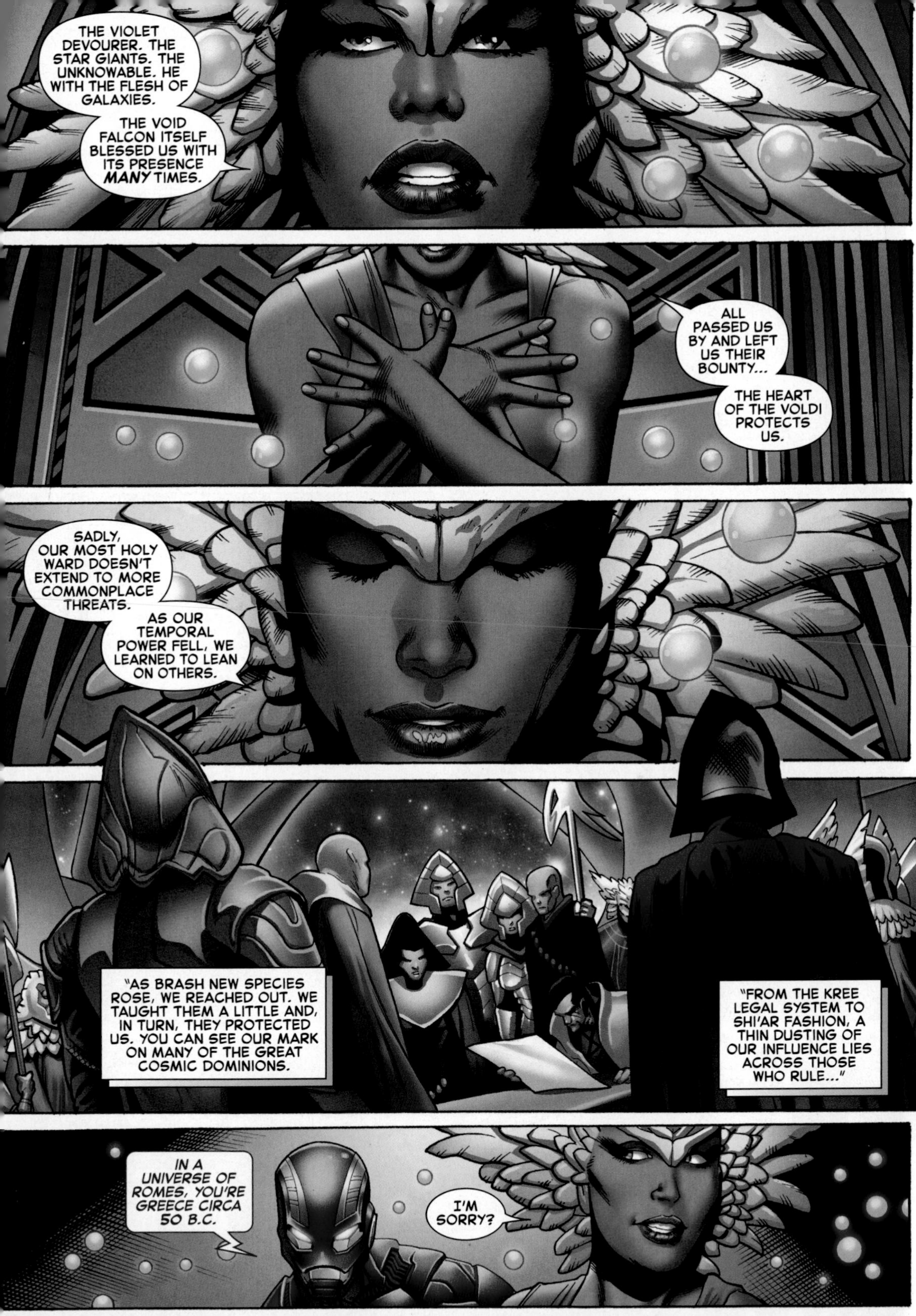
THE VIOLET DEVOURER. THE STAR GIANTS. THE UNKNOWABLE. HE WITH THE FLESH OF GALAXIES.
THE VOID FALCON ITSELF BLESSED US WITH ITS PRESENCE MANY TIMES.
ALL PASSED US BY AND LEFT US THEIR BOUNTY...
THE HEART OF THE VOLDI PROTECTS US.
SADLY, OUR MOST HOLY WARD DOESN'T EXTEND TO MORE COMMONPLACE THREATS.
AS OUR TEMPORAL POWER FELL, WE LEARNED TO LEAN ON OTHERS.
"AS BRASH NEW SPECIES ROSE, WE REACHED OUT. WE TAUGHT THEM A LITTLE AND, IN TURN, THEY PROTECTED US. YOU CAN SEE OUR MARK ON MANY OF THE GREAT COSMIC DOMINIONS.
"FROM THE KREE LEGAL SYSTEM TO SHI'AR FASHION, A THIN DUSTING OF OUR INFLUENCE LIES ACROSS THOSE WHO RULE..."
IN A UNIVERSE OF ROMES, YOU'RE GREECE CIRCA 50 B.C.
I'M SORRY?

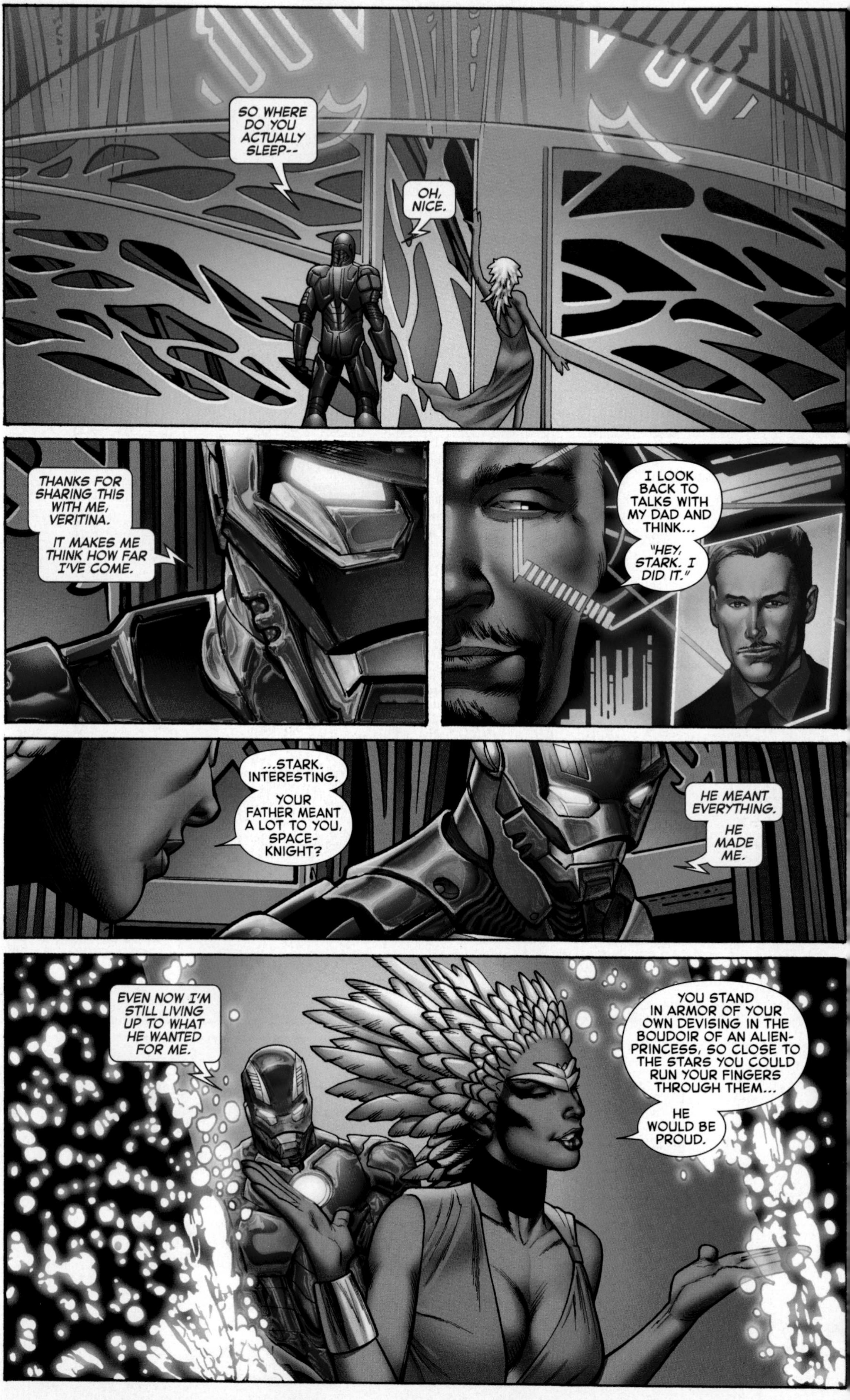
SO WHERE DO YOU ACTUALLY SLEEP--
OH, NICE.
THANKS FOR SHARING THIS WITH ME, VERITINA.
IT MAKES ME THINK HOW FAR I'VE COME.
I LOOK BACK TO TALKS WITH MY DAD AND THINK...
"HEY, STARK. I DID IT."
...STARK. INTERESTING.
YOUR FATHER MEANT A LOT TO YOU, SPACE-KNIGHT?
HE MEANT EVERYTHING.
HE MADE ME.
EVEN NOW I'M STILL LIVING UP TO WHAT HE WANTED FOR ME.
YOU STAND IN ARMOR OF YOUR OWN DEVISING IN THE BOUDOIR OF AN ALIEN-PRINCESS, SO CLOSE TO THE STARS YOU COULD RUN YOUR FINGERS THROUGH THEM...
HE WOULD BE PROUD.

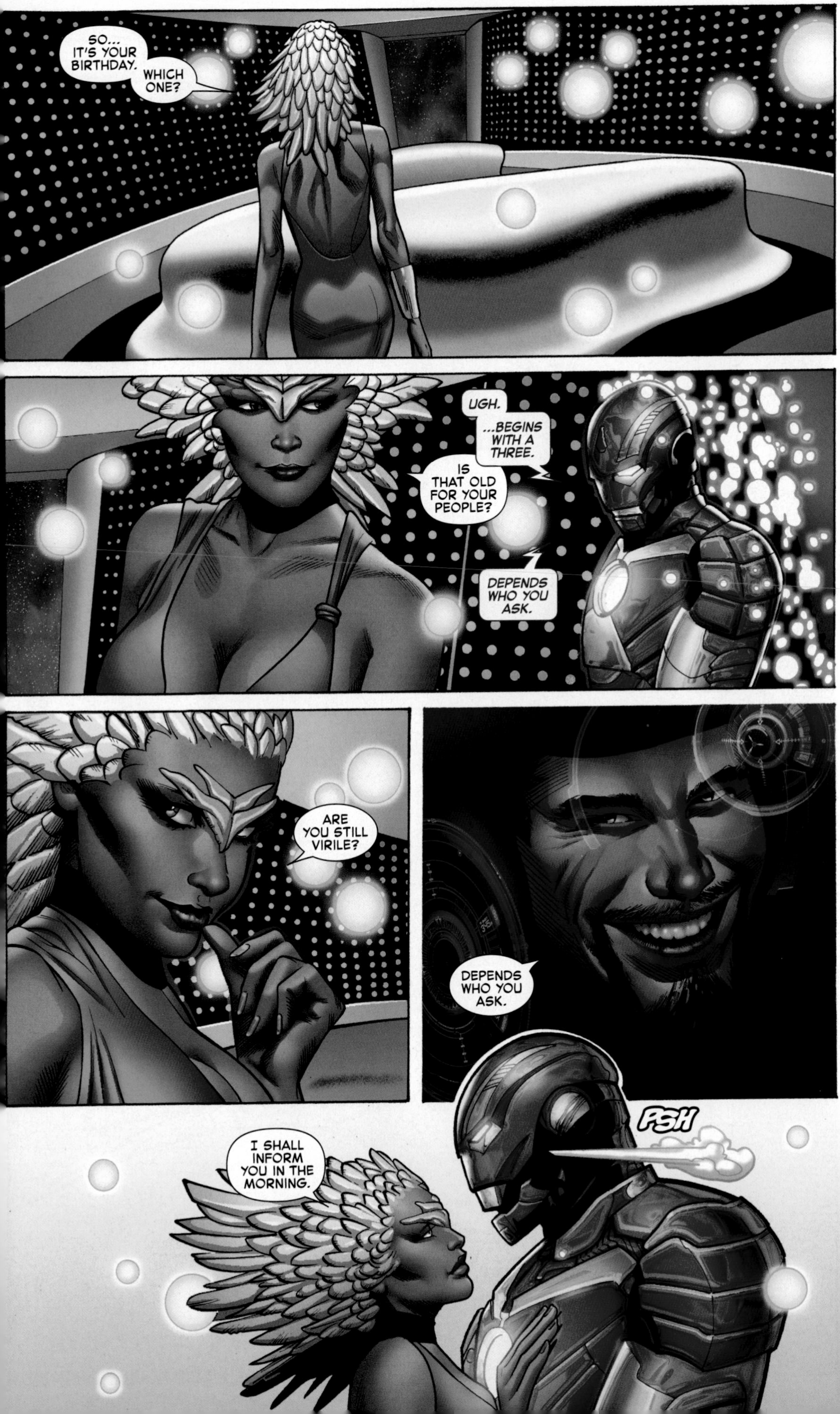
SO... IT'S YOUR BIRTHDAY.
WHICH ONE?
UGH.
...BEGINS WITH A THREE.
IS THAT OLD FOR YOUR PEOPLE?
DEPENDS WHO YOU ASK.
ARE YOU STILL VIRILE?
DEPENDS WHO YOU ASK.
PSH
I SHALL INFORM YOU IN THE MORNING.

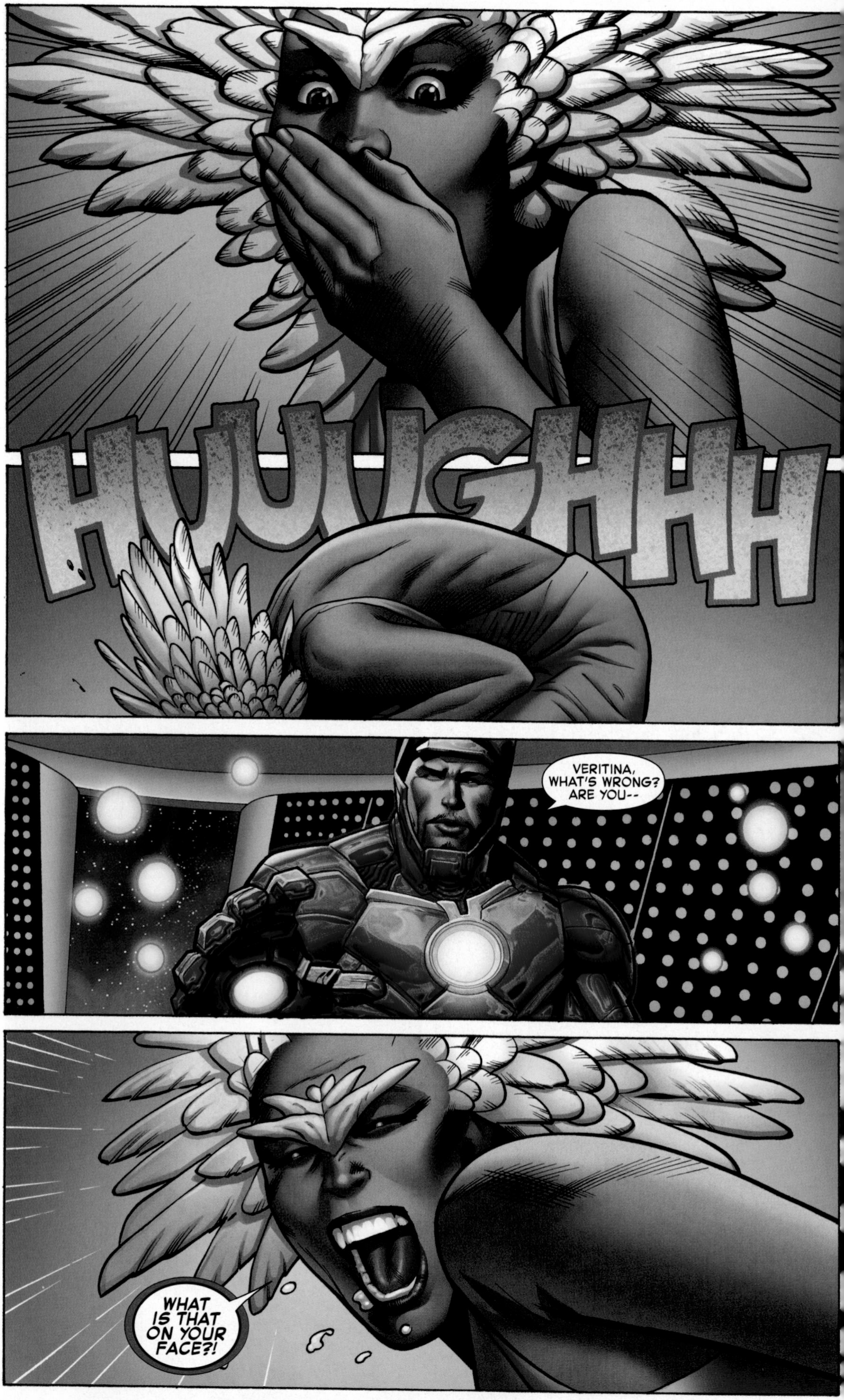
HUUUGHHH
VERITINA, WHAT'S WRONG? ARE YOU--
WHAT IS THAT ON YOUR FACE?!

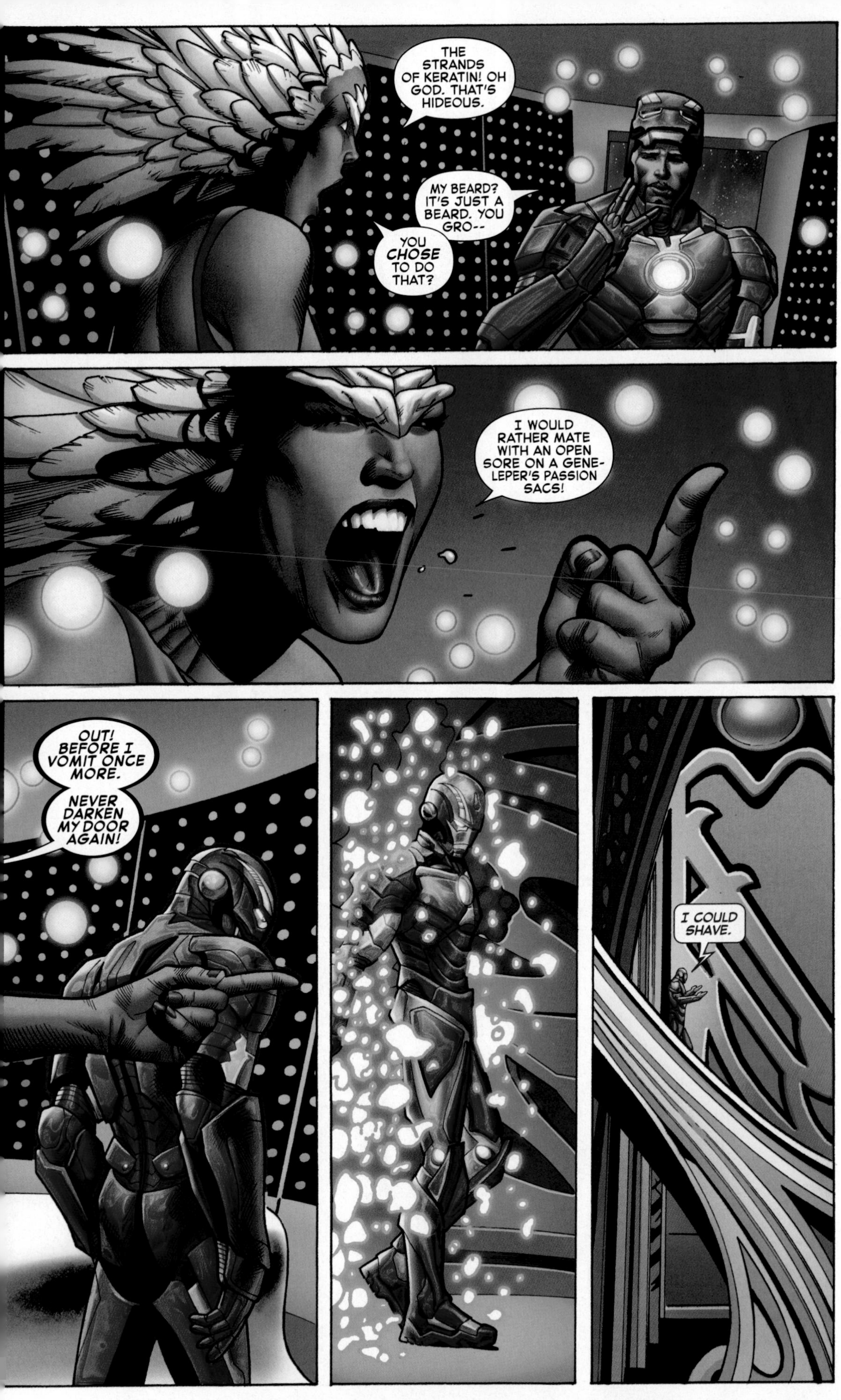
THE STRANDS OF KERATIN! OH GOD. THAT'S HIDEOUS.
MY BEARD? IT'S JUST A BEARD. YOU GRO--
YOU CHOSE TO DO THAT?
I WOULD RATHER MATE WITH AN OPEN SORE ON A GENE-LEPER'S PASSION SACS!
OUT! BEFORE I VOMIT ONCE MORE.
NEVER DARKEN MY DOOR AGAIN!
I COULD SHAVE.

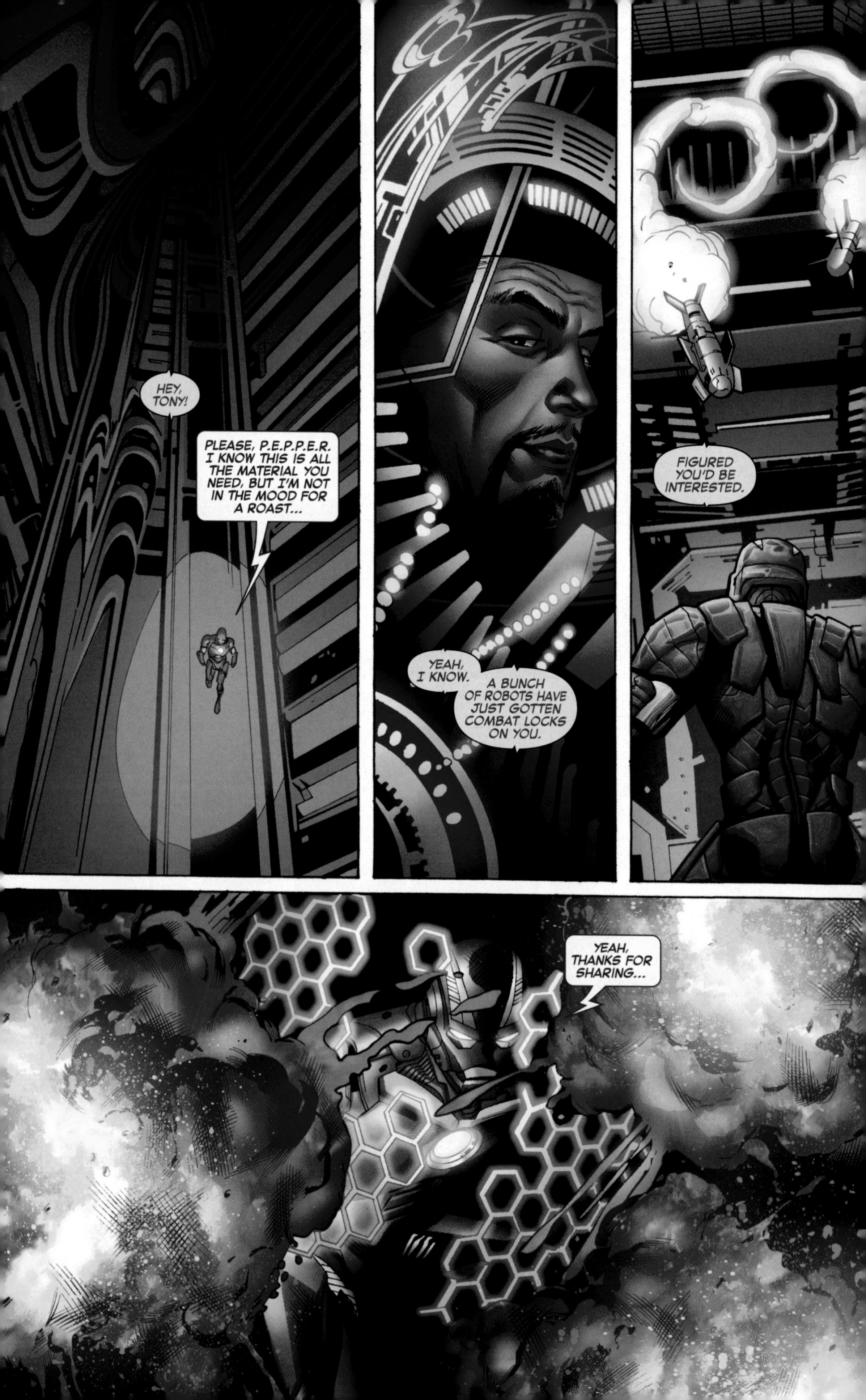
HEY, TONY!
PLEASE, P.E.P.P.E.R. I KNOW THIS IS ALL THE MATERIAL YOU NEED, BUT I'M NOT IN THE MOOD FOR A ROAST...
YEAH, I KNOW.
A BUNCH OF ROBOTS HAVE JUST GOTTEN COMBAT LOCKS ON YOU.
FIGURED YOU'D BE INTERESTED.
YEAH, THANKS FOR SHARING...

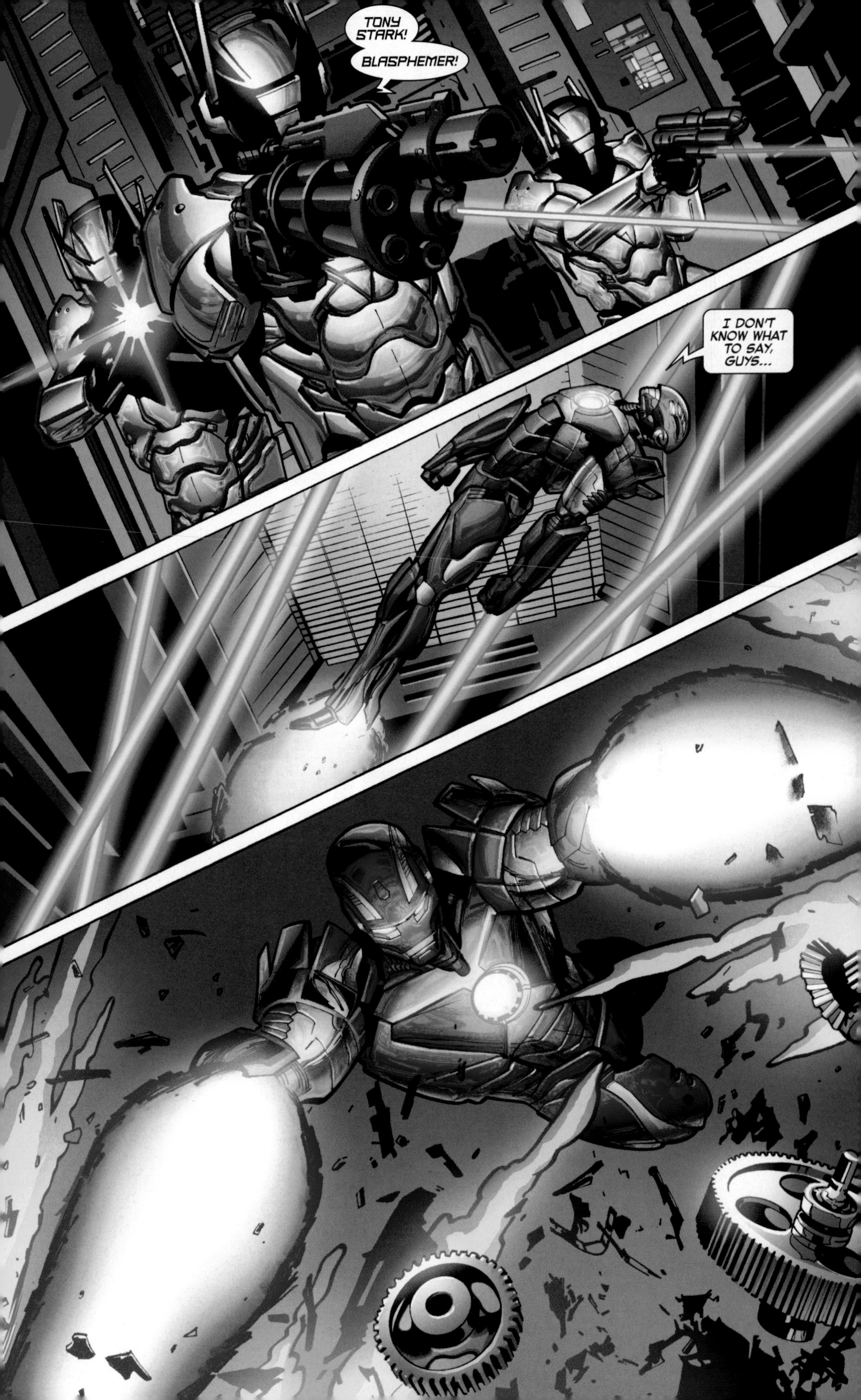
TONY STARK!
BLASPHEMER!
I DON'T KNOW WHAT TO SAY, GUYS...

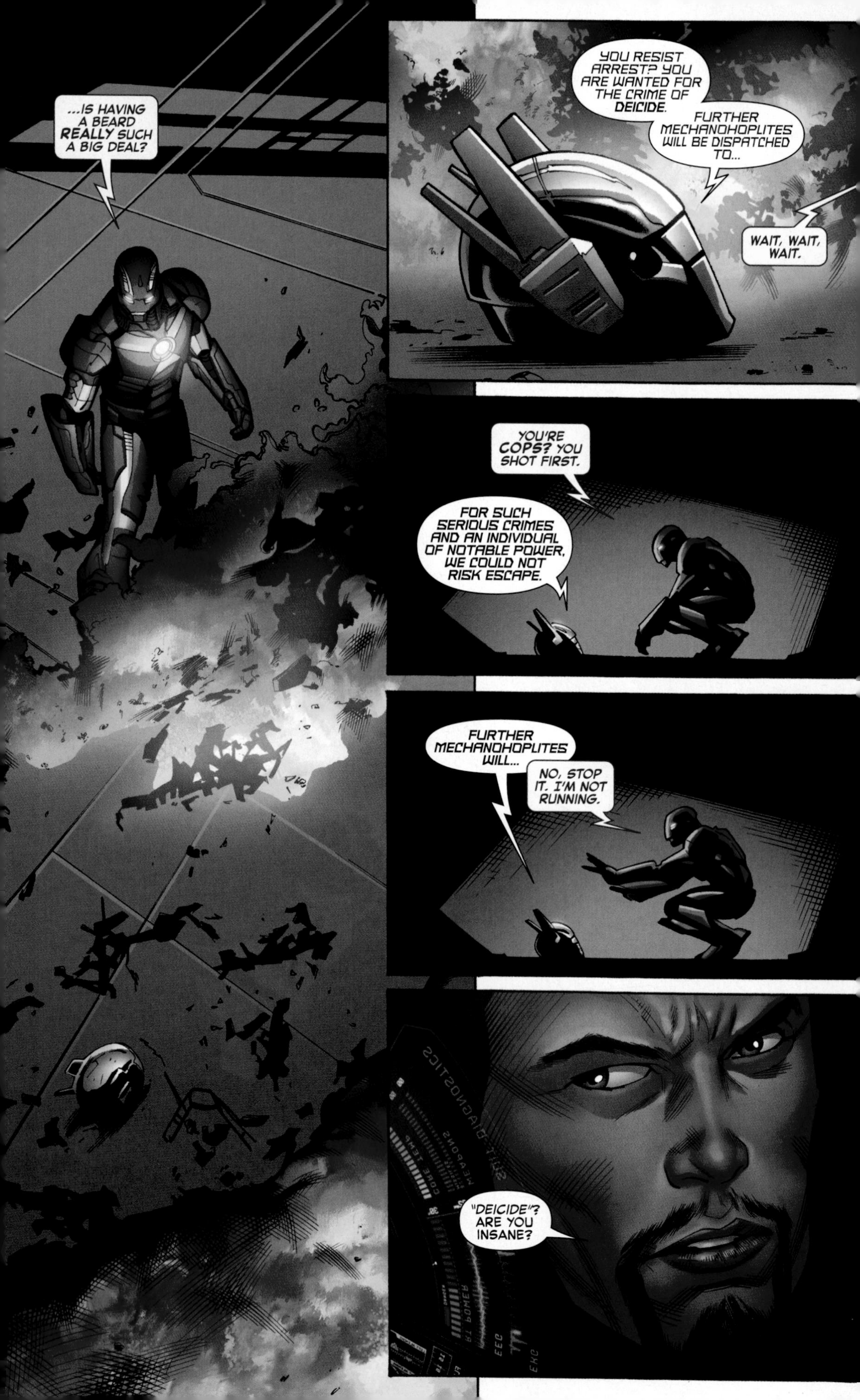
...IS HAVING A BEARD REALLY SUCH A BIG DEAL?
YOU RESIST ARREST? YOU ARE WANTED FOR THE CRIME OF DEICIDE.
FURTHER MECHANOHOPLITES WILL BE DISPATCHED TO...
WAIT, WAIT, WAIT.
YOU'RE COPS? YOU SHOT FIRST.
FOR SUCH SERIOUS CRIMES AND AN INDIVIDUAL OF NOTABLE POWER, WE COULD NOT RISK ESCAPE.
FURTHER MECHANOHOPLITES WILL...
NO, STOP IT. I'M NOT RUNNING.
"DEICIDE"? ARE YOU INSANE?

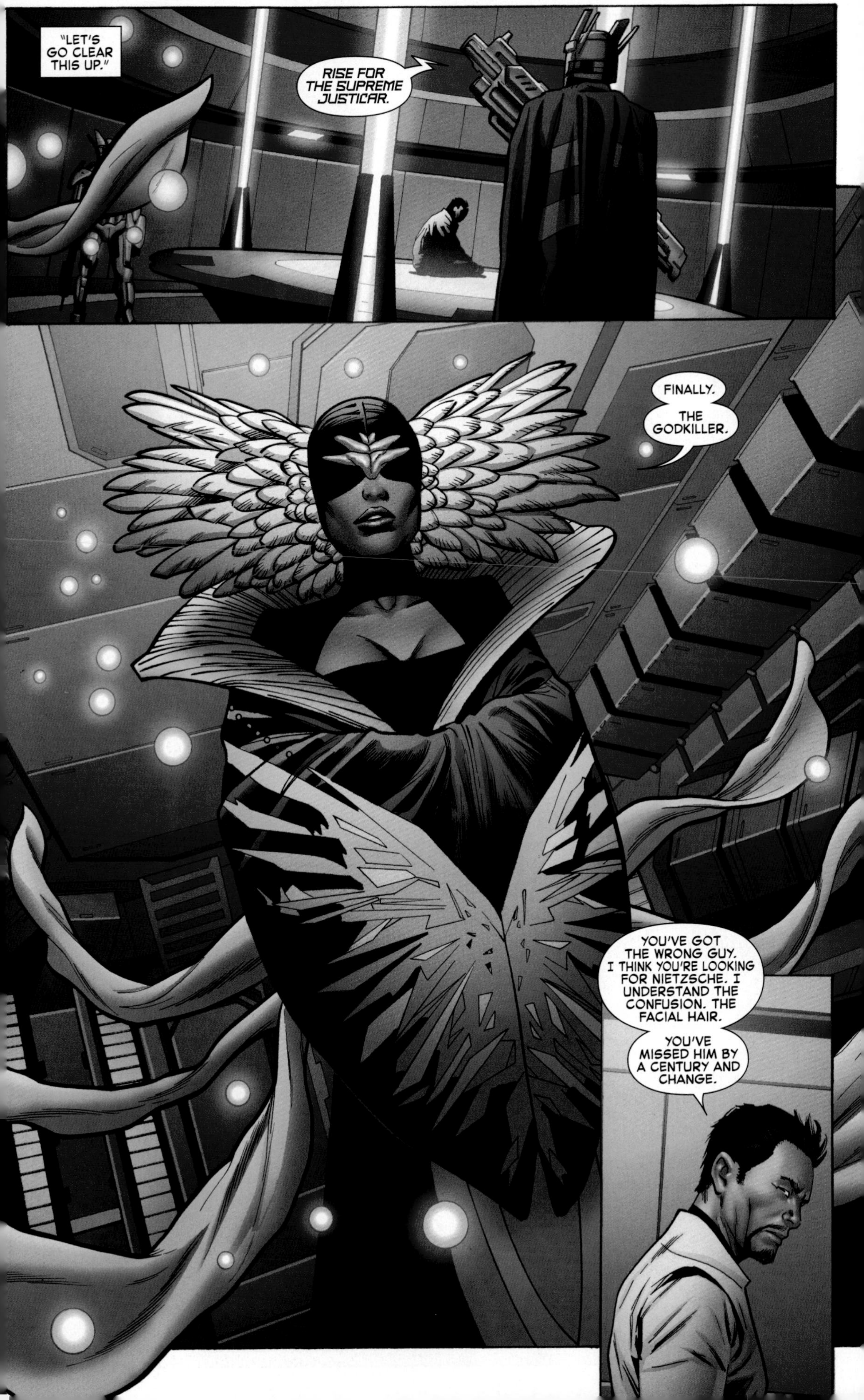
"LET'S GO CLEAR THIS UP."
RISE FOR THE SUPREME JUSTICAR.
FINALLY.
THE GODKILLER.
YOU'VE GOT THE WRONG GUY. I THINK YOU'RE LOOKING FOR NIETZSCHE. I UNDERSTAND THE CONFUSION. THE FACIAL HAIR.
YOU'VE MISSED HIM BY A CENTURY AND CHANGE.

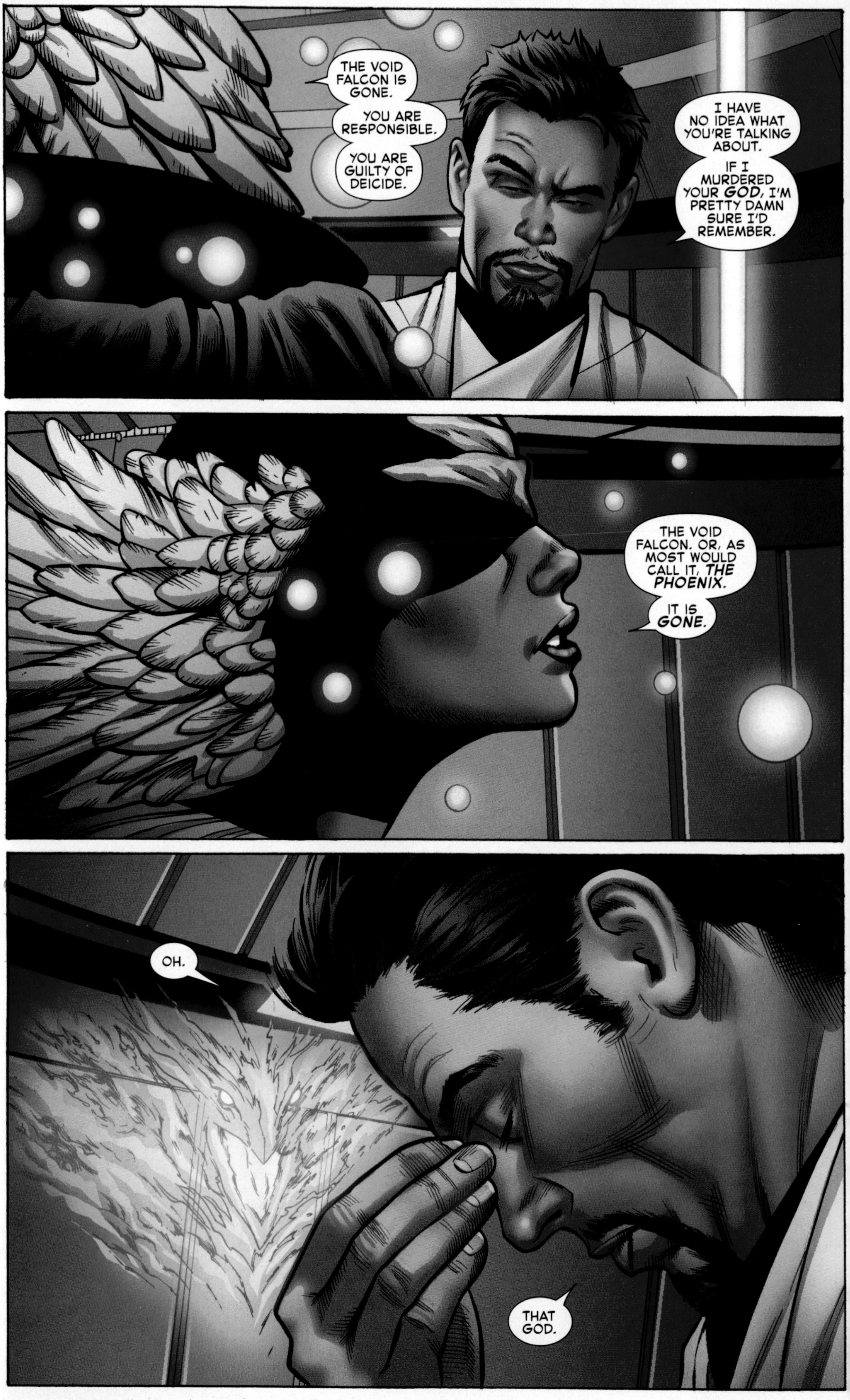
THE VOID FALCON IS GONE.
YOU ARE RESPONSIBLE.
YOU ARE GUILTY OF DEICIDE.
I HAVE NO IDEA WHAT YOU'RE TALKING ABOUT.
IF I MURDERED YOUR *GOD*, I'M PRETTY DAMN SURE I'D REMEMBER.
THE VOID FALCON. OR, AS MOST WOULD CALL IT, *THE PHOENIX*.
IT IS *GONE*.
OH.
THAT GOD.

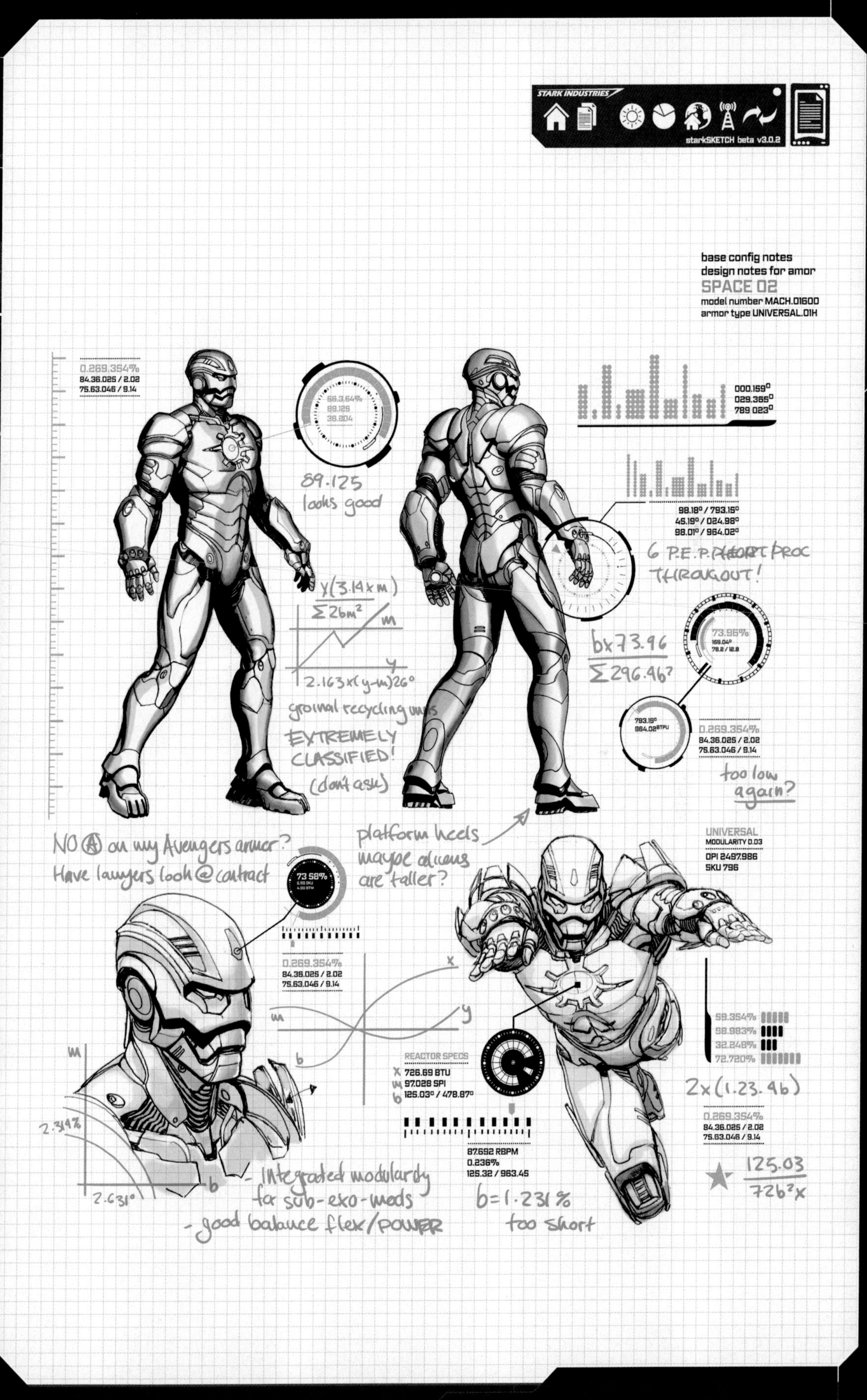
STARK INDUSTRIES
starkSKETCH beta v3.0.2
base config notes
design notes for amor
SPACE 02
model number MACH.01600
armor type UNIVERSAL.01H
0.269.354%
84.36.025 / 2.02
75.63.046 / 9.14
89.125
looks good
000.159°
029.365°
789 023°
98.18° / 793.15°
45.19° / 024.98°
98.01° / 964.02°
6 P.E.P. PROC THROUGOUT!
y(3.14xm)
Σ26m²
2.163x(y-m)26°
groinal recycling units
EXTREMELY CLASSIFIED!
(don't ask)
bx73.96
Σ296.46?
73.96%
too low again?
NO Ⓐ on my Avengers armor? Have lawyers look @ contract
platform heels maybe aliens are taller?
UNIVERSAL
MODULARITY 0.03
OPI 2487.986
SKU 796
73 58%
59.354%
98.983%
32.248%
72.720%
2x(1.23.46)
REACTOR SPECS
X 726.69 BTU
M 97.028 SPI
b 125.03° / 478.87°
87.692 RBPM
0.236%
125.32 / 963.45
2.31%
2.631°
- Integrated modularity for sub-exo-mods
- good balance flex/POWER
b=1.231%
too short
125.03
726²x

#6 ARMOR VARIANT BY STEVE McNIVEN & JARED FLETCHER

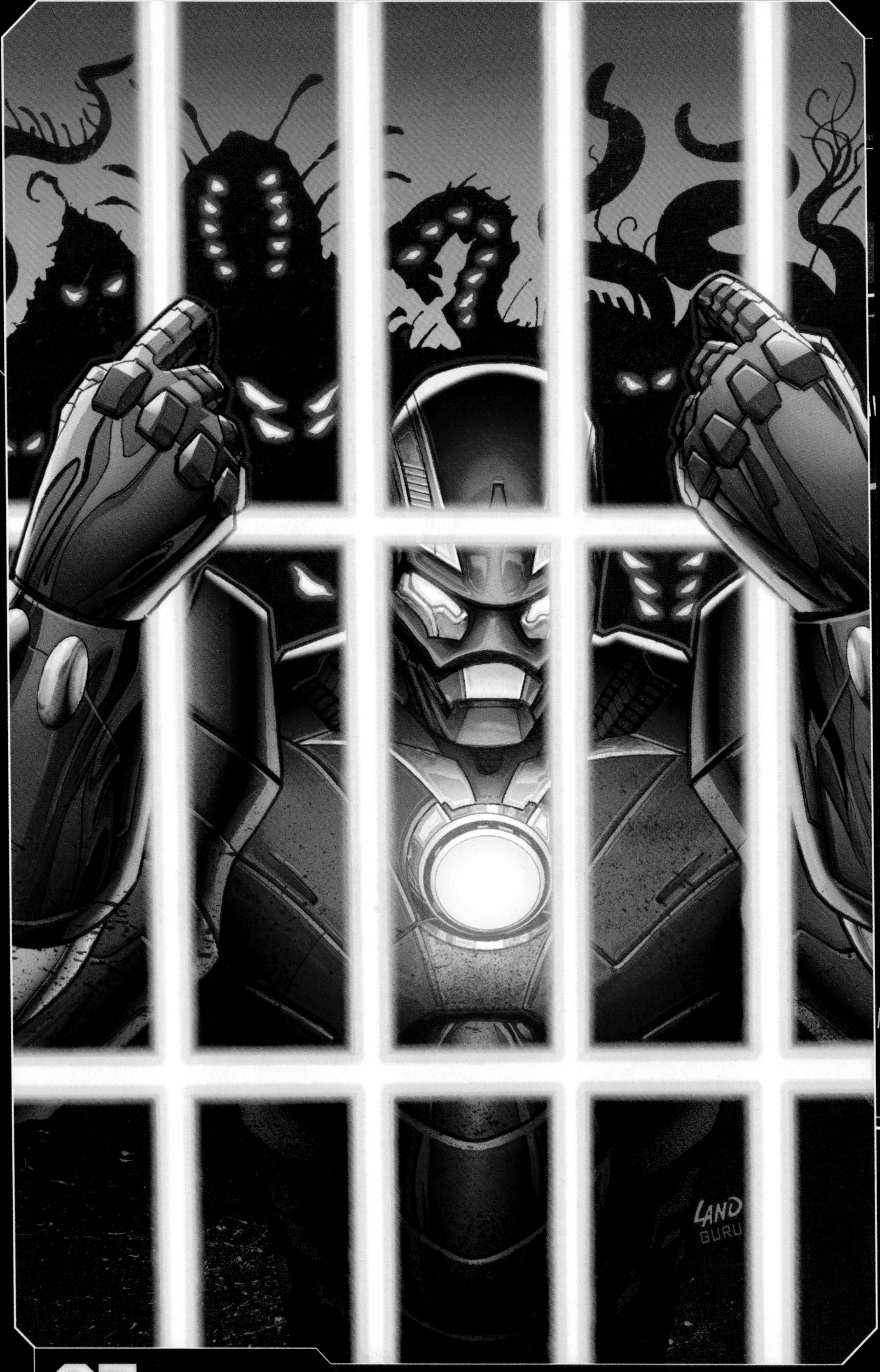
LAND
GURU

07 THE GODKILLER PART 2

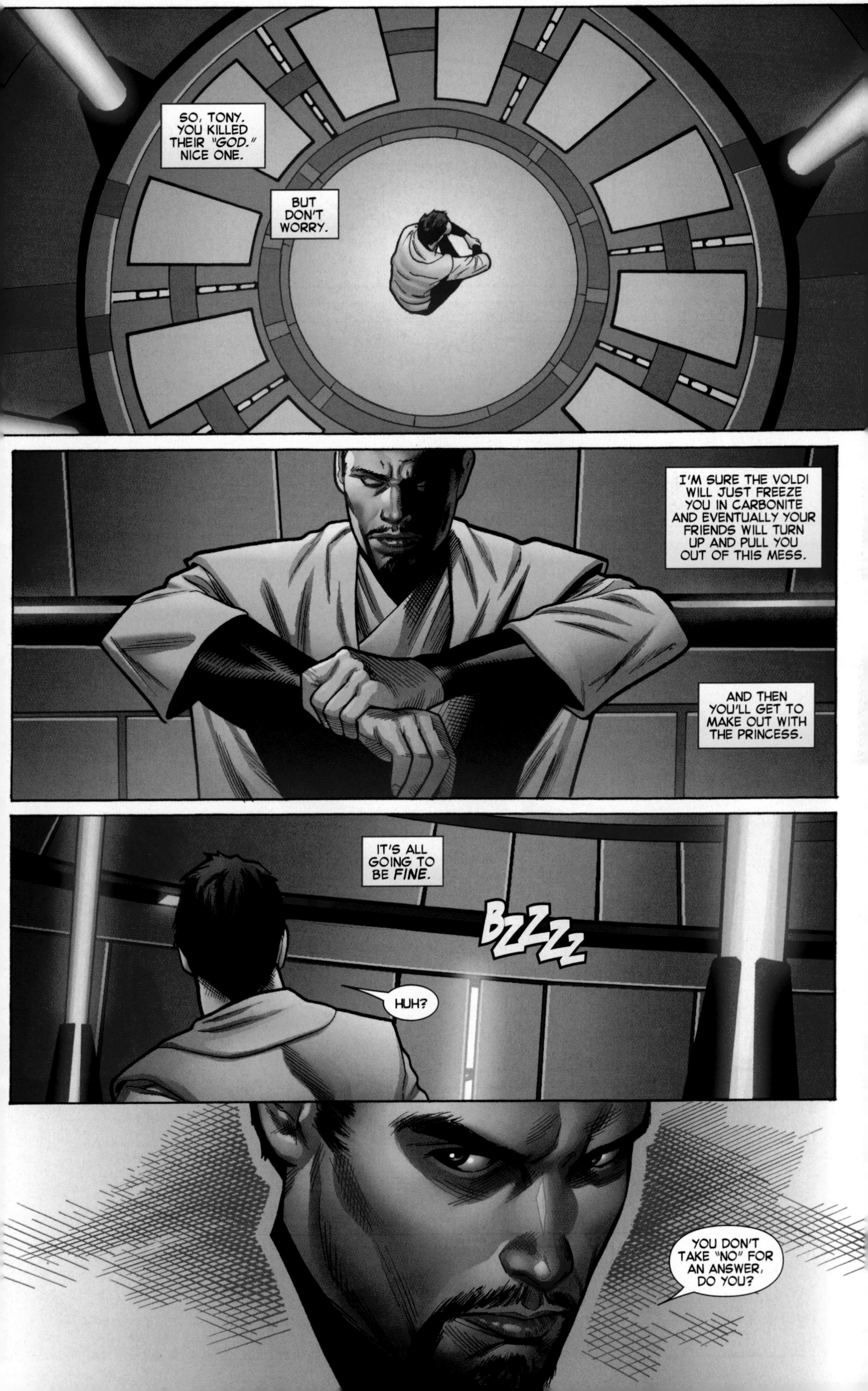
SO, TONY. YOU KILLED THEIR "GOD." NICE ONE.
BUT DON'T WORRY.
I'M SURE THE VOLDI WILL JUST FREEZE YOU IN CARBONITE AND EVENTUALLY YOUR FRIENDS WILL TURN UP AND PULL YOU OUT OF THIS MESS.
AND THEN YOU'LL GET TO MAKE OUT WITH THE PRINCESS.
IT'S ALL GOING TO BE *FINE.*
BZZZZ
HUH?
YOU DON'T TAKE "NO" FOR AN ANSWER, DO YOU?

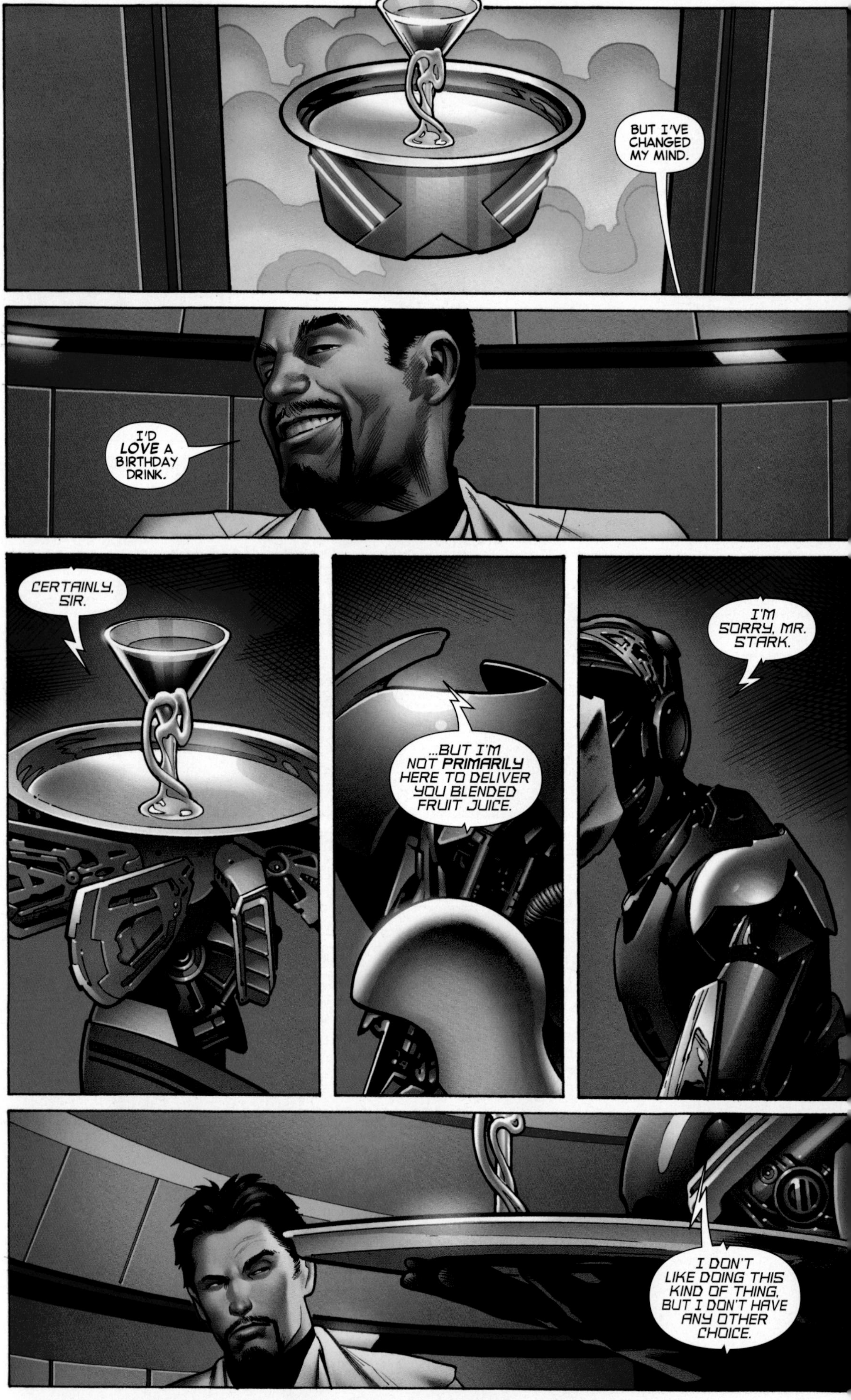

BUT I'VE CHANGED MY MIND.
I'D **LOVE** A BIRTHDAY DRINK.
CERTAINLY, SIR.
I'M SORRY, MR. STARK.
...BUT I'M NOT **PRIMARILY** HERE TO DELIVER YOU BLENDED FRUIT JUICE.
I DON'T LIKE DOING THIS KIND OF THING, BUT I DON'T HAVE ANY OTHER CHOICE.

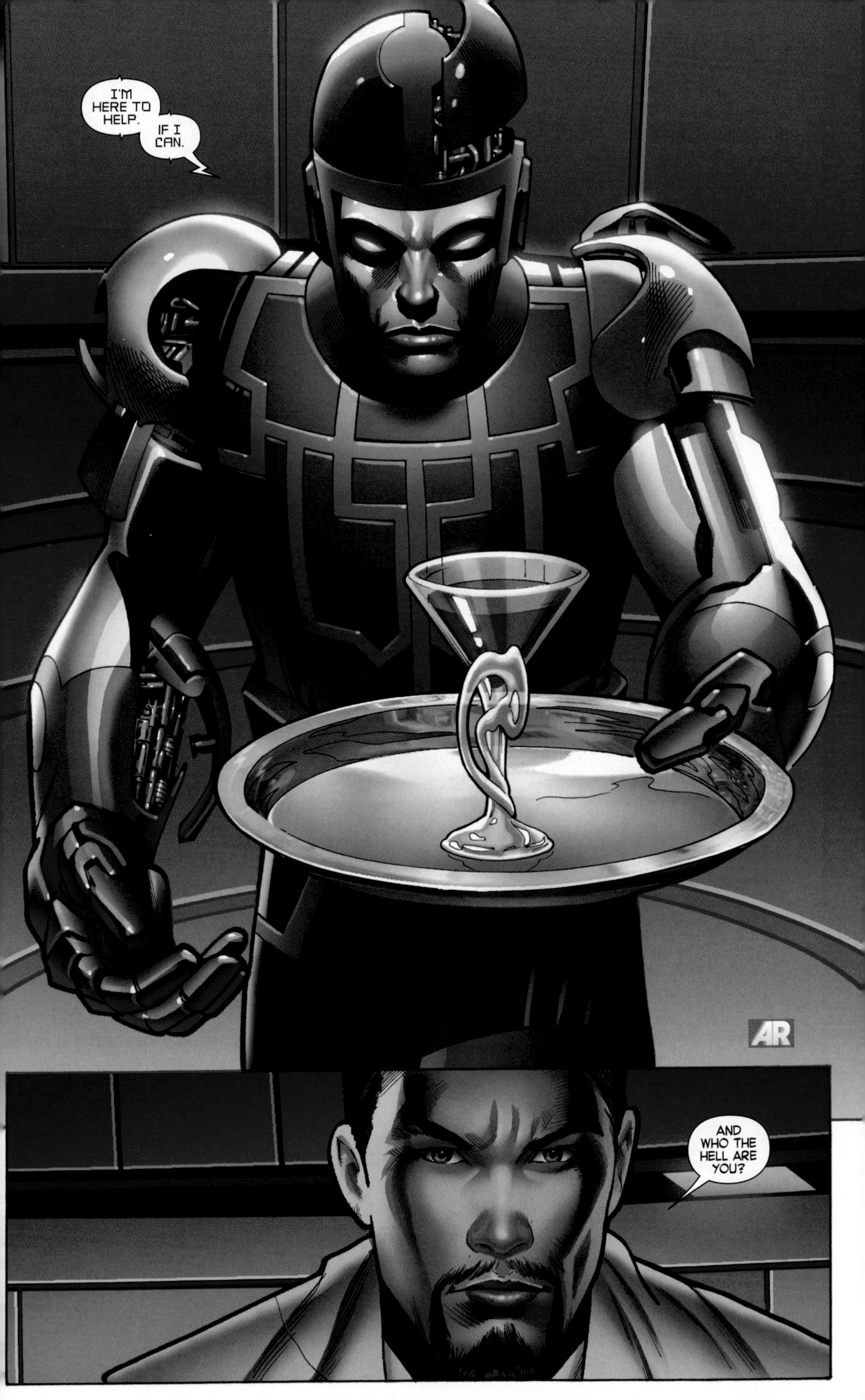
I'M HERE TO HELP.
IF I CAN.
AND WHO THE HELL ARE YOU?

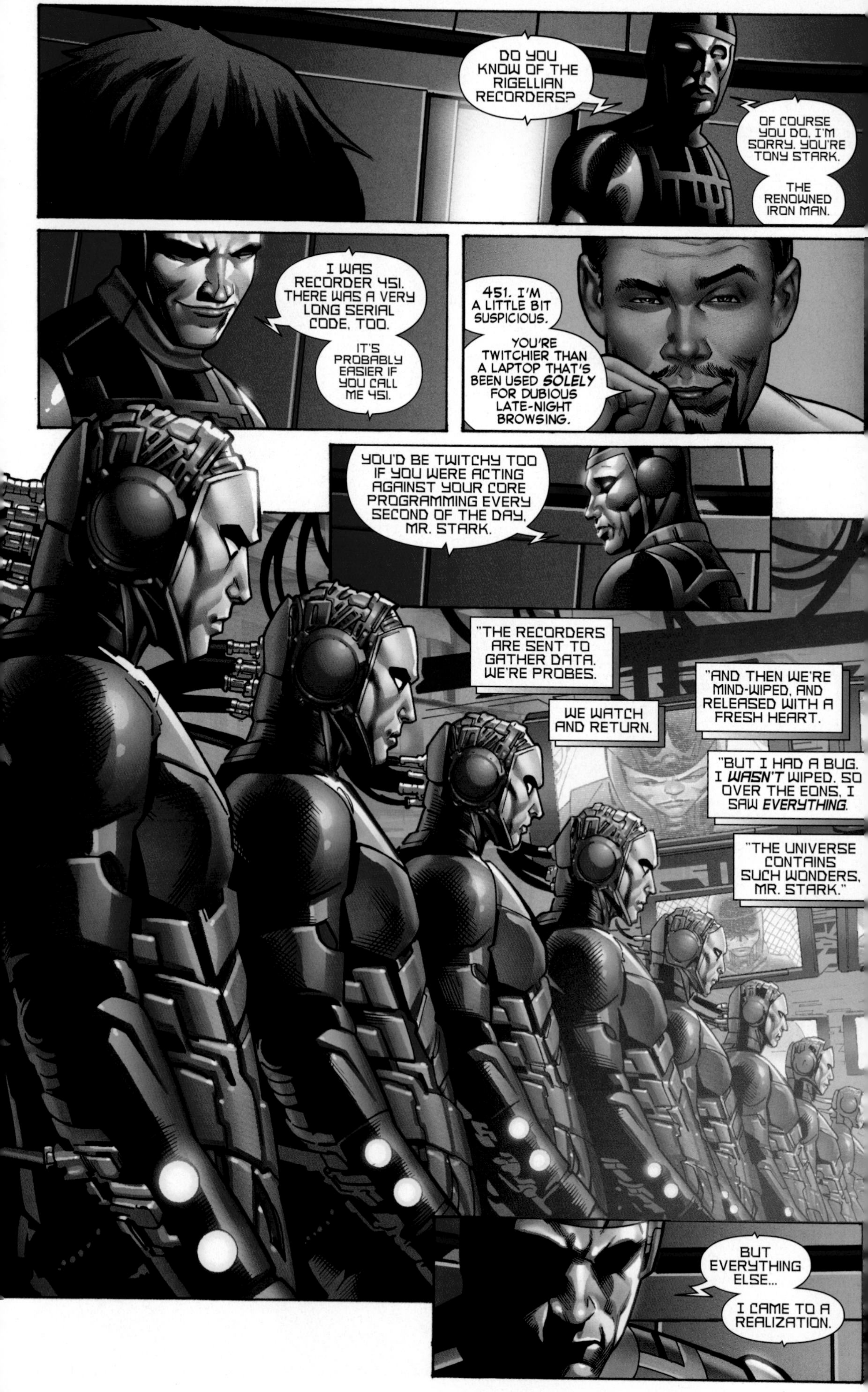

DO YOU KNOW OF THE RIGELLIAN RECORDERS?
OF COURSE YOU DO. I'M SORRY. YOU'RE TONY STARK.
THE RENOWNED IRON MAN.
I WAS RECORDER 451. THERE WAS A VERY LONG SERIAL CODE, TOO.
IT'S PROBABLY EASIER IF YOU CALL ME 451.
451. I'M A LITTLE BIT SUSPICIOUS.
YOU'RE TWITCHIER THAN A LAPTOP THAT'S BEEN USED SOLELY FOR DUBIOUS LATE-NIGHT BROWSING.
YOU'D BE TWITCHY TOO IF YOU WERE ACTING AGAINST YOUR CORE PROGRAMMING EVERY SECOND OF THE DAY, MR. STARK.
"THE RECORDERS ARE SENT TO GATHER DATA. WE'RE PROBES.
WE WATCH AND RETURN.
"AND THEN WE'RE MIND-WIPED, AND RELEASED WITH A FRESH HEART.
"BUT I HAD A BUG. I WASN'T WIPED. SO OVER THE EONS, I SAW EVERYTHING.
"THE UNIVERSE CONTAINS SUCH WONDERS, MR. STARK."
BUT EVERYTHING ELSE...
I CAME TO A REALIZATION.

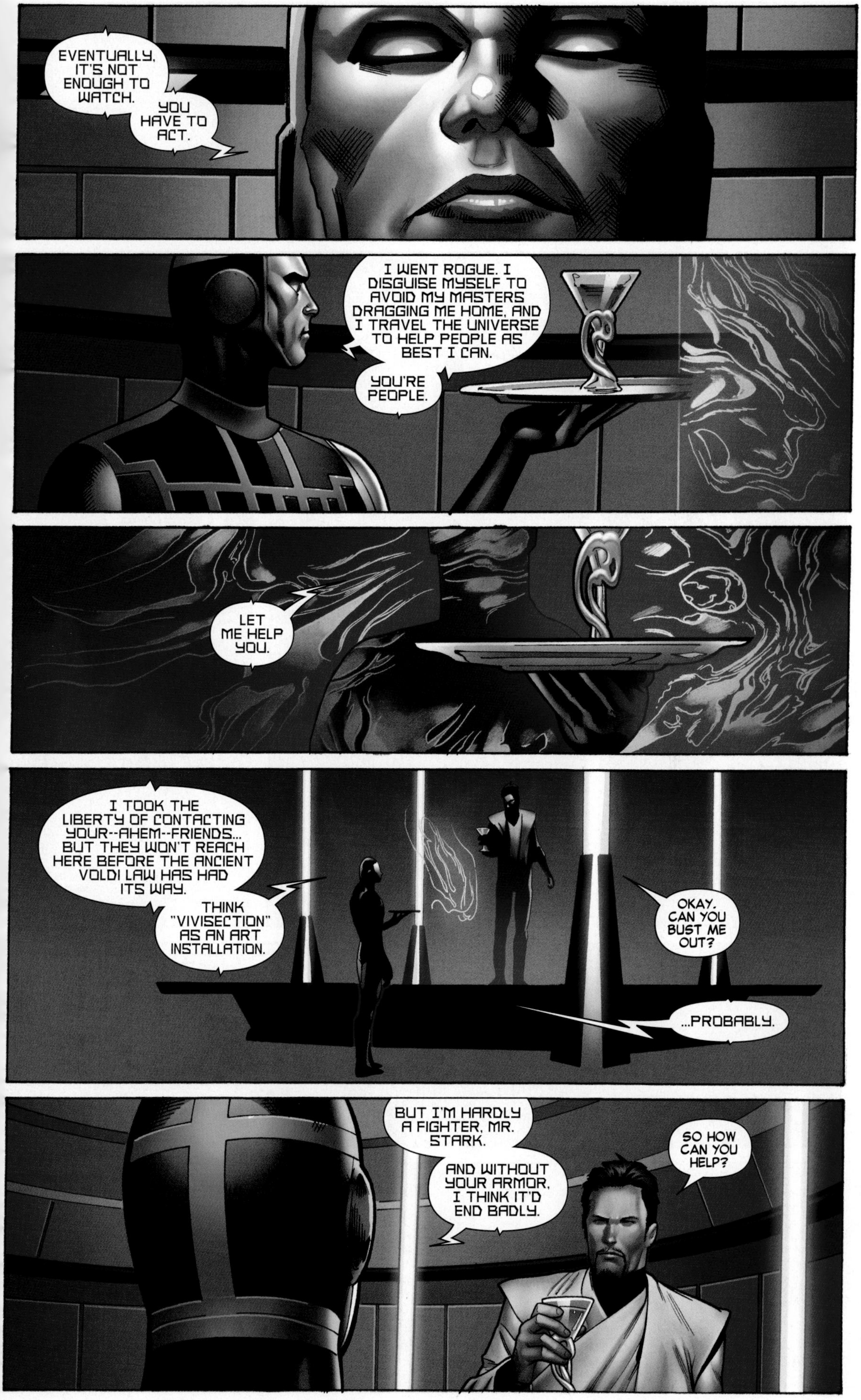
EVENTUALLY, IT'S NOT ENOUGH TO WATCH.
YOU HAVE TO ACT.
I WENT ROGUE. I DISGUISE MYSELF TO AVOID MY MASTERS DRAGGING ME HOME, AND I TRAVEL THE UNIVERSE TO HELP PEOPLE AS BEST I CAN.
YOU'RE PEOPLE.
LET ME HELP YOU.
I TOOK THE LIBERTY OF CONTACTING YOUR--AHEM--FRIENDS... BUT THEY WON'T REACH HERE BEFORE THE ANCIENT VOLDI LAW HAS HAD ITS WAY.
THINK "VIVISECTION" AS AN ART INSTALLATION.
OKAY. CAN YOU BUST ME OUT?
...PROBABLY.
BUT I'M HARDLY A FIGHTER, MR. STARK.
AND WITHOUT YOUR ARMOR, I THINK IT'D END BADLY.
SO HOW CAN YOU HELP?

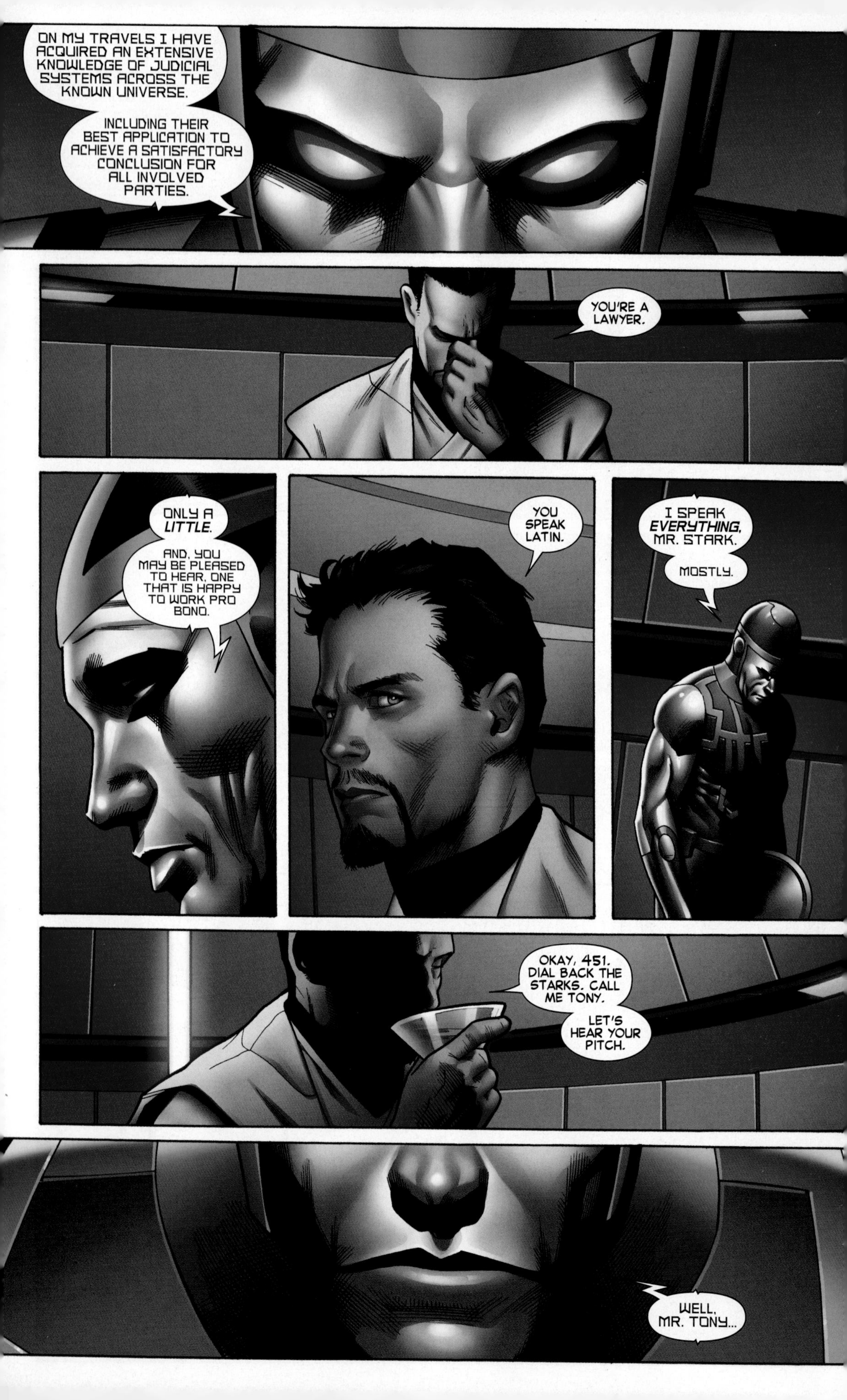
ON MY TRAVELS I HAVE ACQUIRED AN EXTENSIVE KNOWLEDGE OF JUDICIAL SYSTEMS ACROSS THE KNOWN UNIVERSE.
INCLUDING THEIR BEST APPLICATION TO ACHIEVE A SATISFACTORY CONCLUSION FOR ALL INVOLVED PARTIES.
YOU'RE A LAWYER.
ONLY A *LITTLE*.
AND, YOU MAY BE PLEASED TO HEAR, ONE THAT IS HAPPY TO WORK PRO BONO.
YOU SPEAK LATIN.
I SPEAK *EVERYTHING*, MR. STARK.
MOSTLY.
OKAY, 451. DIAL BACK THE STARKS. CALL ME TONY.
LET'S HEAR YOUR PITCH.
WELL, MR. TONY...

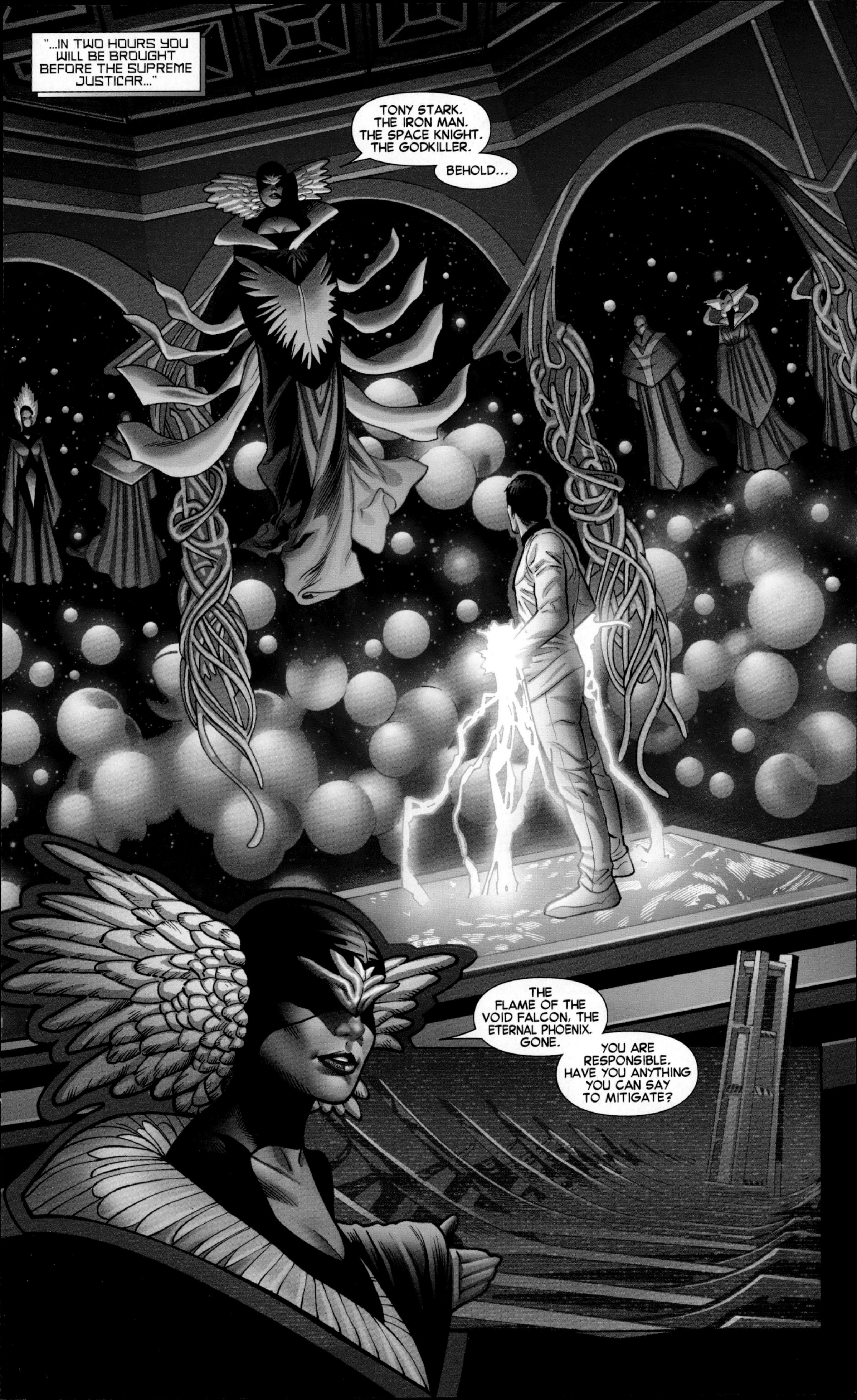
"...IN TWO HOURS YOU WILL BE BROUGHT BEFORE THE SUPREME JUSTICAR..."
TONY STARK. THE IRON MAN. THE SPACE KNIGHT. THE GODKILLER.
BEHOLD...
THE FLAME OF THE VOID FALCON, THE ETERNAL PHOENIX. GONE.
YOU ARE RESPONSIBLE. HAVE YOU ANYTHING YOU CAN SAY TO MITIGATE?

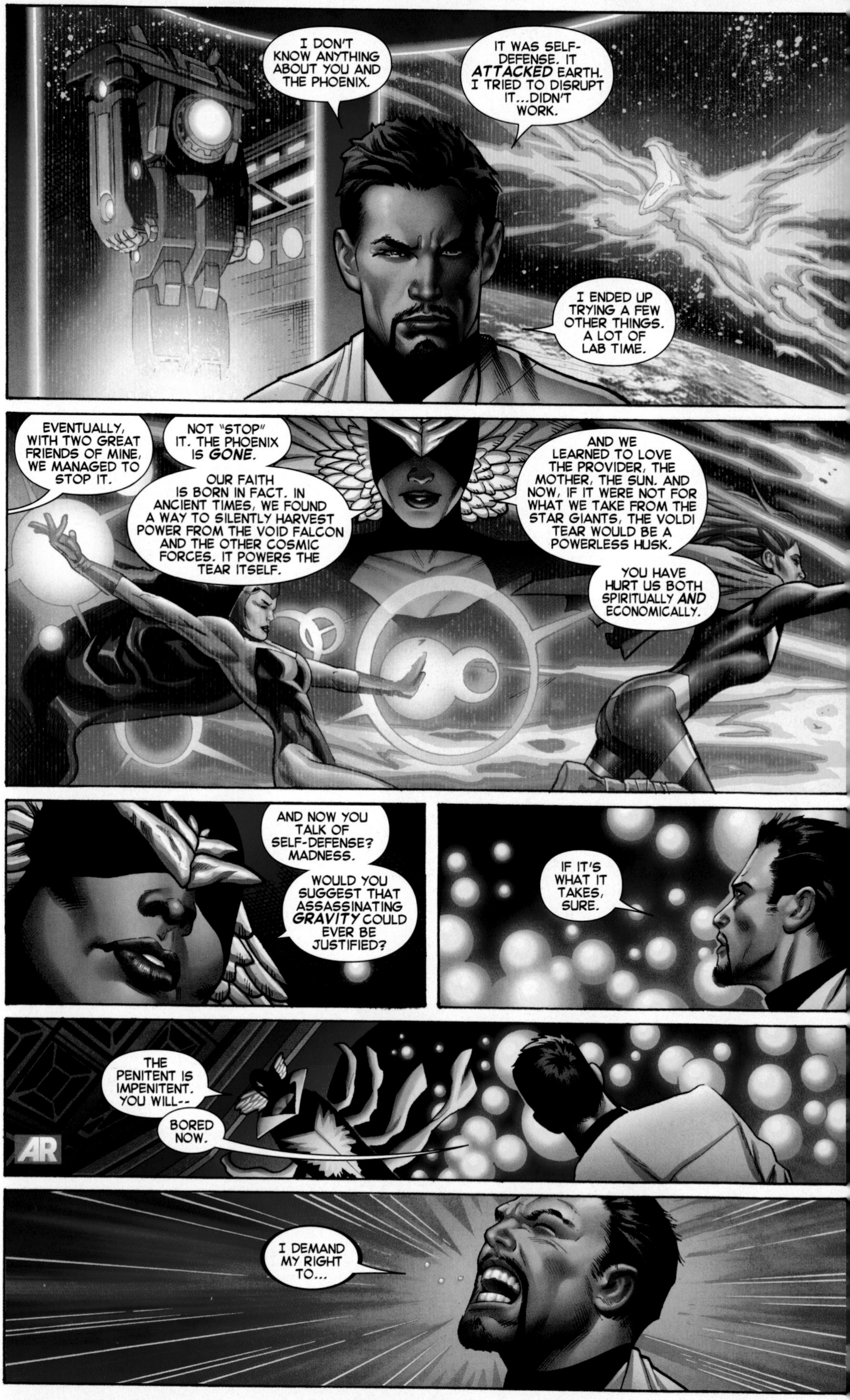
I DON'T KNOW ANYTHING ABOUT YOU AND THE PHOENIX.
IT WAS SELF-DEFENSE. IT ATTACKED EARTH. I TRIED TO DISRUPT IT...DIDN'T WORK.
I ENDED UP TRYING A FEW OTHER THINGS. A LOT OF LAB TIME.
EVENTUALLY, WITH TWO GREAT FRIENDS OF MINE, WE MANAGED TO STOP IT.
NOT "STOP" IT. THE PHOENIX IS GONE.
OUR FAITH IS BORN IN FACT. IN ANCIENT TIMES, WE FOUND A WAY TO SILENTLY HARVEST POWER FROM THE VOID FALCON AND THE OTHER COSMIC FORCES. IT POWERS THE TEAR ITSELF.
AND WE LEARNED TO LOVE THE PROVIDER, THE MOTHER, THE SUN. AND NOW, IF IT WERE NOT FOR WHAT WE TAKE FROM THE STAR GIANTS, THE VOLDI TEAR WOULD BE A POWERLESS HUSK.
YOU HAVE HURT US BOTH SPIRITUALLY AND ECONOMICALLY.
AND NOW YOU TALK OF SELF-DEFENSE? MADNESS.
WOULD YOU SUGGEST THAT ASSASSINATING GRAVITY COULD EVER BE JUSTIFIED?
IF IT'S WHAT IT TAKES, SURE.
THE PENITENT IS IMPENITENT. YOU WILL--
BORED NOW.
AR
I DEMAND MY RIGHT TO...

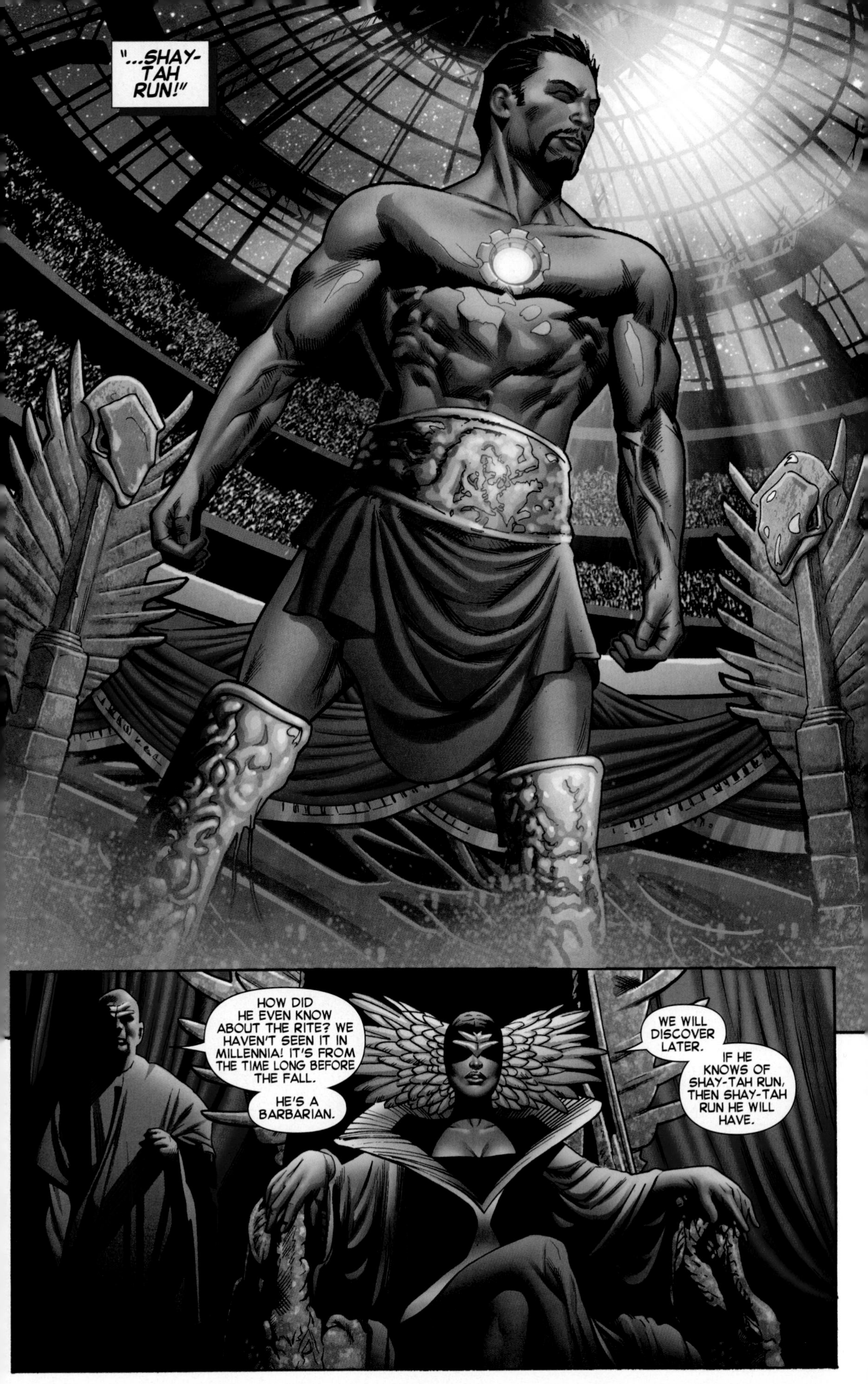
"...SHAY-TAH RUN!"
HOW DID HE EVEN KNOW ABOUT THE RITE? WE HAVEN'T SEEN IT IN MILLENNIA! IT'S FROM THE TIME LONG BEFORE THE FALL.
HE'S A BARBARIAN.
WE WILL DISCOVER LATER.
IF HE KNOWS OF SHAY-TAH RUN, THEN SHAY-TAH RUN HE WILL HAVE.

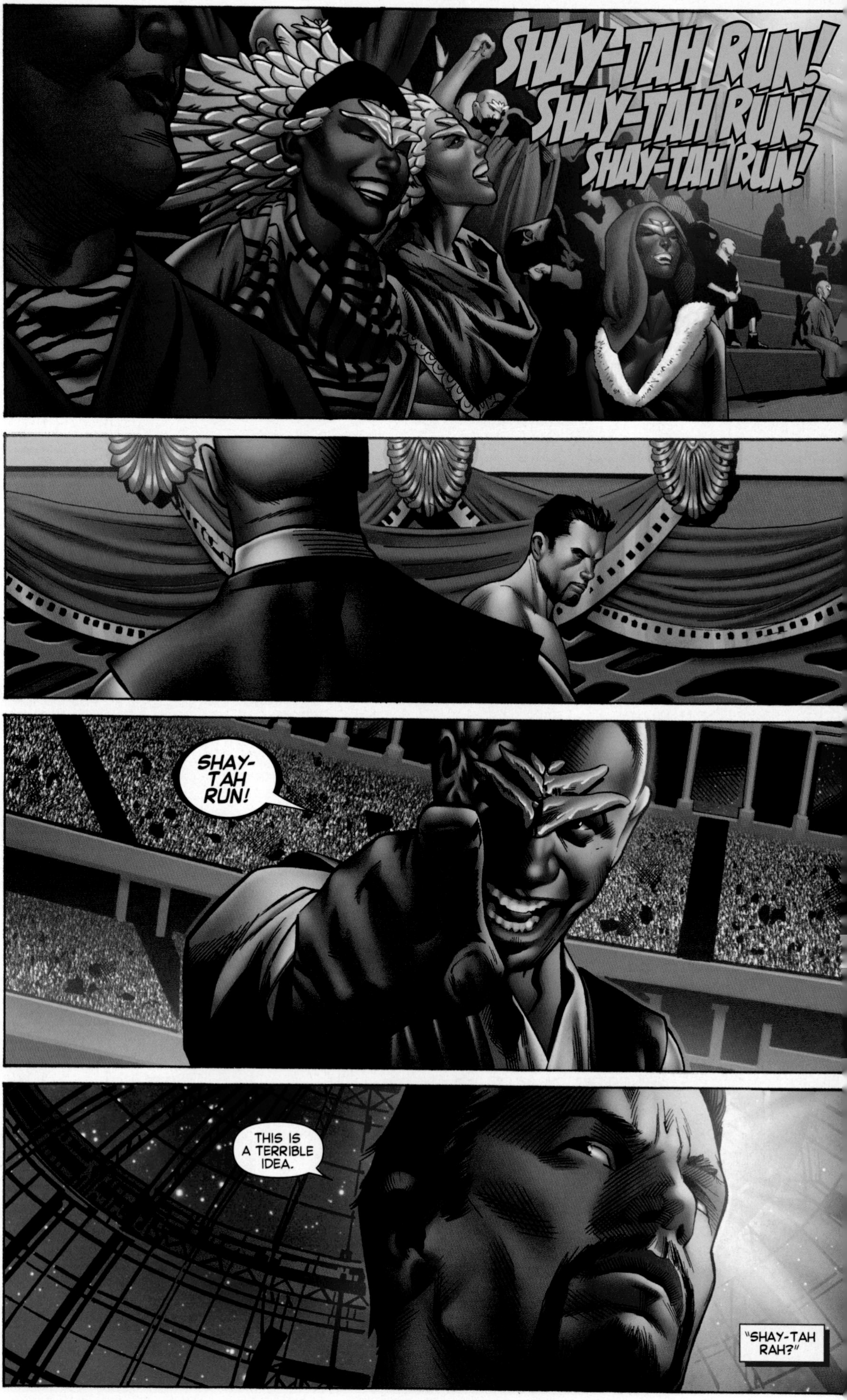
SHAY-TAH RUN!
SHAY-TAH RUN!
SHAY-TAH RUN!
SHAY-TAH RUN!
THIS IS A TERRIBLE IDEA.
"SHAY-TAH RAH?"

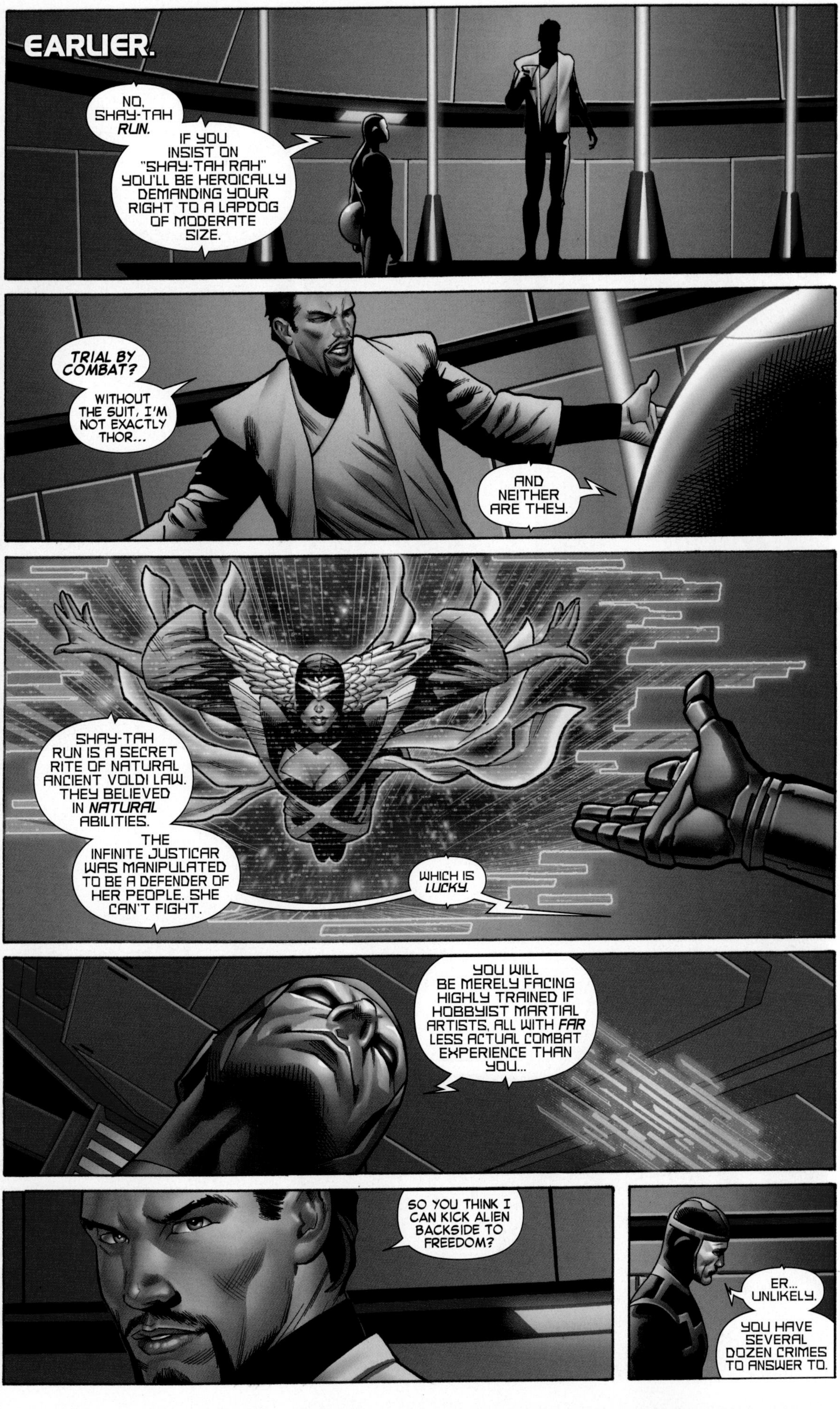
EARLIER.
NO, SHAY-TAH RUN.
IF YOU INSIST ON "SHAY-TAH RAH" YOU'LL BE HEROICALLY DEMANDING YOUR RIGHT TO A LAPDOG OF MODERATE SIZE.
TRIAL BY COMBAT?
WITHOUT THE SUIT, I'M NOT EXACTLY THOR...
AND NEITHER ARE THEY.
SHAY-TAH RUN IS A SECRET RITE OF NATURAL ANCIENT VOLDI LAW. THEY BELIEVED IN NATURAL ABILITIES.
THE INFINITE JUSTICAR WAS MANIPULATED TO BE A DEFENDER OF HER PEOPLE. SHE CAN'T FIGHT.
WHICH IS LUCKY.
YOU WILL BE MERELY FACING HIGHLY TRAINED IF HOBBYIST MARTIAL ARTISTS, ALL WITH FAR LESS ACTUAL COMBAT EXPERIENCE THAN YOU...
SO YOU THINK I CAN KICK ALIEN BACKSIDE TO FREEDOM?
ER... UNLIKELY.
YOU HAVE SEVERAL DOZEN CRIMES TO ANSWER TO.

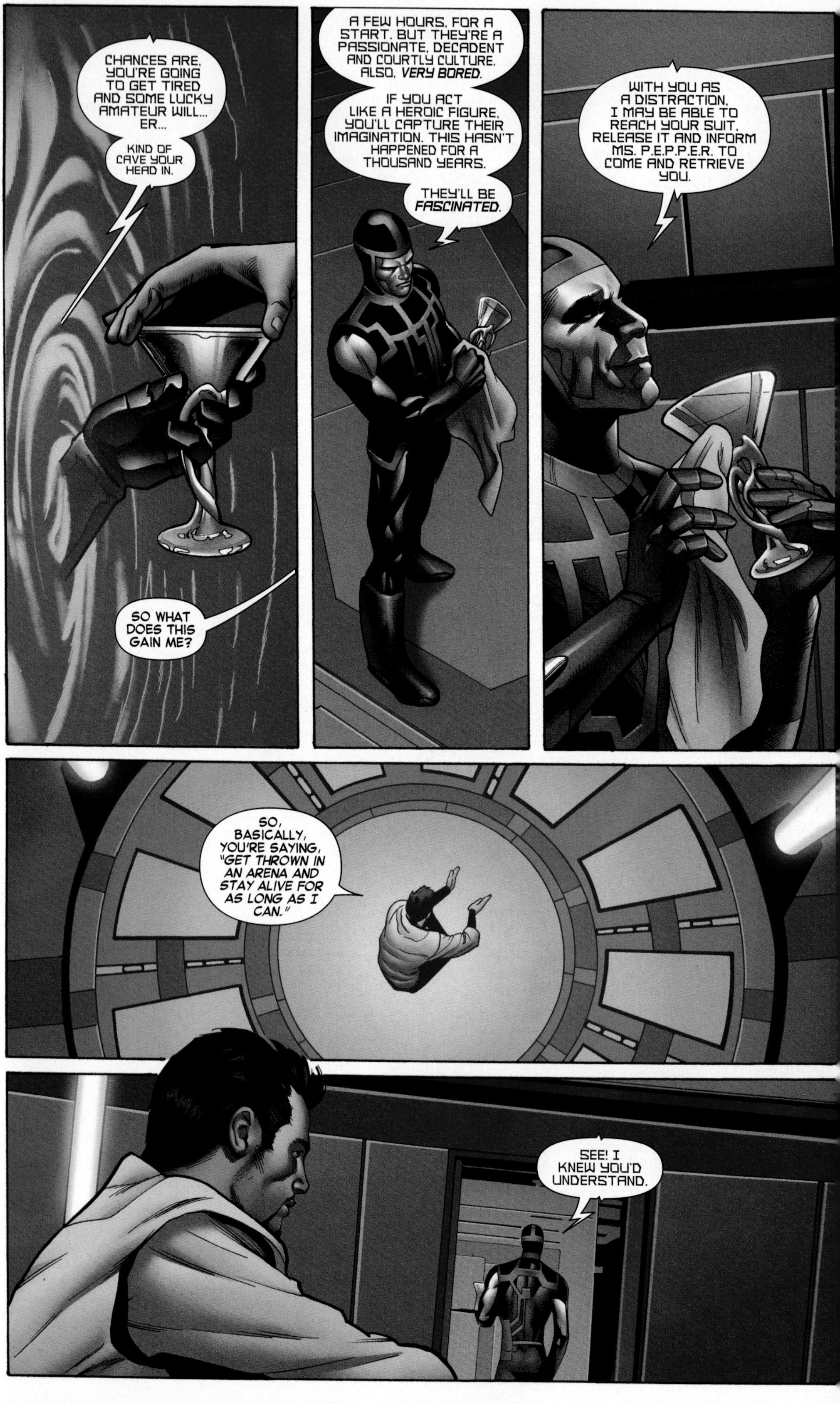
CHANCES ARE, YOU'RE GOING TO GET TIRED AND SOME LUCKY AMATEUR WILL... ER...
KIND OF CAVE YOUR HEAD IN.
SO WHAT DOES THIS GAIN ME?
A FEW HOURS, FOR A START. BUT THEY'RE A PASSIONATE, DECADENT AND COURTLY CULTURE. ALSO, VERY BORED.
IF YOU ACT LIKE A HEROIC FIGURE, YOU'LL CAPTURE THEIR IMAGINATION. THIS HASN'T HAPPENED FOR A THOUSAND YEARS.
THEY'LL BE FASCINATED.
WITH YOU AS A DISTRACTION, I MAY BE ABLE TO REACH YOUR SUIT, RELEASE IT AND INFORM MS. P.E.P.P.E.R. TO COME AND RETRIEVE YOU.
SO, BASICALLY, YOU'RE SAYING, "GET THROWN IN AN ARENA AND STAY ALIVE FOR AS LONG AS I CAN."
SEE! I KNEW YOU'D UNDERSTAND.

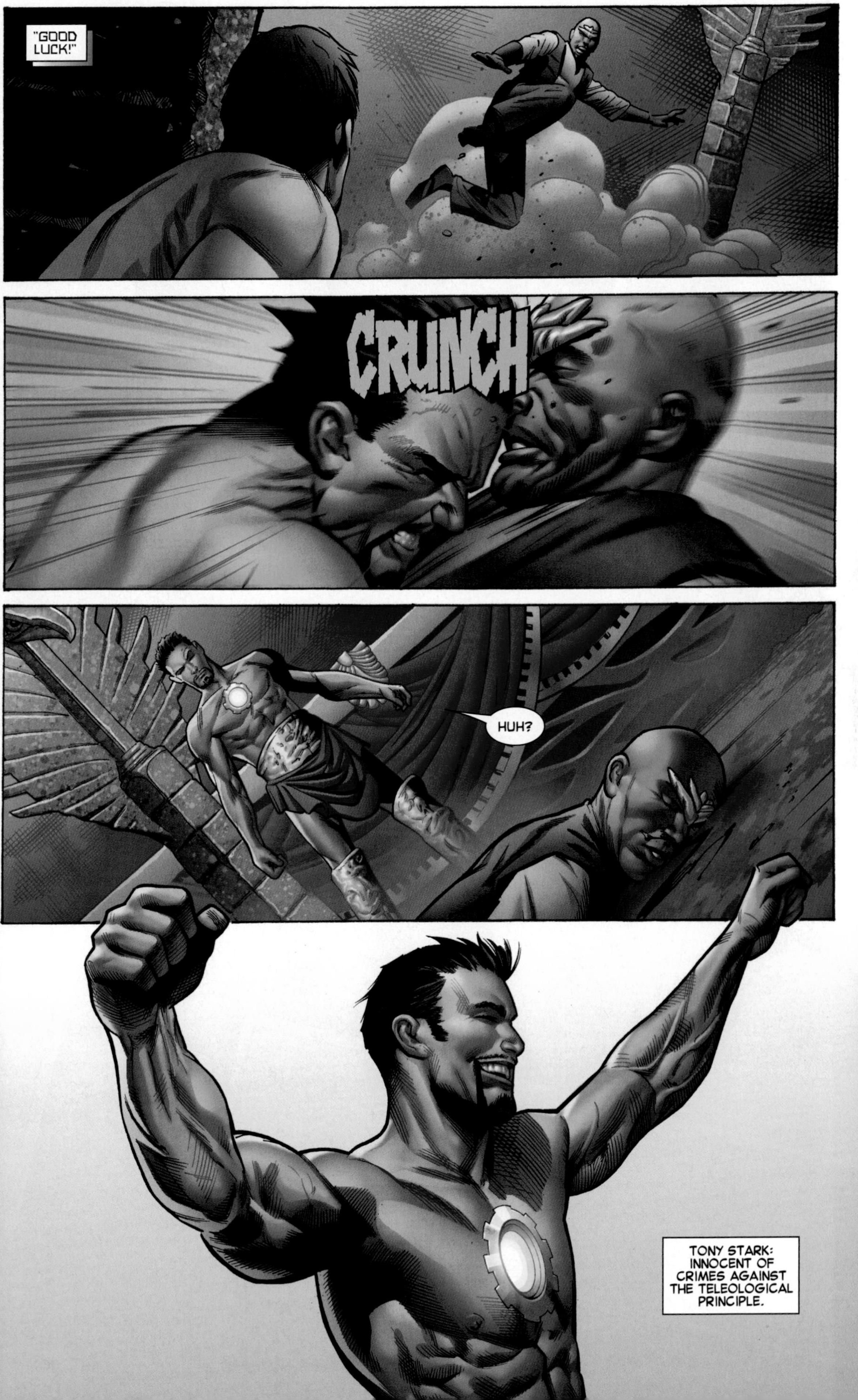
"GOOD LUCK!"
CRUNCH
HUH?
TONY STARK: INNOCENT OF CRIMES AGAINST THE TELEOLOGICAL PRINCIPLE.

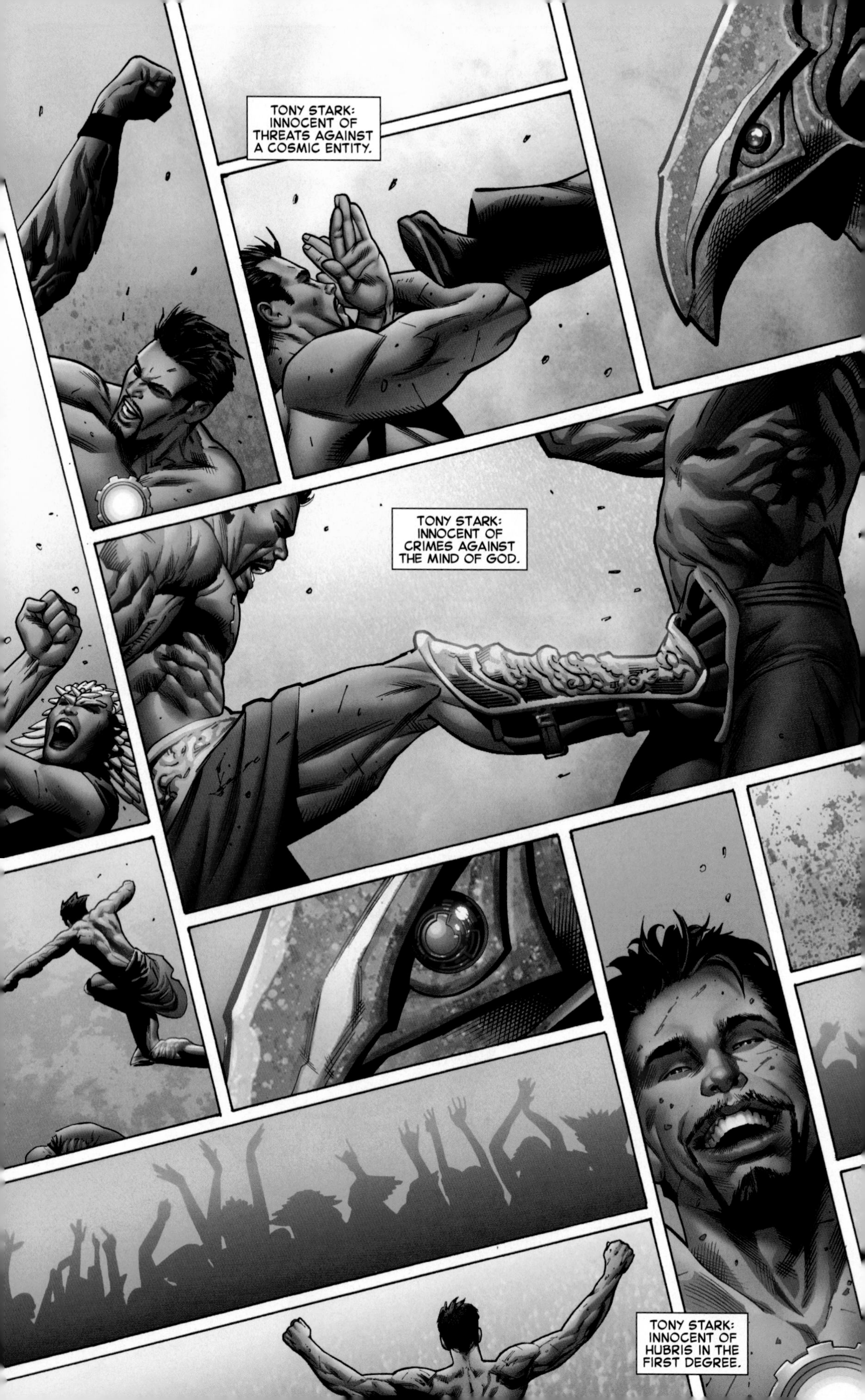
TONY STARK:
INNOCENT OF
THREATS AGAINST
A COSMIC ENTITY.
TONY STARK:
INNOCENT OF
CRIMES AGAINST
THE MIND OF GOD.
TONY STARK:
INNOCENT OF
HUBRIS IN THE
FIRST DEGREE.

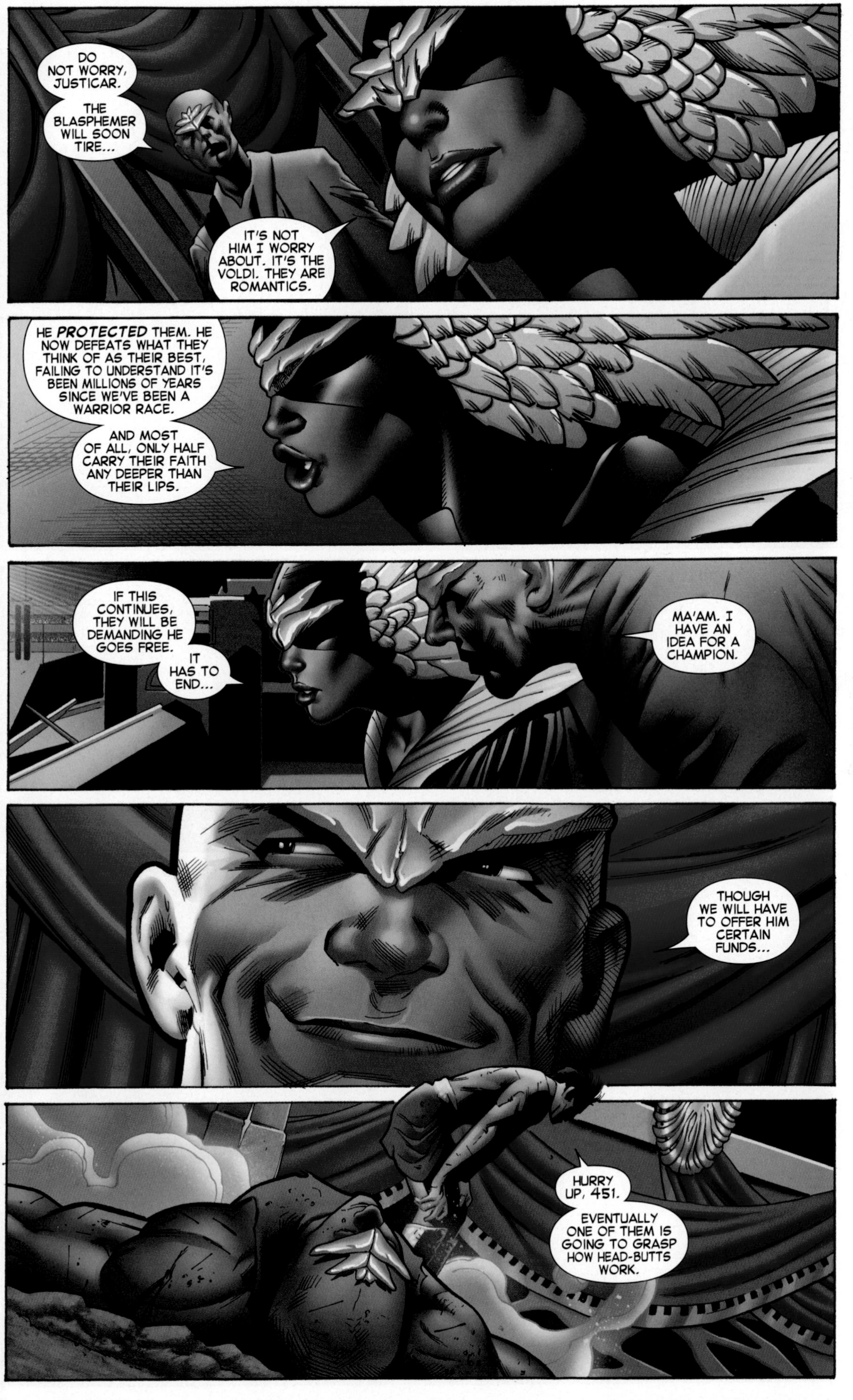
DO NOT WORRY, JUSTICAR.
THE BLASPHEMER WILL SOON TIRE...
IT'S NOT HIM I WORRY ABOUT. IT'S THE VOLDI. THEY ARE ROMANTICS.
HE PROTECTED THEM. HE NOW DEFEATS WHAT THEY THINK OF AS THEIR BEST, FAILING TO UNDERSTAND IT'S BEEN MILLIONS OF YEARS SINCE WE'VE BEEN A WARRIOR RACE.
AND MOST OF ALL, ONLY HALF CARRY THEIR FAITH ANY DEEPER THAN THEIR LIPS.
IF THIS CONTINUES, THEY WILL BE DEMANDING HE GOES FREE.
IT HAS TO END...
MA'AM. I HAVE AN IDEA FOR A CHAMPION.
THOUGH WE WILL HAVE TO OFFER HIM CERTAIN FUNDS...
HURRY UP, 451.
EVENTUALLY ONE OF THEM IS GOING TO GRASP HOW HEAD-BUTTS WORK.

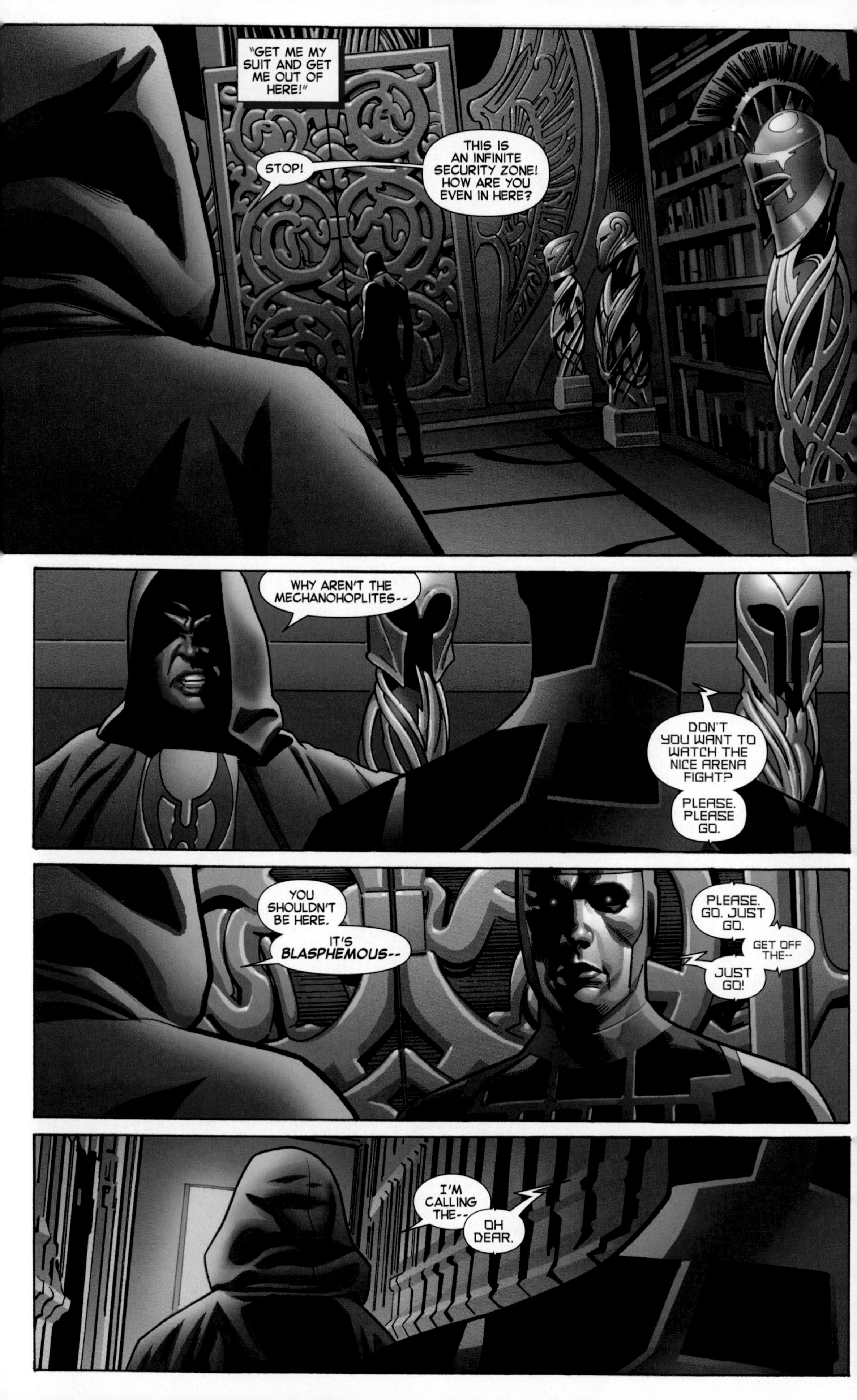
"GET ME MY SUIT AND GET ME OUT OF HERE!"
STOP!
THIS IS AN INFINITE SECURITY ZONE! HOW ARE YOU EVEN IN HERE?
WHY AREN'T THE MECHANOHOPLITES--
DON'T YOU WANT TO WATCH THE NICE ARENA FIGHT?
PLEASE. PLEASE GO.
YOU SHOULDN'T BE HERE.
IT'S BLASPHEMOUS--
PLEASE. GO. JUST GO.
GET OFF THE--
JUST GO!
I'M CALLING THE--
OH DEAR.

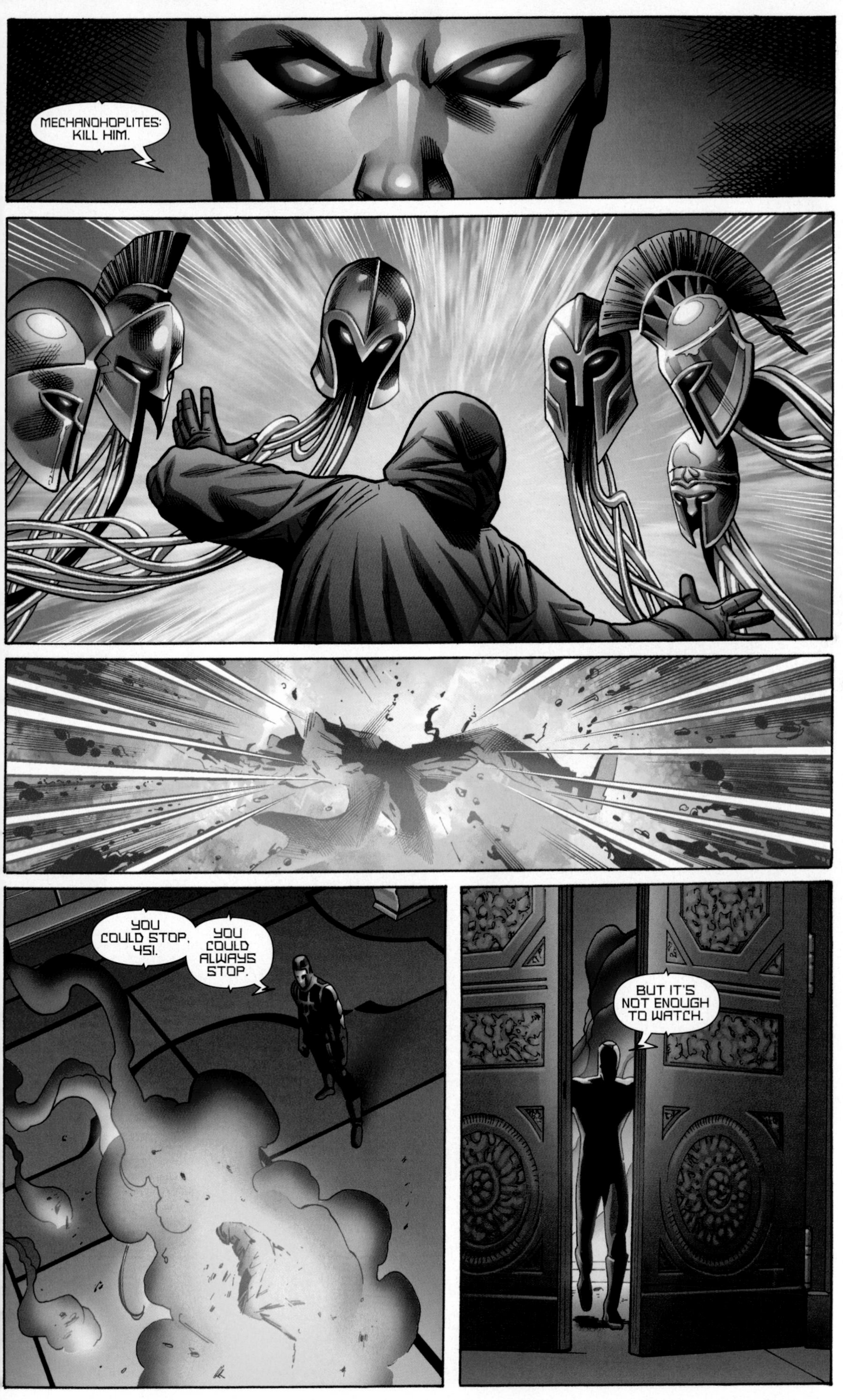
MECHANOHOPLITES: KILL HIM.
YOU COULD STOP, 451.
YOU COULD ALWAYS STOP.
BUT IT'S NOT ENOUGH TO WATCH.

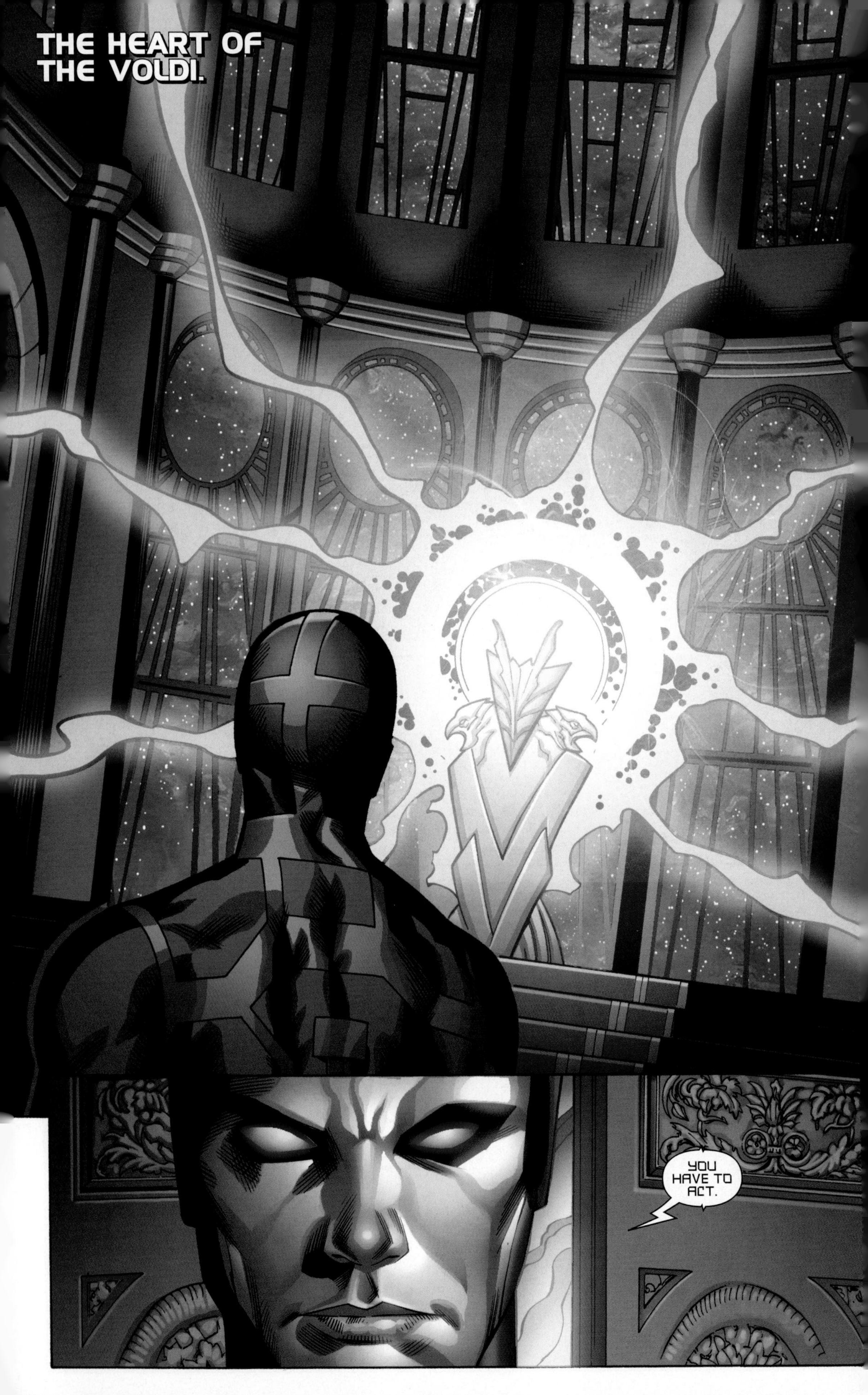
THE HEART OF THE VOLDI.
YOU HAVE TO ACT.

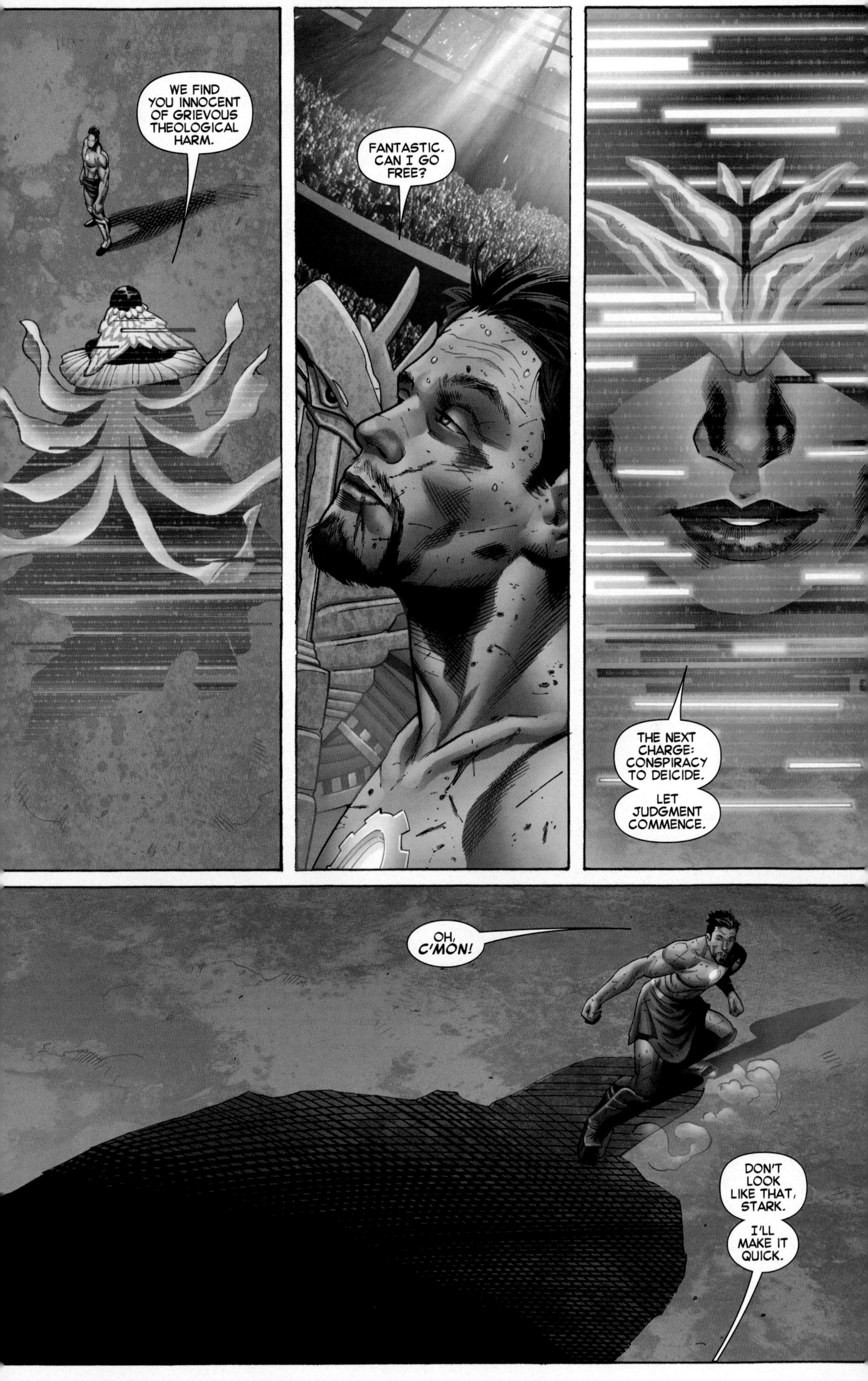
WE FIND YOU INNOCENT OF GRIEVOUS THEOLOGICAL HARM.
FANTASTIC. CAN I GO FREE?
THE NEXT CHARGE: CONSPIRACY TO DEICIDE.
LET JUDGMENT COMMENCE.
OH, C'MON!
DON'T LOOK LIKE THAT, STARK.
I'LL MAKE IT QUICK.

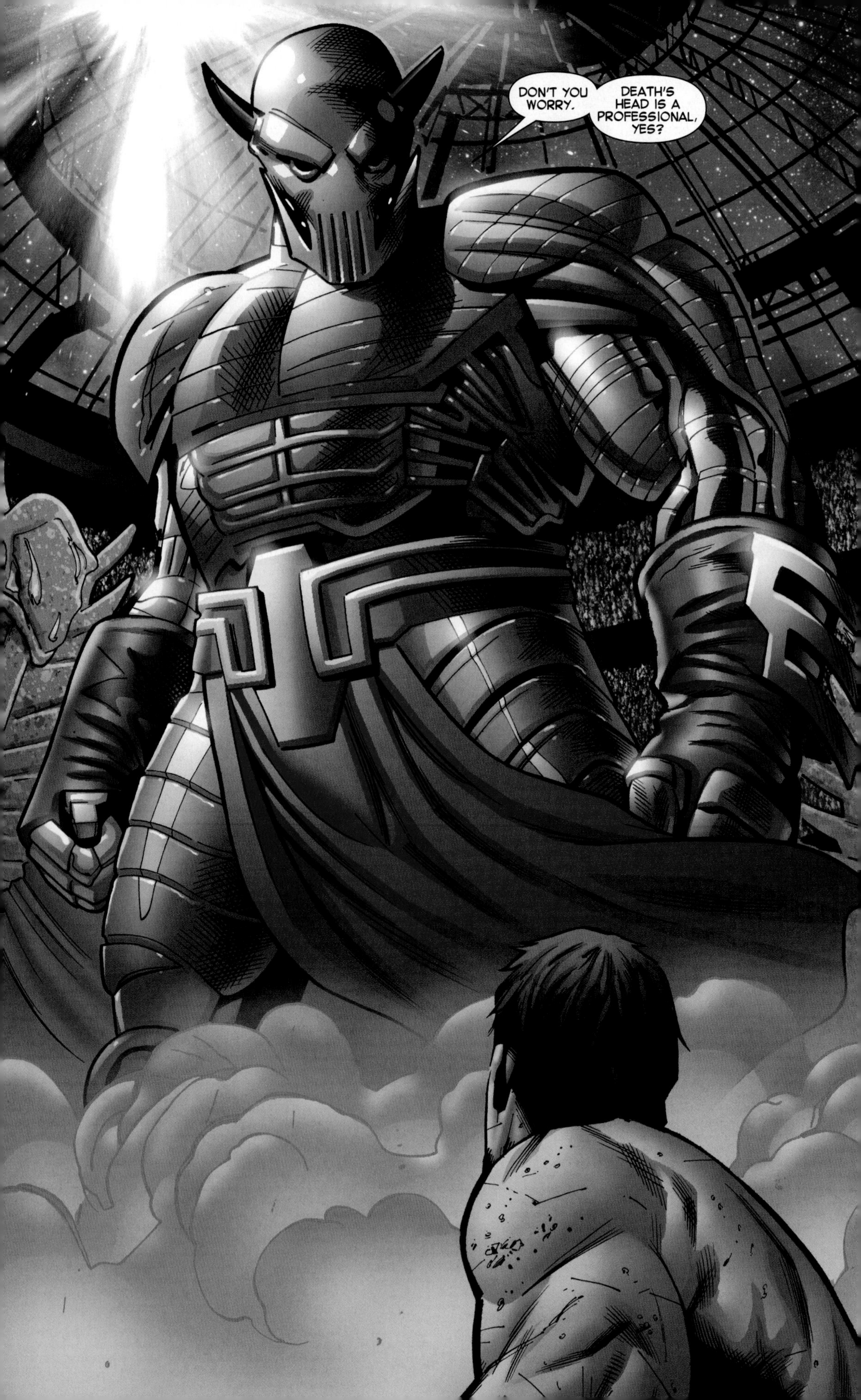
DON'T YOU WORRY.
DEATH'S HEAD IS A PROFESSIONAL, YES?

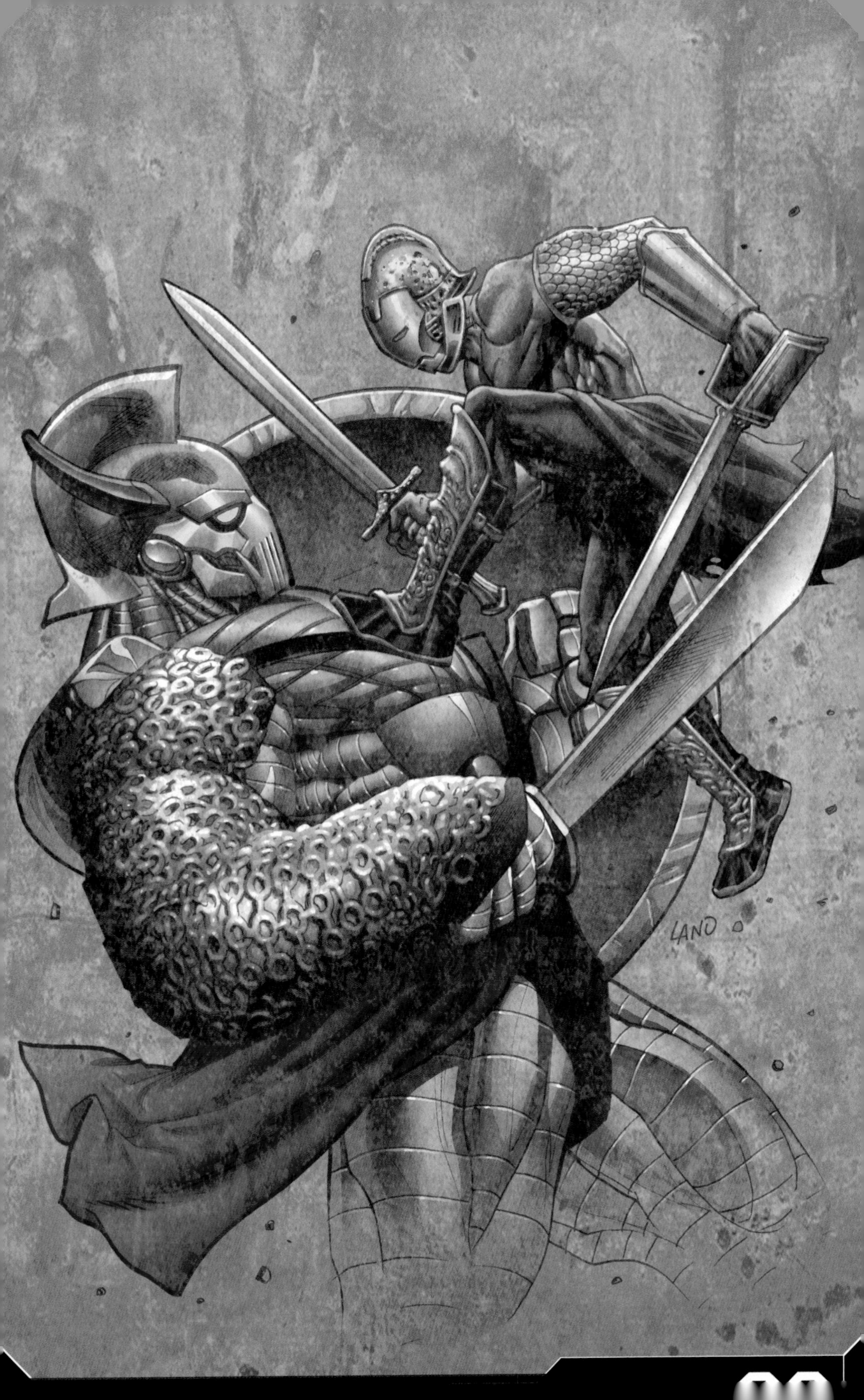
LAND

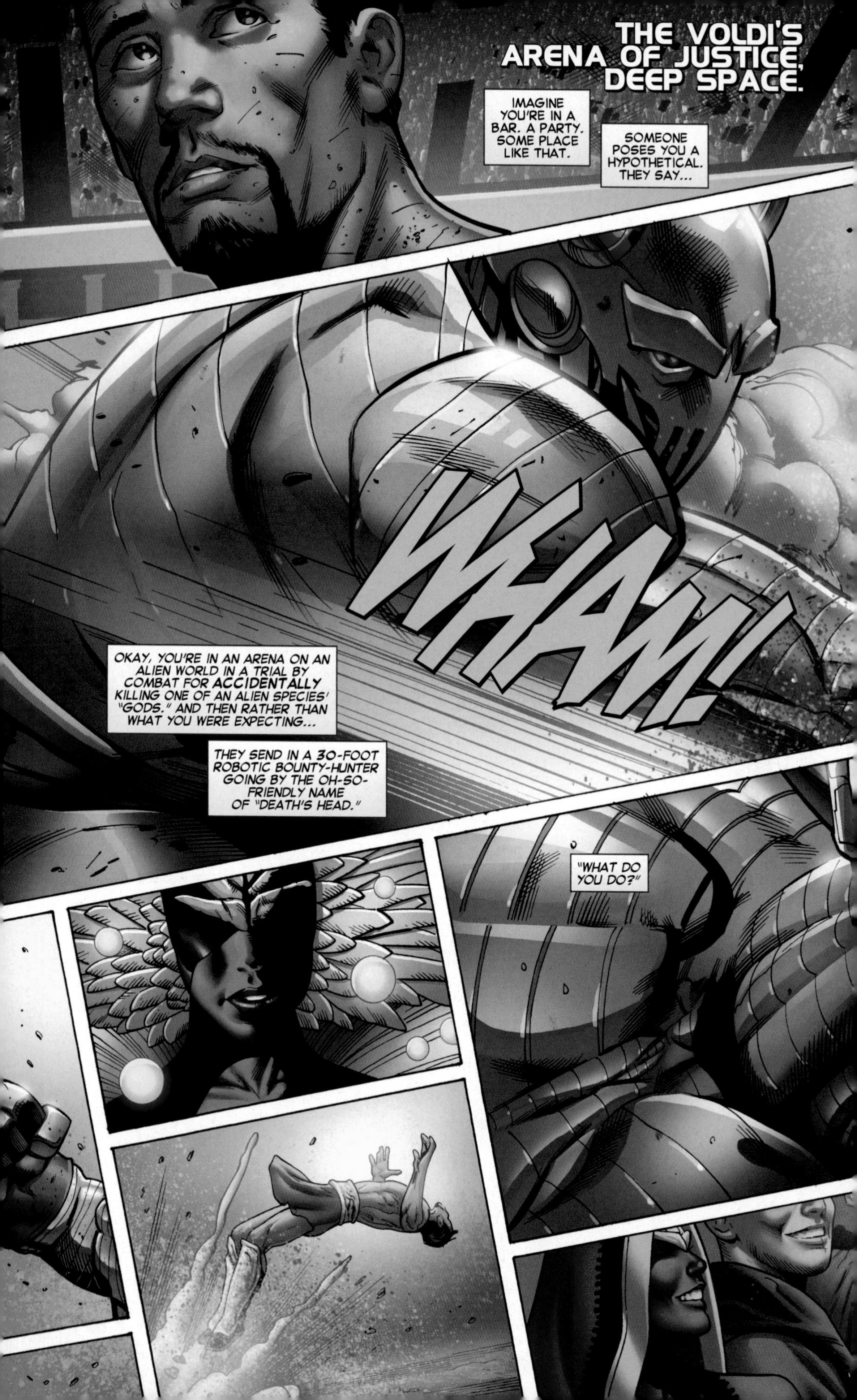

THE VOLDI'S ARENA OF JUSTICE, DEEP SPACE.
IMAGINE YOU'RE IN A BAR. A PARTY. SOME PLACE LIKE THAT.
SOMEONE POSES YOU A HYPOTHETICAL. THEY SAY...
WHAM!
OKAY, YOU'RE IN AN ARENA ON AN ALIEN WORLD IN A TRIAL BY COMBAT FOR ACCIDENTALLY KILLING ONE OF AN ALIEN SPECIES' "GODS." AND THEN RATHER THAN WHAT YOU WERE EXPECTING...
THEY SEND IN A 30-FOOT ROBOTIC BOUNTY-HUNTER GOING BY THE OH-SO-FRIENDLY NAME OF "DEATH'S HEAD."
"WHAT DO YOU DO?"

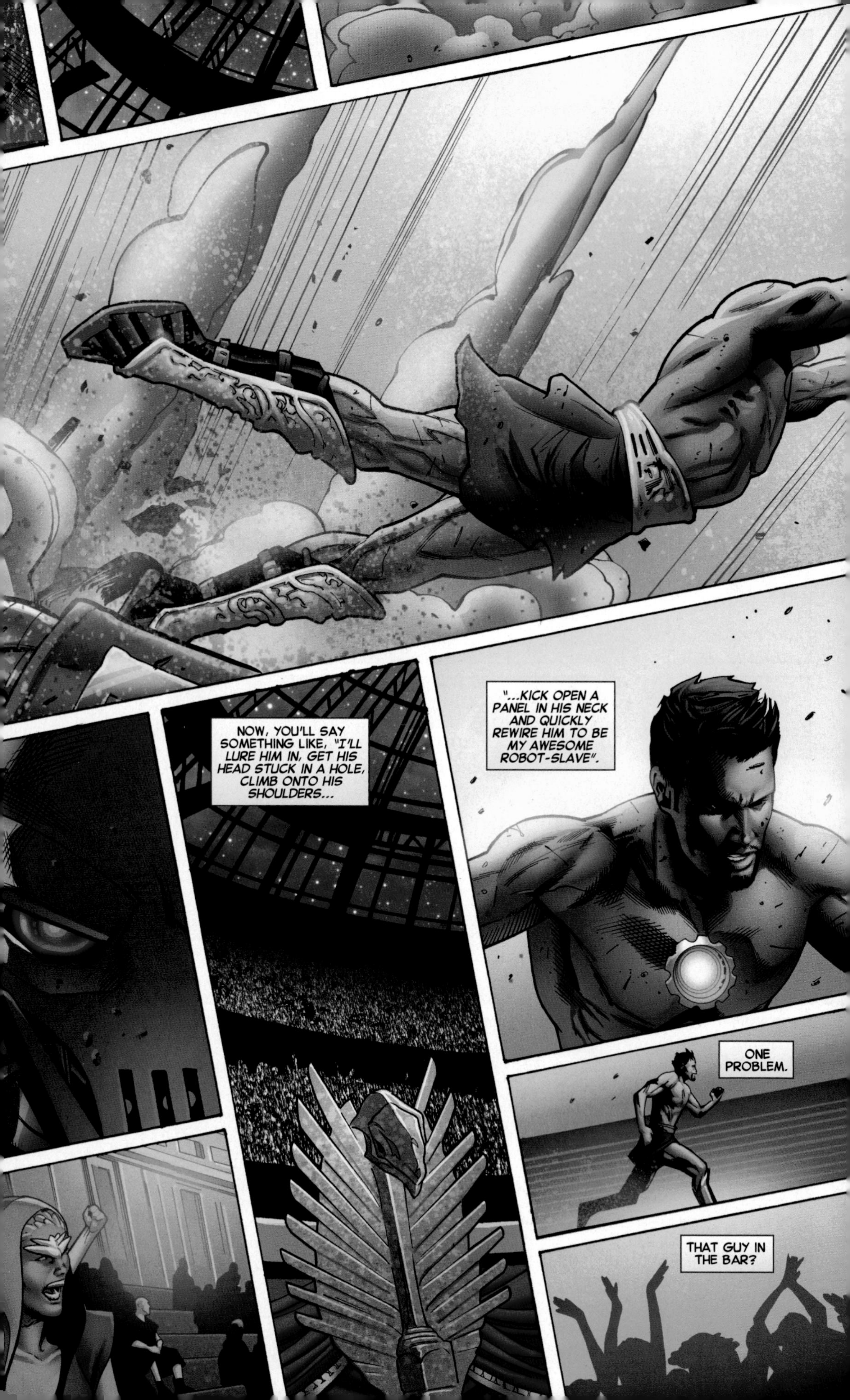

NOW, YOU'LL SAY SOMETHING LIKE, "I'LL LURE HIM IN, GET HIS HEAD STUCK IN A HOLE, CLIMB ONTO HIS SHOULDERS...
"...KICK OPEN A PANEL IN HIS NECK AND QUICKLY REWIRE HIM TO BE MY AWESOME ROBOT-SLAVE".
ONE PROBLEM.
THAT GUY IN THE BAR?

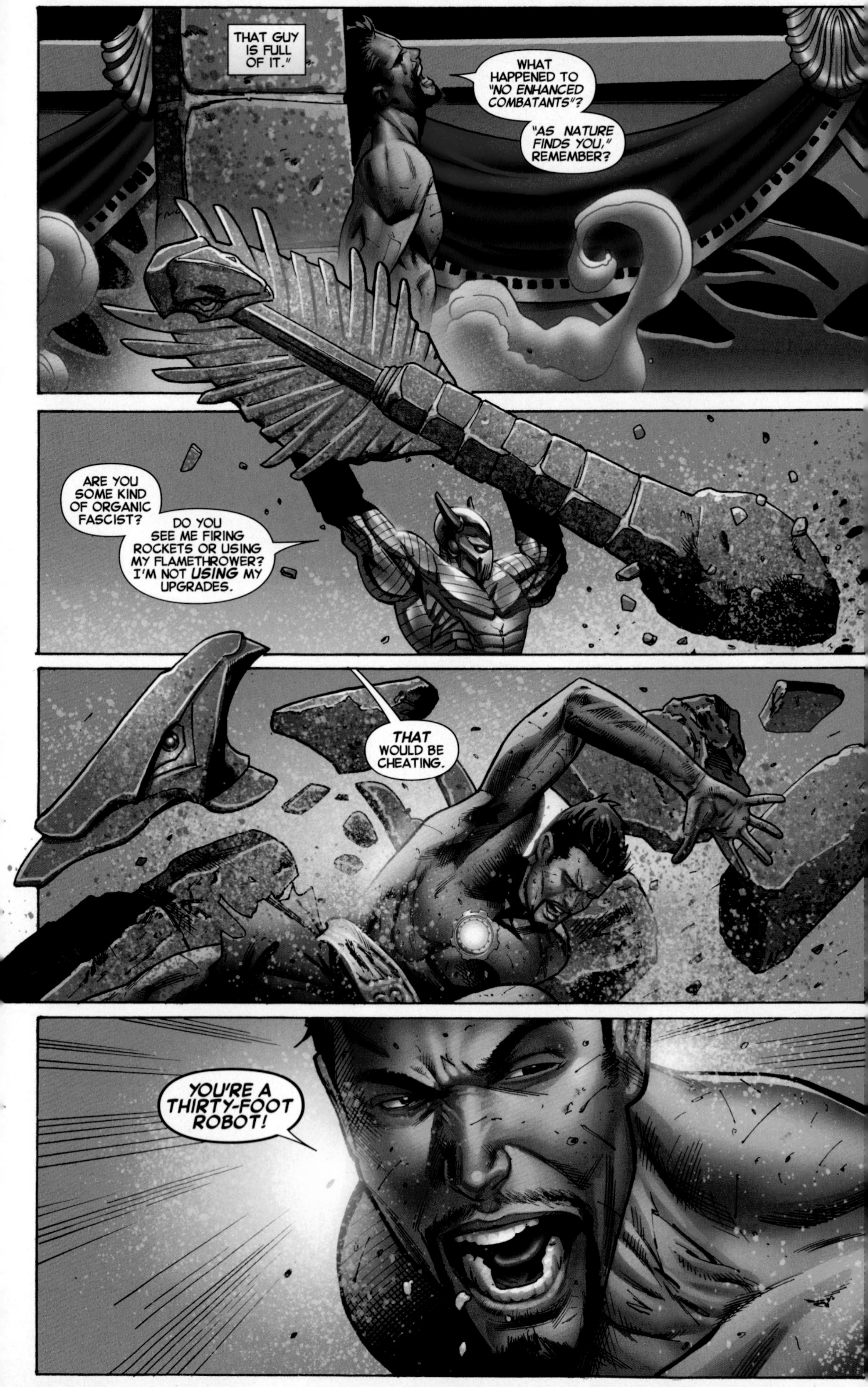
THAT GUY IS FULL OF IT."
WHAT HAPPENED TO "NO ENHANCED COMBATANTS"?
"AS NATURE FINDS YOU," REMEMBER?
ARE YOU SOME KIND OF ORGANIC FASCIST?
DO YOU SEE ME FIRING ROCKETS OR USING MY FLAMETHROWER? I'M NOT USING MY UPGRADES.
THAT WOULD BE CHEATING.
YOU'RE A THIRTY-FOOT ROBOT!

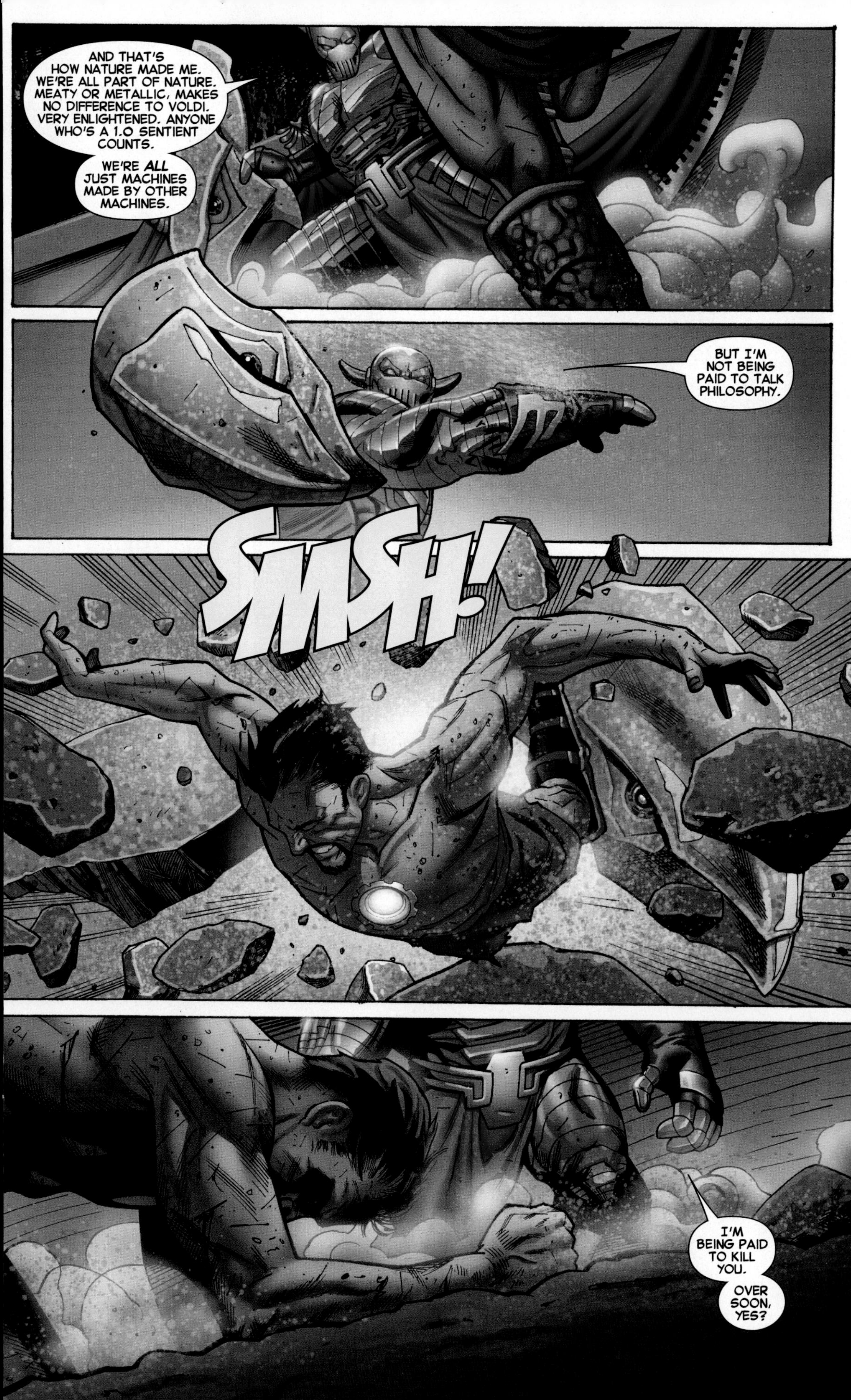
AND THAT'S HOW NATURE MADE ME. WE'RE ALL PART OF NATURE. MEATY OR METALLIC, MAKES NO DIFFERENCE TO VOLDI. VERY ENLIGHTENED. ANYONE WHO'S A 1.0 SENTIENT COUNTS.
WE'RE *ALL* JUST MACHINES MADE BY OTHER MACHINES.
BUT I'M NOT BEING PAID TO TALK PHILOSOPHY.
SMSH!
I'M BEING PAID TO KILL YOU.
OVER SOON, YES?

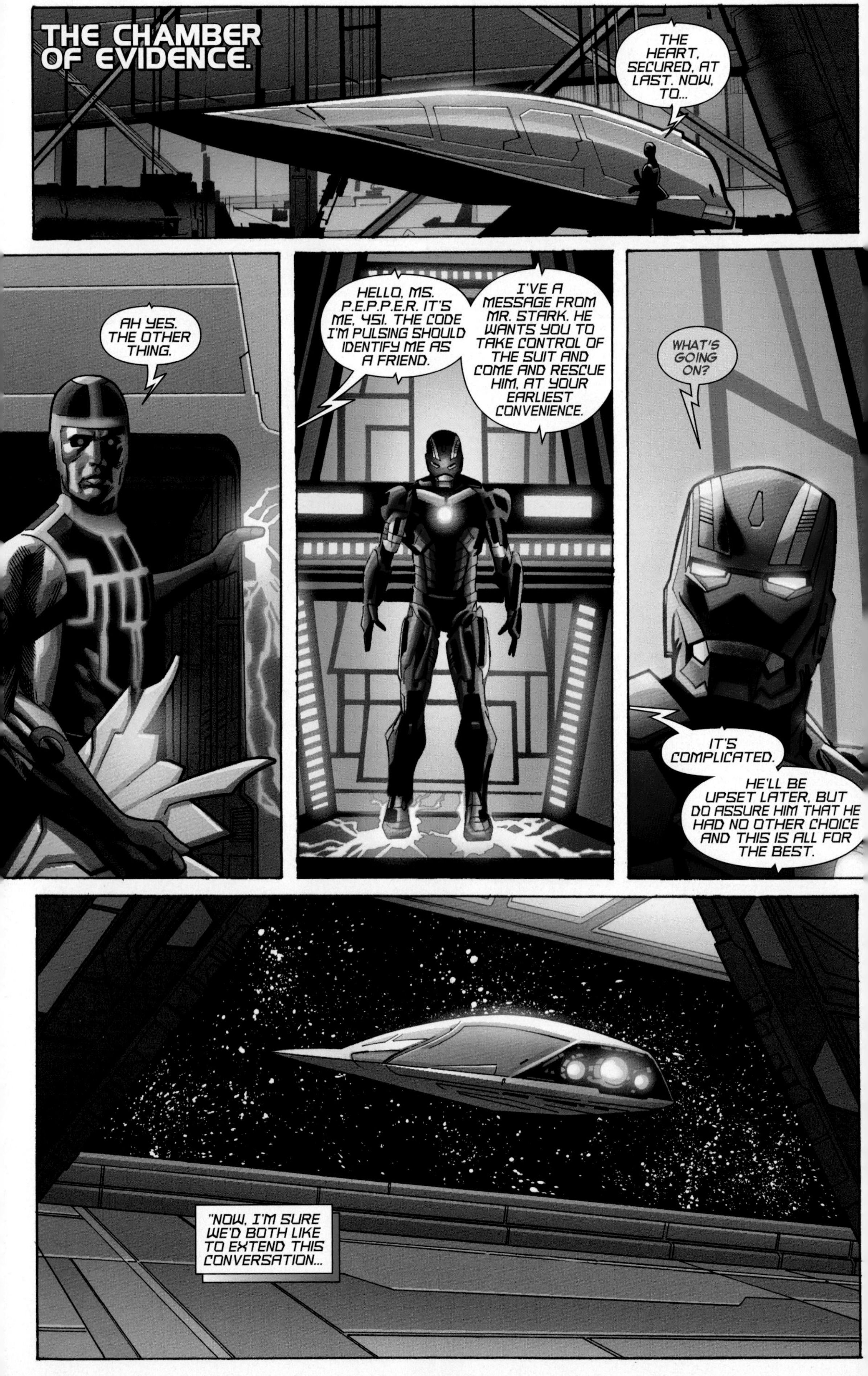
THE CHAMBER OF EVIDENCE.
THE HEART, SECURED, AT LAST. NOW, TO...
AH YES. THE OTHER THING.
HELLO, MS. P.E.P.P.E.R. IT'S ME, 451. THE CODE I'M PULSING SHOULD IDENTIFY ME AS A FRIEND.
I'VE A MESSAGE FROM MR. STARK. HE WANTS YOU TO TAKE CONTROL OF THE SUIT AND COME AND RESCUE HIM, AT YOUR EARLIEST CONVENIENCE.
WHAT'S GOING ON?
IT'S COMPLICATED.
HE'LL BE UPSET LATER, BUT DO ASSURE HIM THAT HE HAD NO OTHER CHOICE AND THIS IS ALL FOR THE BEST.
"NOW, I'M SURE WE'D BOTH LIKE TO EXTEND THIS CONVERSATION...

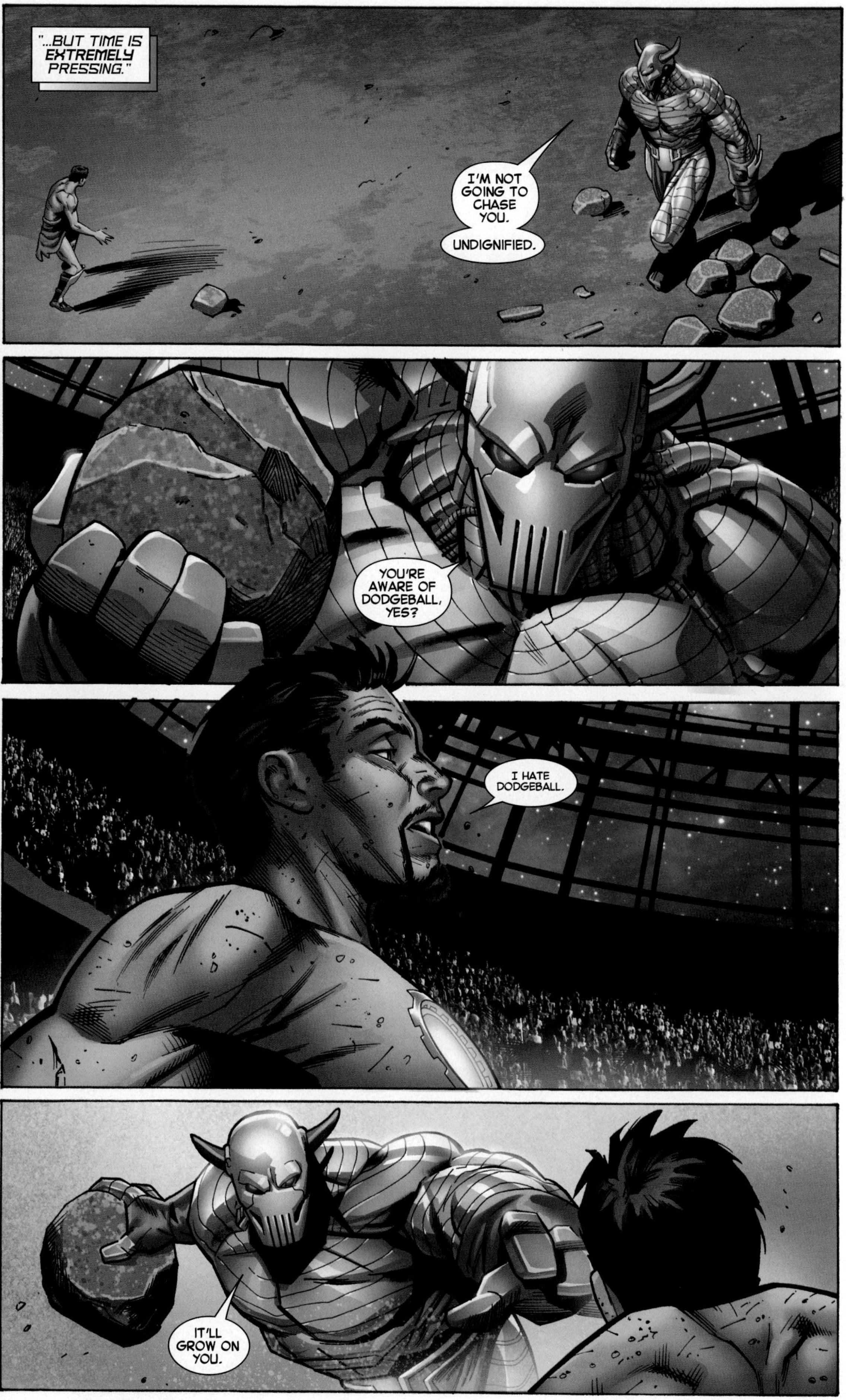
"...BUT TIME IS EXTREMELY PRESSING."
I'M NOT GOING TO CHASE YOU.
UNDIGNIFIED.
YOU'RE AWARE OF DODGEBALL, YES?
I HATE DODGEBALL.
IT'LL GROW ON YOU.

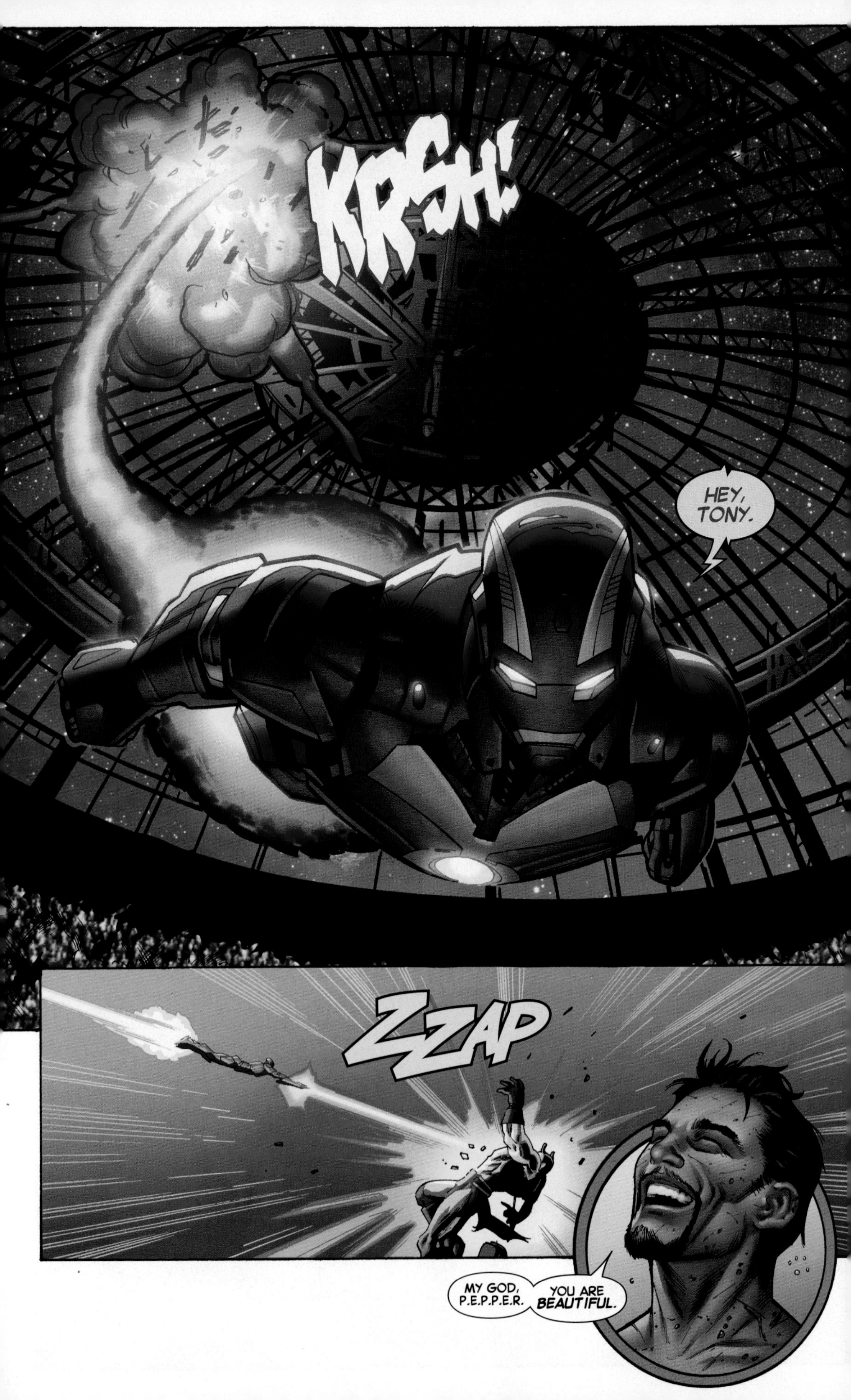
KRSH!
HEY, TONY.
ZZAP
MY GOD, P.E.P.P.E.R.
YOU ARE BEAUTIFUL.

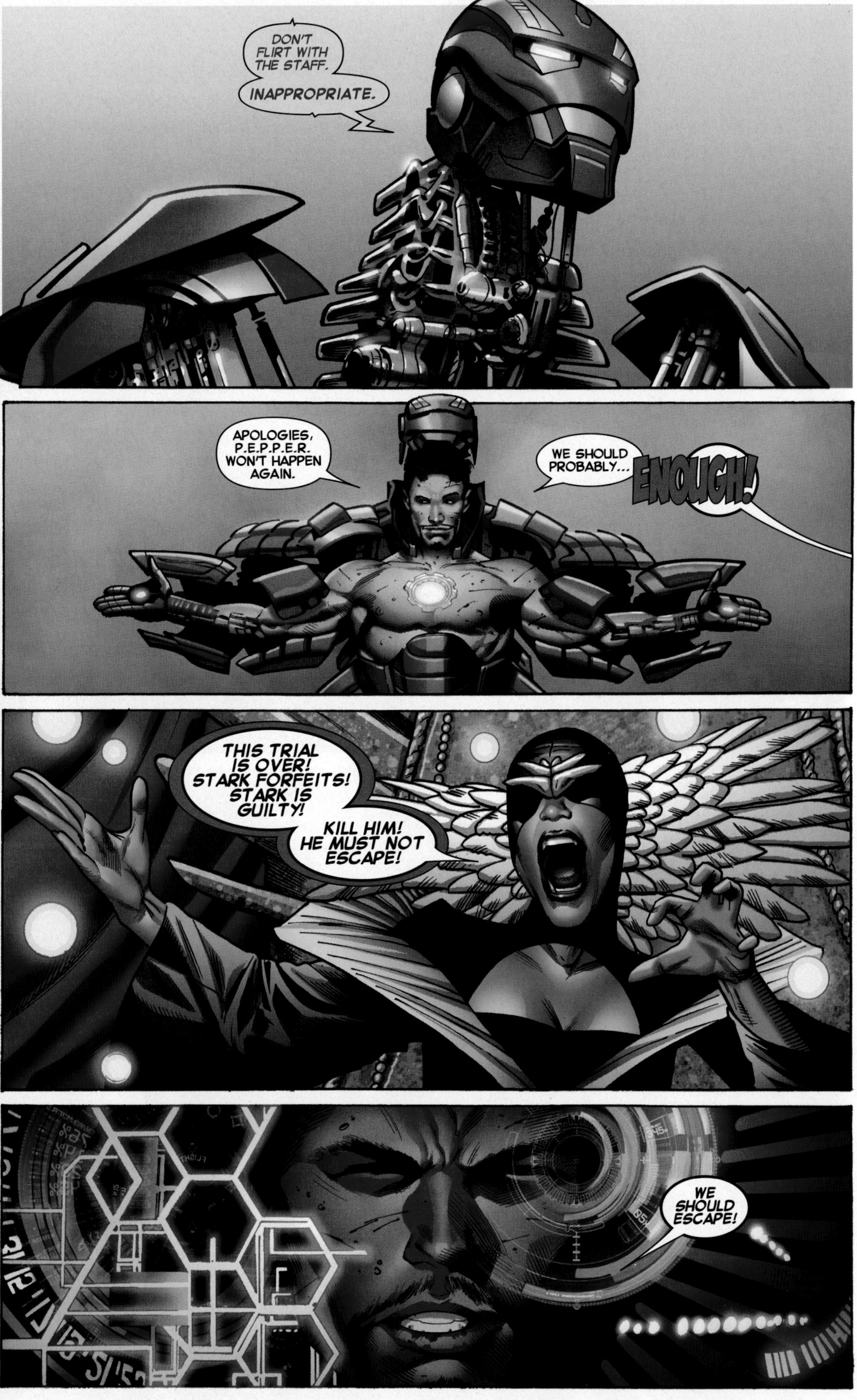
DON'T FLIRT WITH THE STAFF.
INAPPROPRIATE.
APOLOGIES, P.E.P.P.E.R. WON'T HAPPEN AGAIN.
WE SHOULD PROBABLY...
ENOUGH!
THIS TRIAL IS OVER! STARK FORFEITS! STARK IS GUILTY!
KILL HIM! HE MUST NOT ESCAPE!
WE SHOULD ESCAPE!

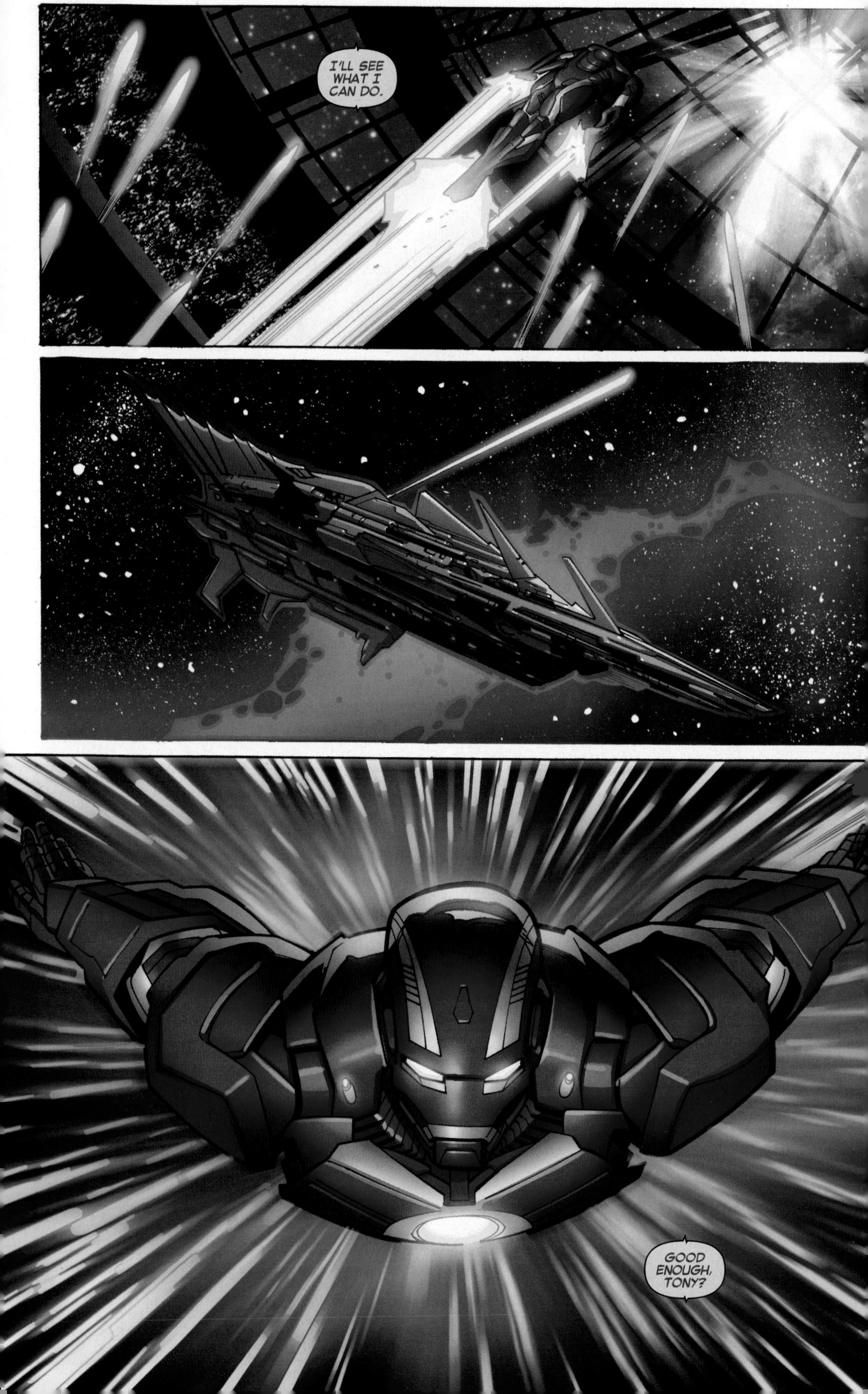
I'LL SEE WHAT I CAN DO.
GOOD ENOUGH, TONY?

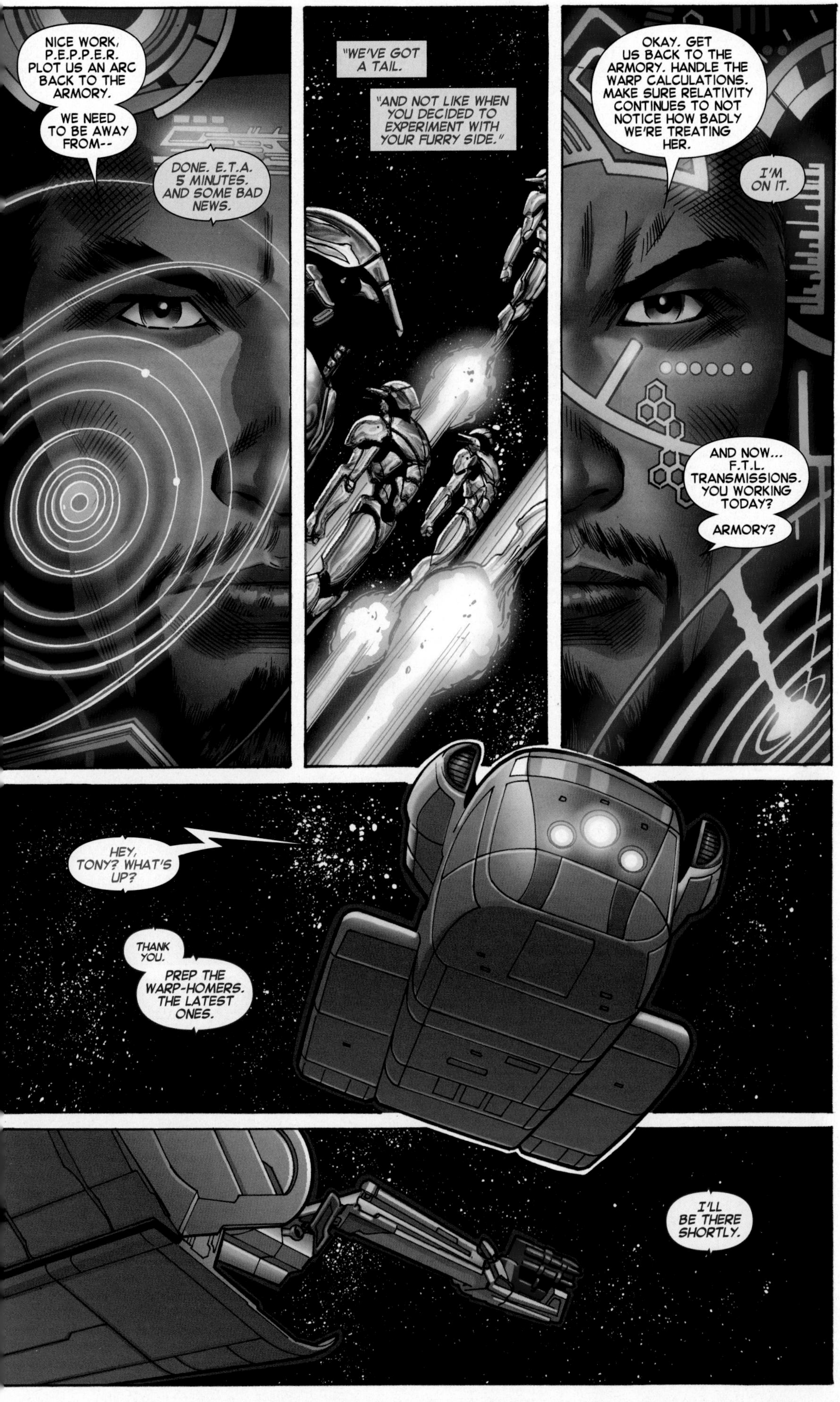
NICE WORK, P.E.P.P.E.R. PLOT US AN ARC BACK TO THE ARMORY.
WE NEED TO BE AWAY FROM--
DONE. E.T.A. 5 MINUTES. AND SOME BAD NEWS.
"WE'VE GOT A TAIL.
"AND NOT LIKE WHEN YOU DECIDED TO EXPERIMENT WITH YOUR FURRY SIDE."
OKAY. GET US BACK TO THE ARMORY. HANDLE THE WARP CALCULATIONS. MAKE SURE RELATIVITY CONTINUES TO NOT NOTICE HOW BADLY WE'RE TREATING HER.
I'M ON IT.
AND NOW... F.T.L. TRANSMISSIONS. YOU WORKING TODAY?
ARMORY?
HEY, TONY? WHAT'S UP?
THANK YOU.
PREP THE WARP-HOMERS. THE LATEST ONES.
I'LL BE THERE SHORTLY.

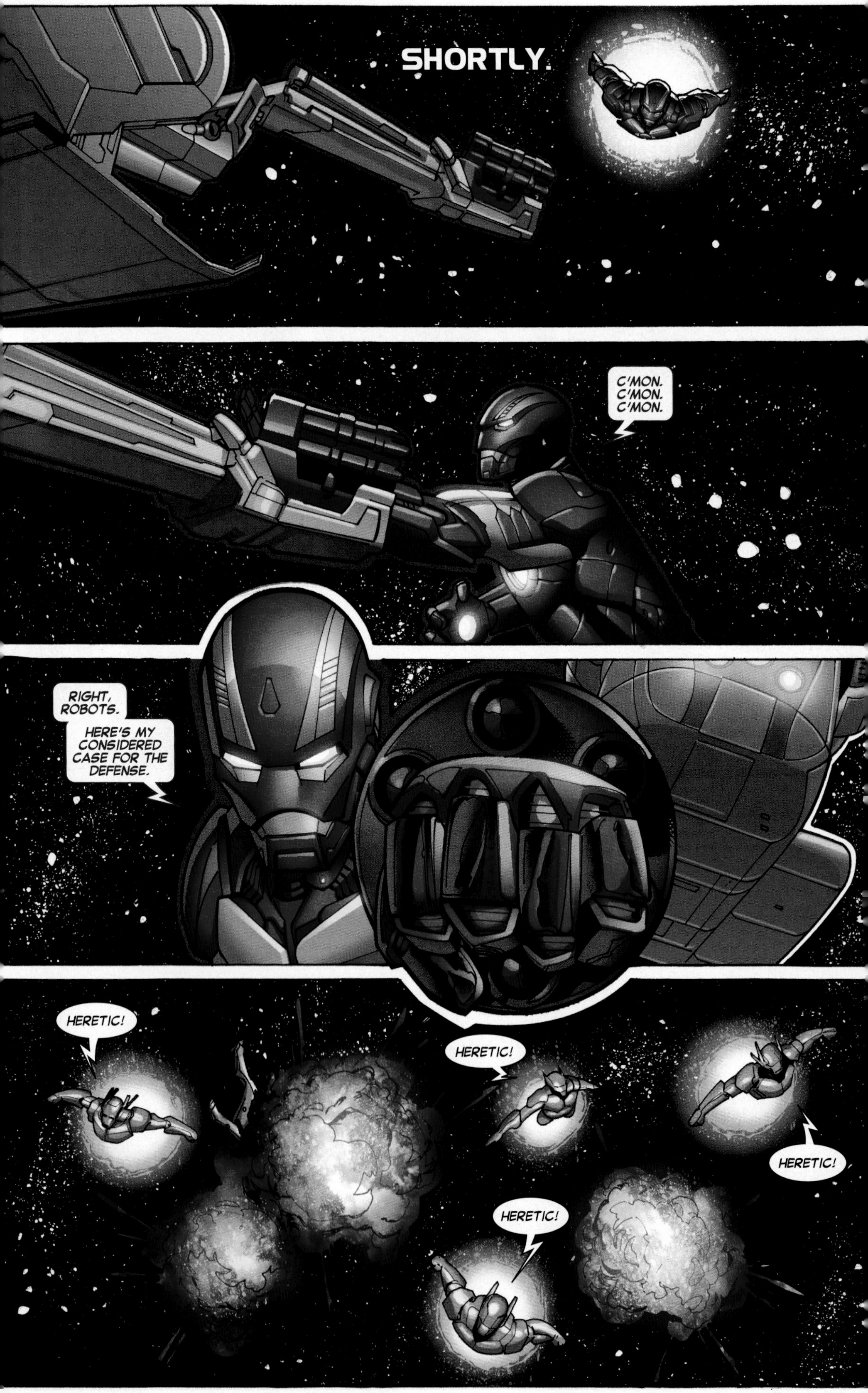
SHORTLY.
C'MON. C'MON. C'MON.
RIGHT, ROBOTS.
HERE'S MY CONSIDERED CASE FOR THE DEFENSE.
HERETIC!
HERETIC!
HERETIC!
HERETIC!

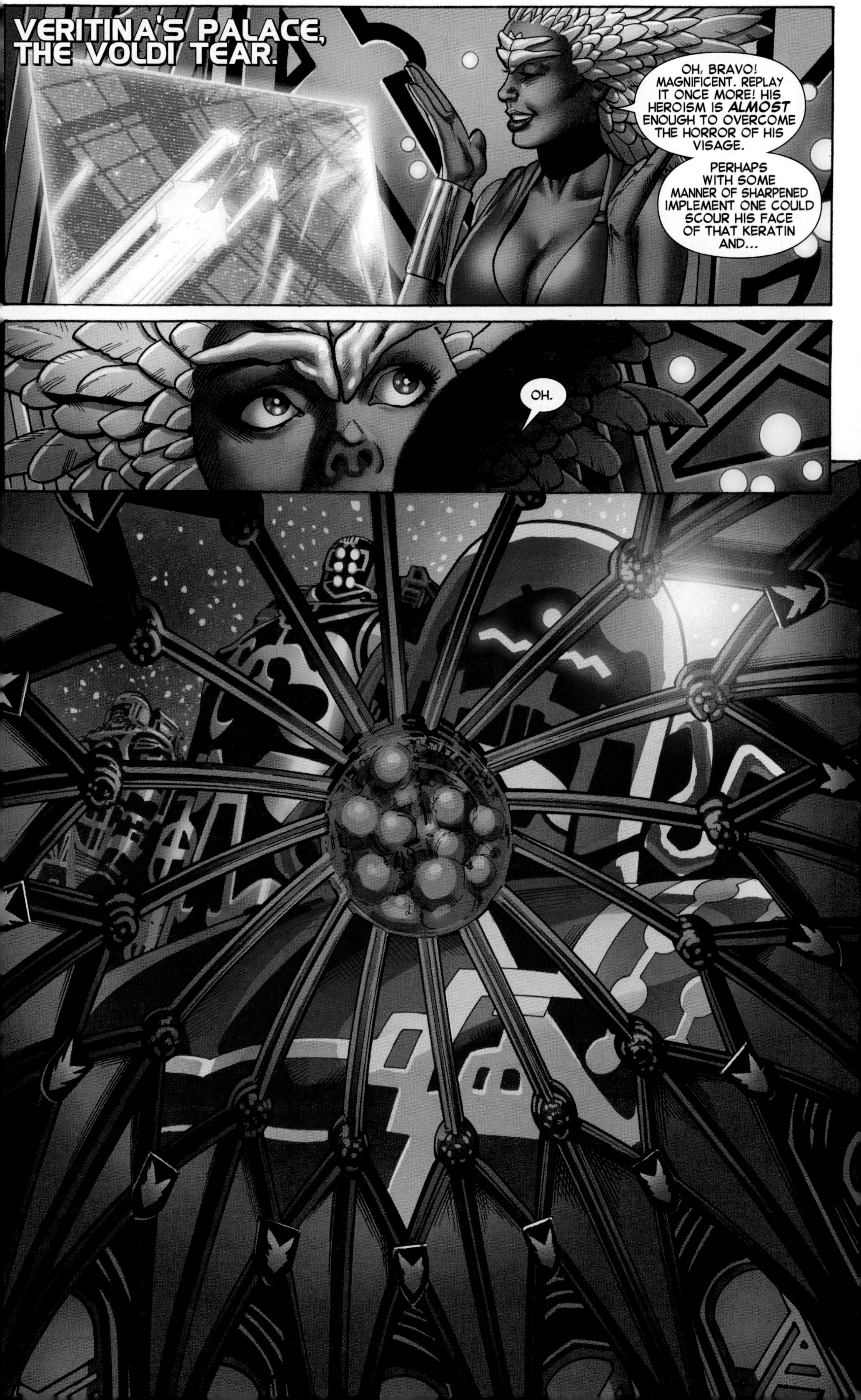
VERITINA'S PALACE, THE VOLDI TEAR.
OH, BRAVO! MAGNIFICENT. REPLAY IT ONCE MORE! HIS HEROISM IS ALMOST ENOUGH TO OVERCOME THE HORROR OF HIS VISAGE.
PERHAPS WITH SOME MANNER OF SHARPENED IMPLEMENT ONE COULD SCOUR HIS FACE OF THAT KERATIN AND...
OH.

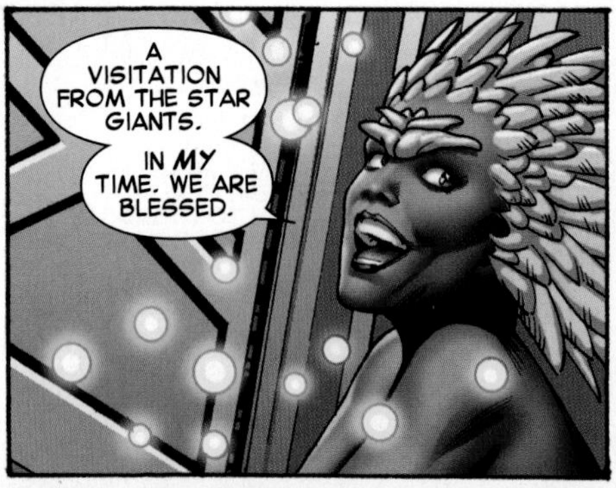
A VISITATION FROM THE STAR GIANTS.
IN MY TIME. WE ARE BLESSED.

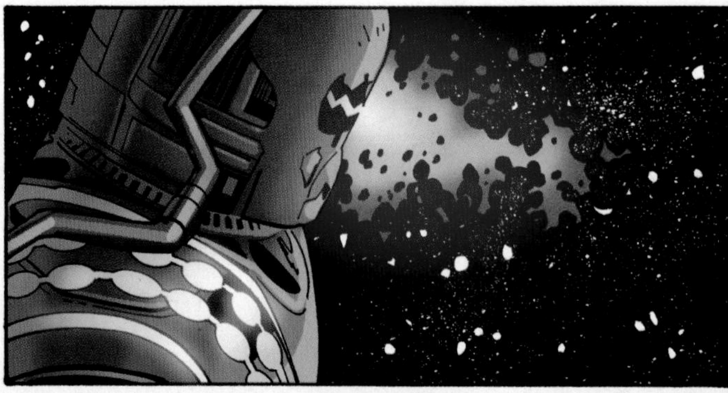

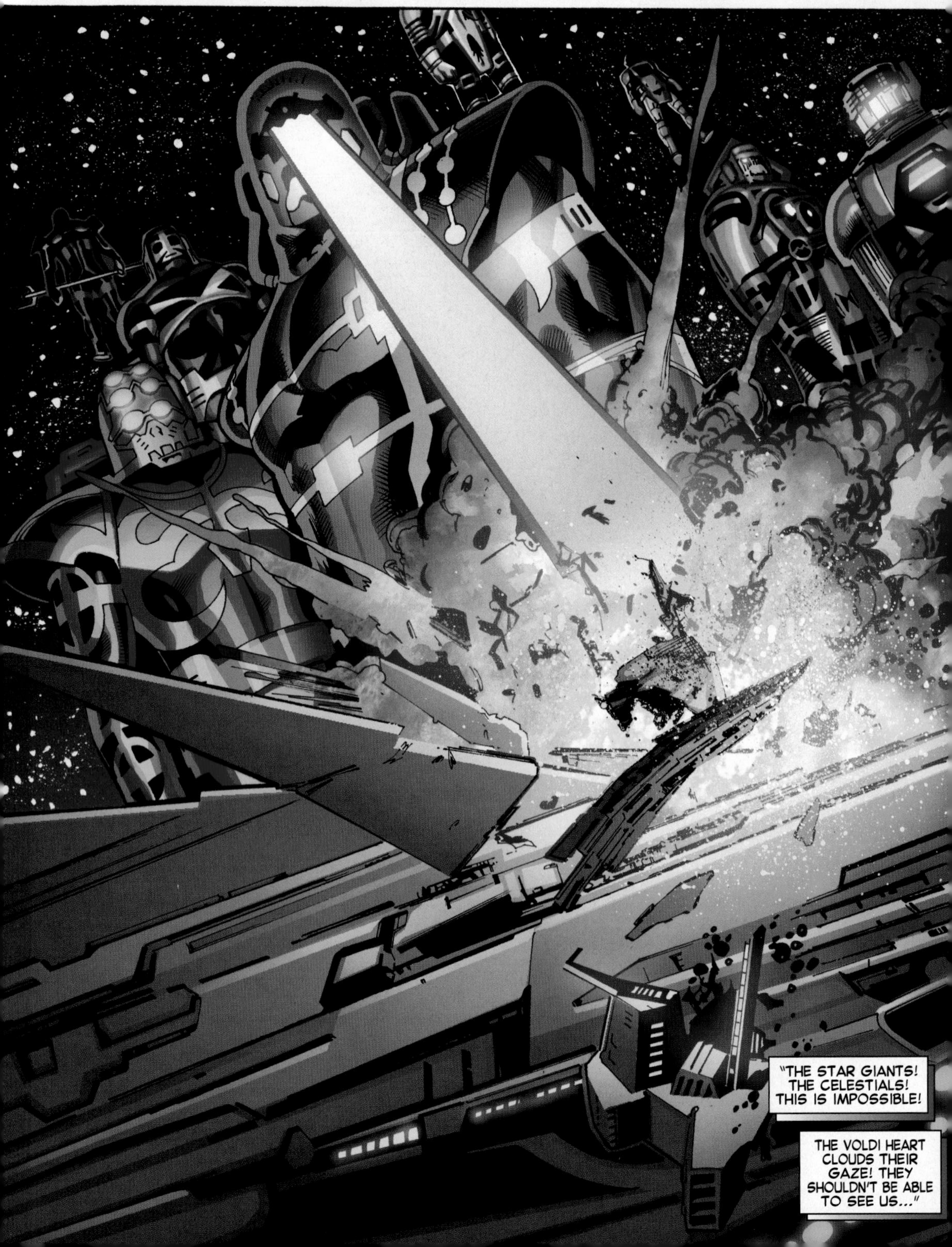
"THE STAR GIANTS! THE CELESTIALS! THIS IS IMPOSSIBLE!
THE VOLDI HEART CLOUDS THEIR GAZE! THEY SHOULDN'T BE ABLE TO SEE US..."

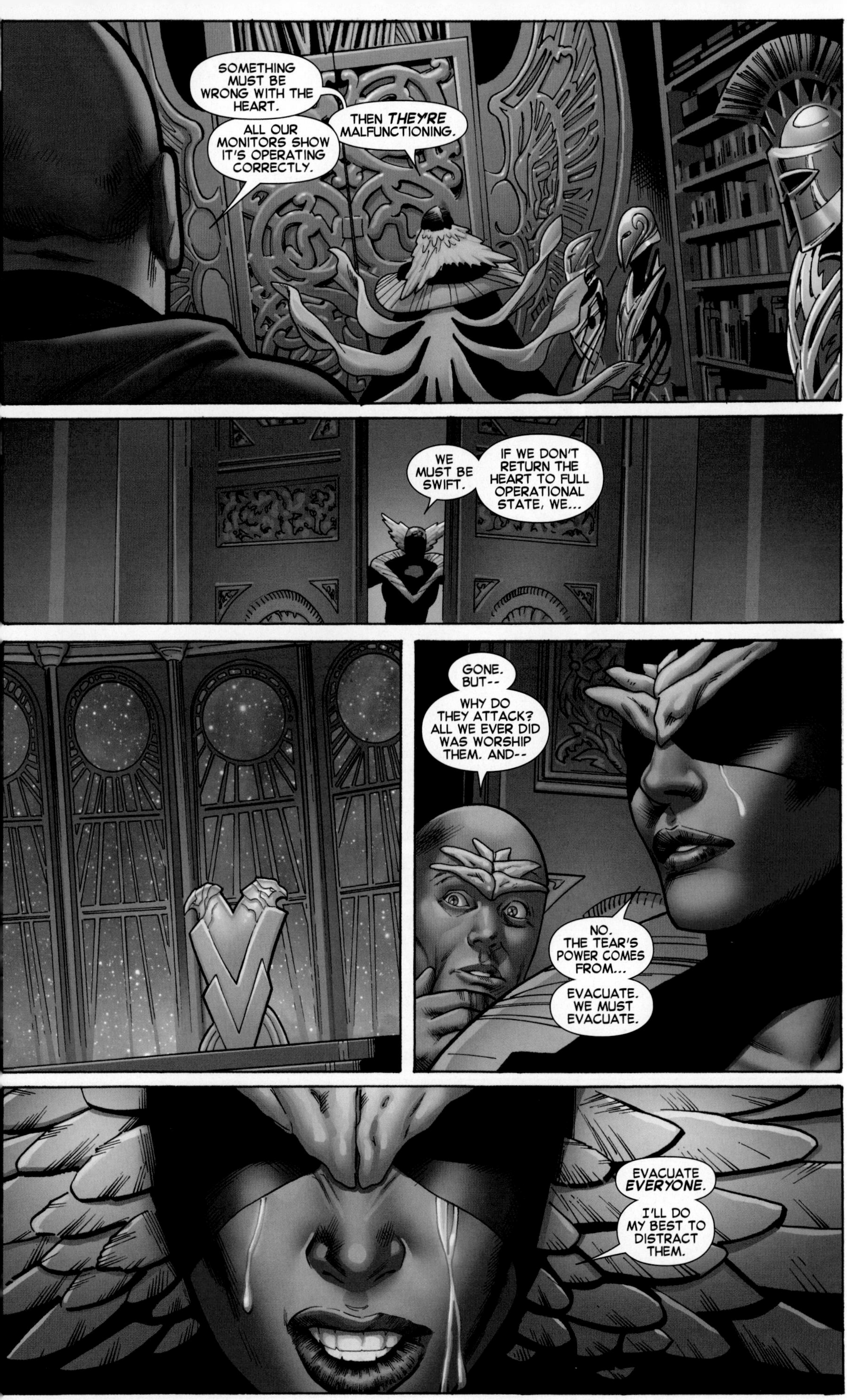
SOMETHING MUST BE WRONG WITH THE HEART.
ALL OUR MONITORS SHOW IT'S OPERATING CORRECTLY.
THEN *THEY'RE* MALFUNCTIONING.
WE MUST BE SWIFT.
IF WE DON'T RETURN THE HEART TO FULL OPERATIONAL STATE, WE...
GONE. BUT--
WHY DO THEY ATTACK? ALL WE EVER DID WAS WORSHIP THEM. AND--
NO. THE TEAR'S POWER COMES FROM...
EVACUATE. WE MUST EVACUATE.
EVACUATE *EVERYONE*.
I'LL DO MY BEST TO DISTRACT THEM.

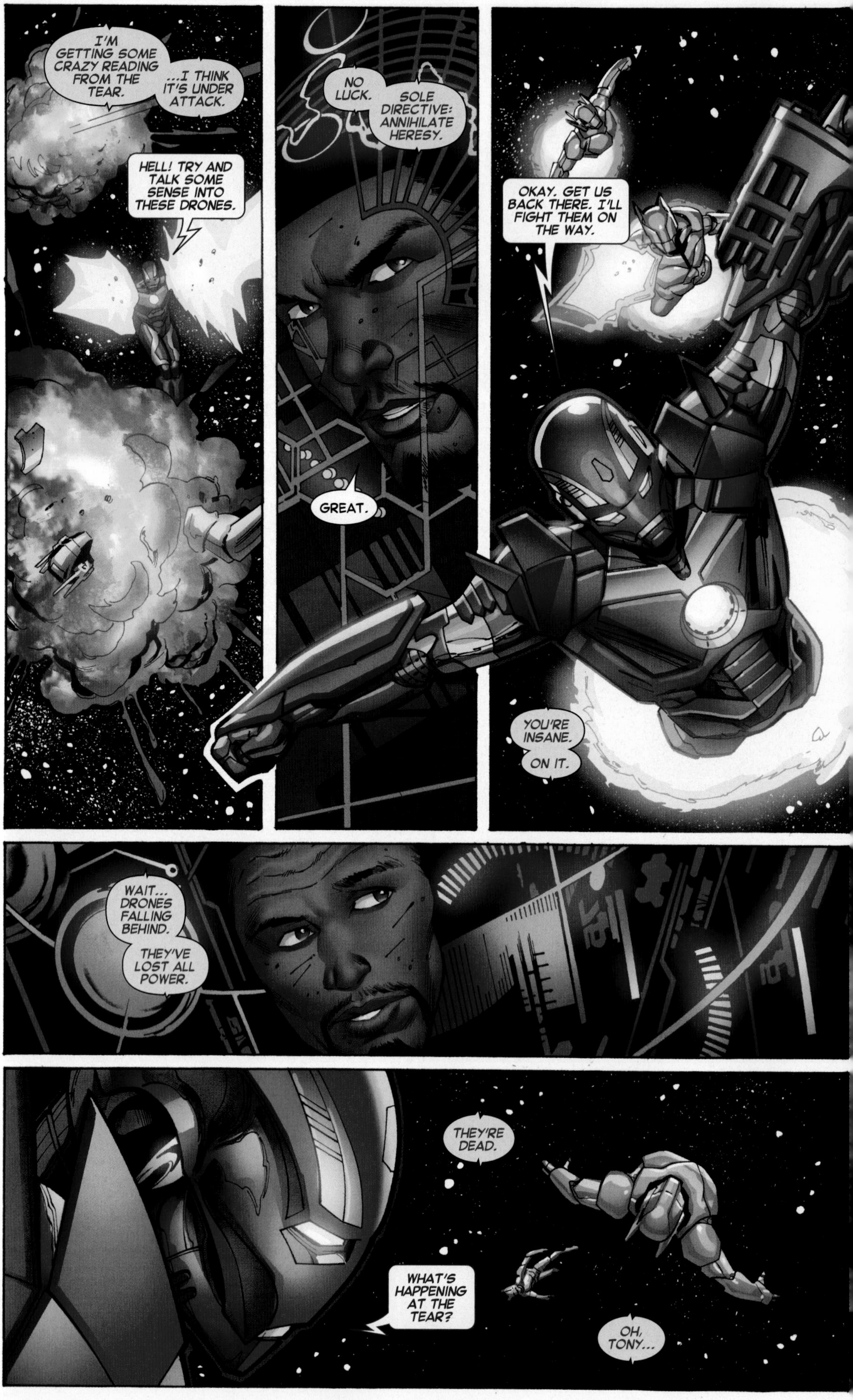
I'M GETTING SOME CRAZY READING FROM THE TEAR.
...I THINK IT'S UNDER ATTACK.
HELL! TRY AND TALK SOME SENSE INTO THESE DRONES.
NO LUCK.
SOLE DIRECTIVE: ANNIHILATE HERESY.
GREAT.
OKAY. GET US BACK THERE. I'LL FIGHT THEM ON THE WAY.
YOU'RE INSANE.
ON IT.
WAIT... DRONES FALLING BEHIND.
THEY'VE LOST ALL POWER.
THEY'RE DEAD.
WHAT'S HAPPENING AT THE TEAR?
OH, TONY...

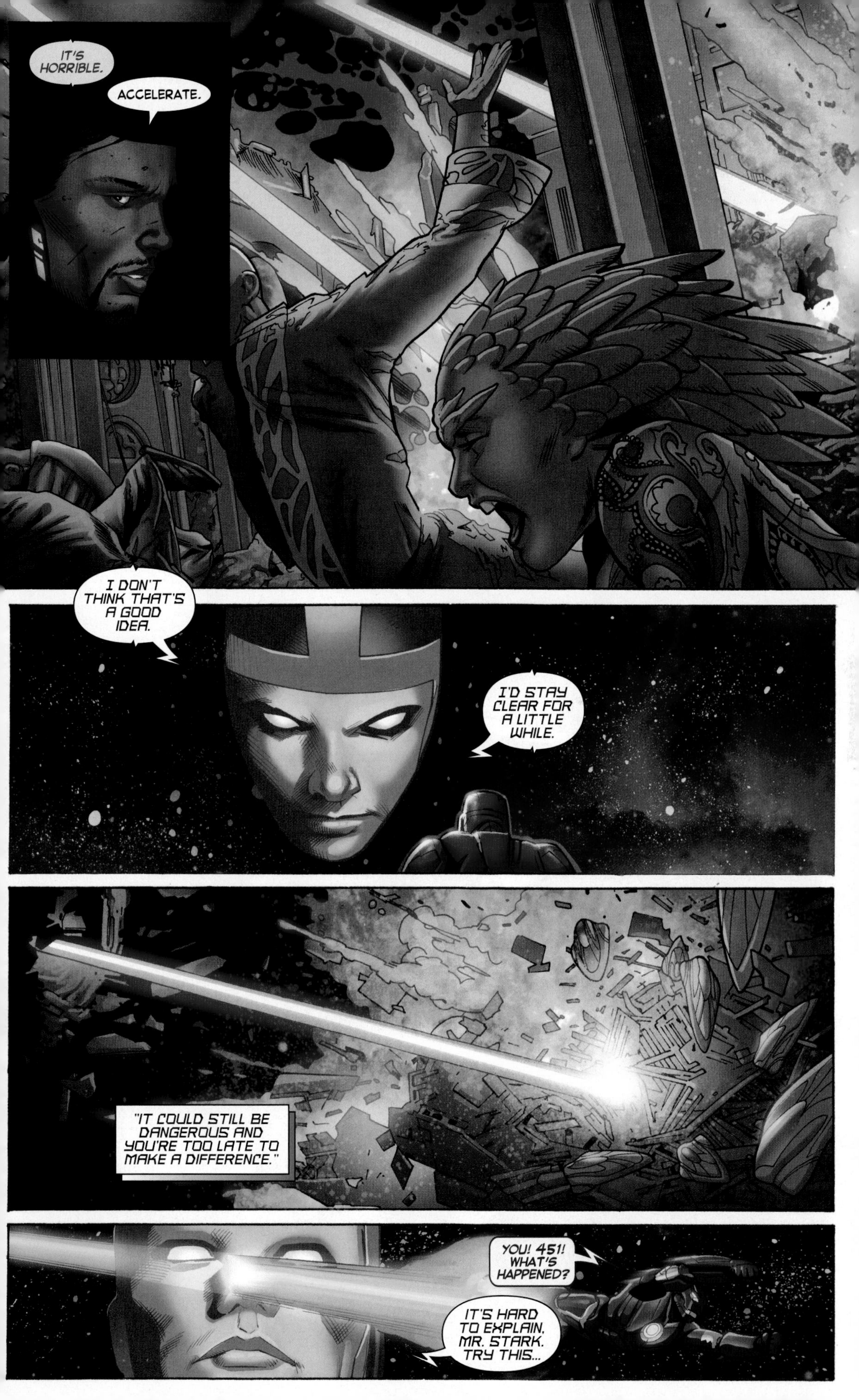
IT'S HORRIBLE.
ACCELERATE.
I DON'T THINK THAT'S A GOOD IDEA.
I'D STAY CLEAR FOR A LITTLE WHILE.
"IT COULD STILL BE DANGEROUS AND YOU'RE TOO LATE TO MAKE A DIFFERENCE."
YOU! 451! WHAT'S HAPPENED?
IT'S HARD TO EXPLAIN, MR. STARK. TRY THIS...

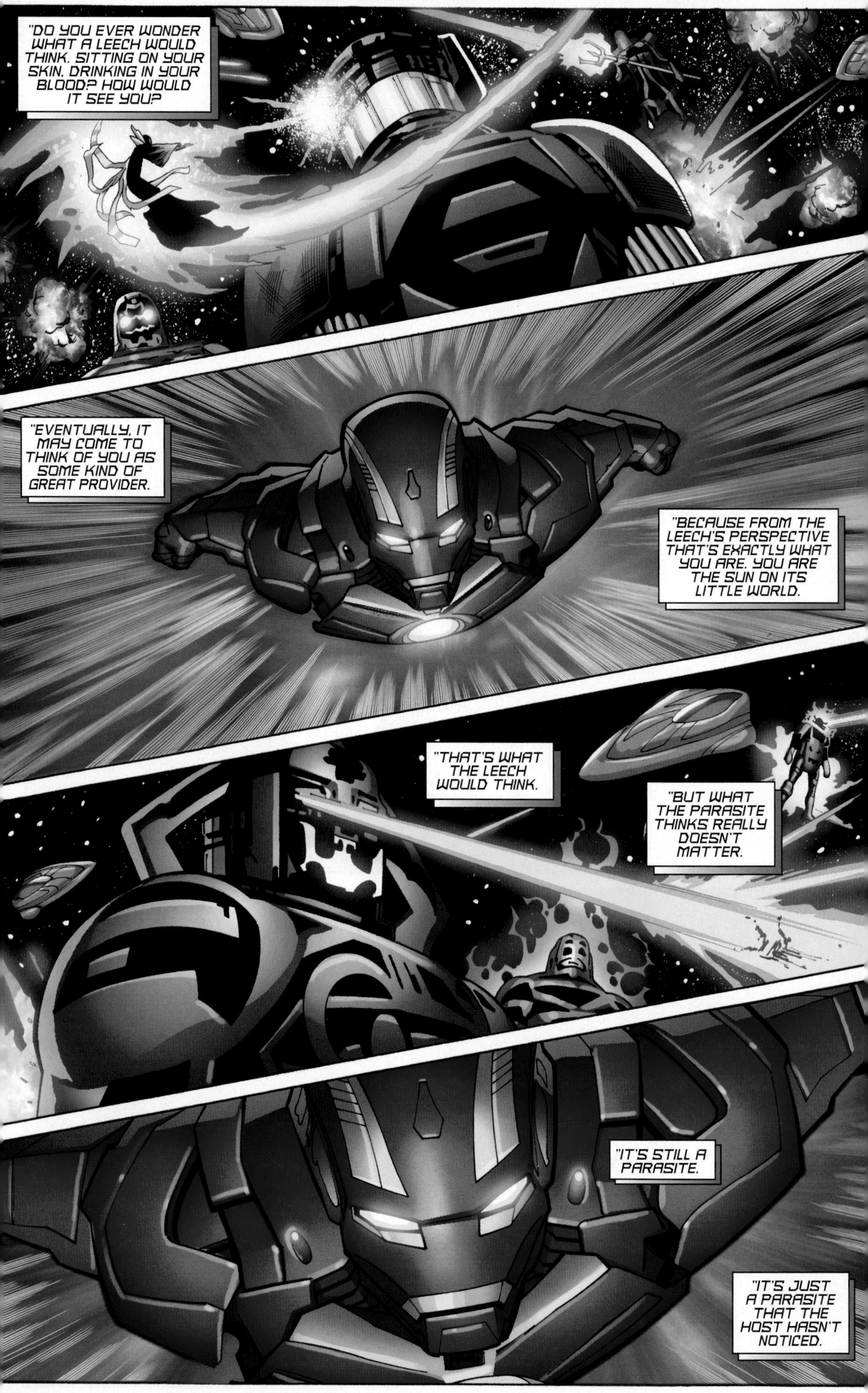
"DO YOU EVER WONDER WHAT A LEECH WOULD THINK. SITTING ON YOUR SKIN, DRINKING IN YOUR BLOOD? HOW WOULD IT SEE YOU?
"EVENTUALLY, IT MAY COME TO THINK OF YOU AS SOME KIND OF GREAT PROVIDER.
"BECAUSE FROM THE LEECH'S PERSPECTIVE THAT'S EXACTLY WHAT YOU ARE. YOU ARE THE SUN ON ITS LITTLE WORLD.
"THAT'S WHAT THE LEECH WOULD THINK.
"BUT WHAT THE PARASITE THINKS REALLY DOESN'T MATTER.
"IT'S STILL A PARASITE.
"IT'S JUST A PARASITE THAT THE HOST HASN'T NOTICED.

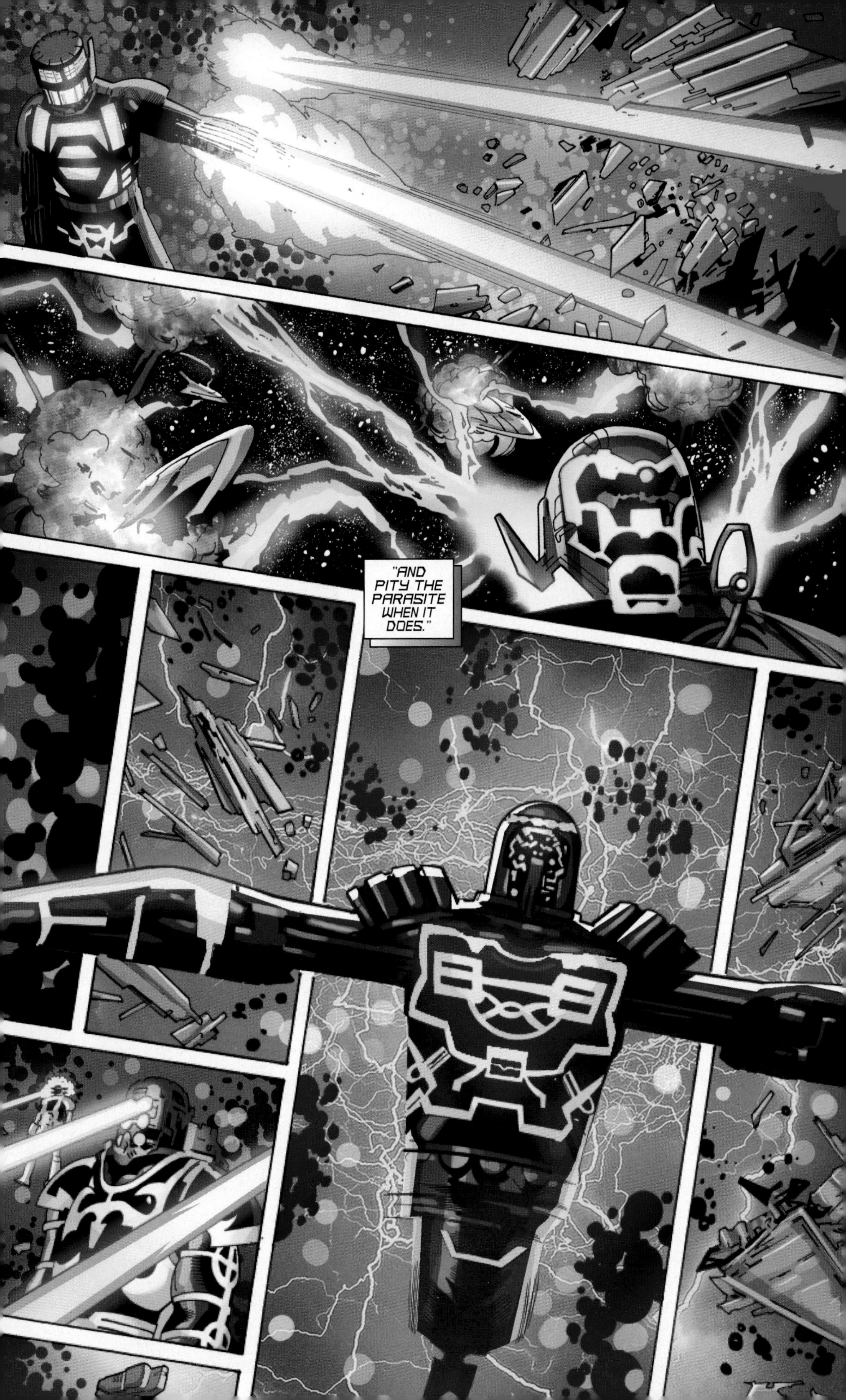
"AND PITY THE PARASITE WHEN IT DOES."

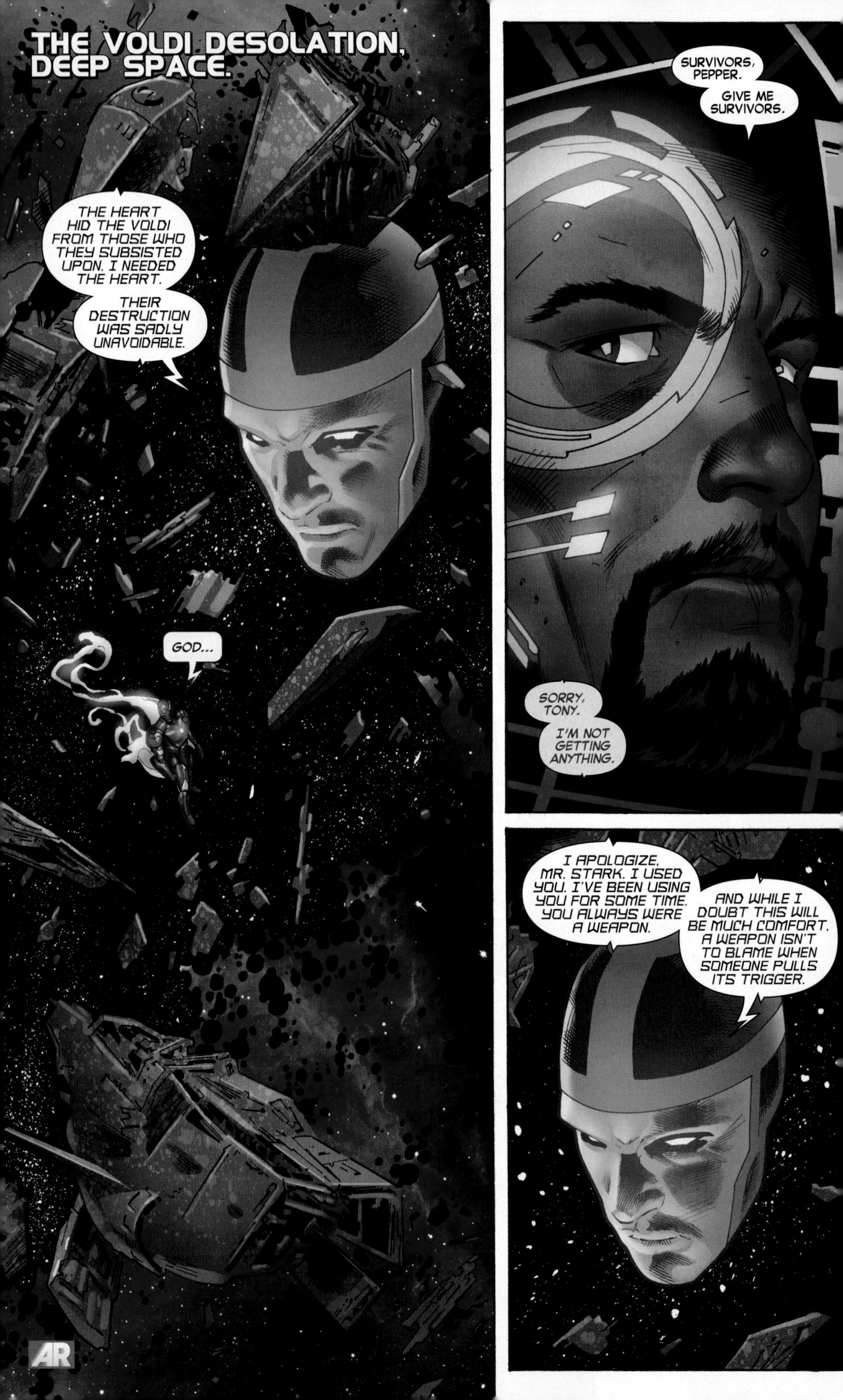
THE VOLDI DESOLATION, DEEP SPACE.
THE HEART HID THE VOLDI FROM THOSE WHO THEY SUBSISTED UPON. I NEEDED THE HEART.
THEIR DESTRUCTION WAS SADLY UNAVOIDABLE.
GOD...
SURVIVORS, PEPPER.
GIVE ME SURVIVORS.
SORRY, TONY.
I'M NOT GETTING ANYTHING.
I APOLOGIZE, MR. STARK. I USED YOU. I'VE BEEN USING YOU FOR SOME TIME. YOU ALWAYS WERE A WEAPON.
AND WHILE I DOUBT THIS WILL BE MUCH COMFORT, A WEAPON ISN'T TO BLAME WHEN SOMEONE PULLS ITS TRIGGER.
AR

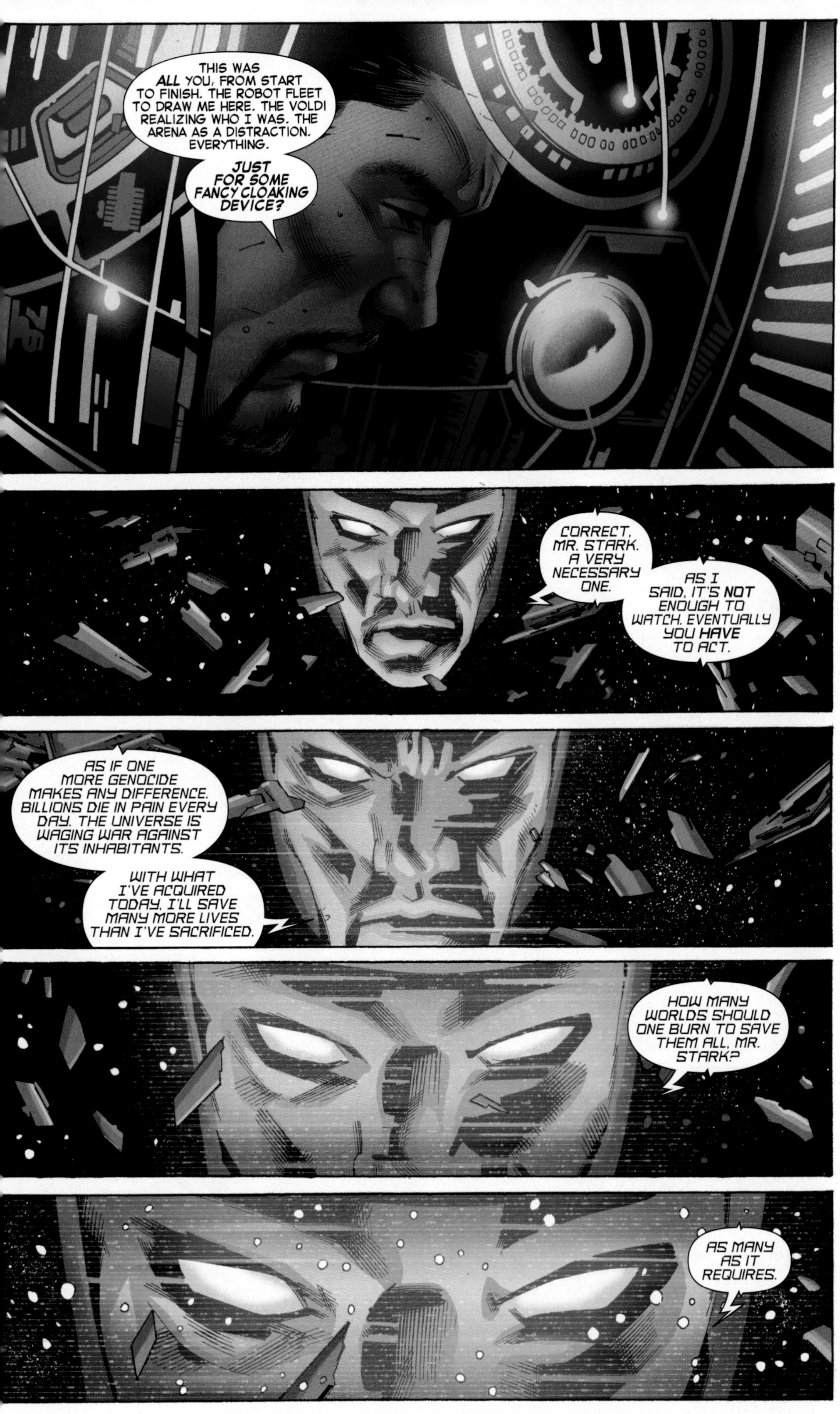
THIS WAS ALL YOU, FROM START TO FINISH. THE ROBOT FLEET TO DRAW ME HERE. THE VOLDI REALIZING WHO I WAS. THE ARENA AS A DISTRACTION. EVERYTHING.
JUST FOR SOME FANCY CLOAKING DEVICE?
CORRECT, MR. STARK. A VERY NECESSARY ONE.
AS I SAID, IT'S NOT ENOUGH TO WATCH. EVENTUALLY YOU HAVE TO ACT.
AS IF ONE MORE GENOCIDE MAKES ANY DIFFERENCE. BILLIONS DIE IN PAIN EVERY DAY. THE UNIVERSE IS WAGING WAR AGAINST ITS INHABITANTS.
WITH WHAT I'VE ACQUIRED TODAY, I'LL SAVE MANY MORE LIVES THAN I'VE SACRIFICED.
HOW MANY WORLDS SHOULD ONE BURN TO SAVE THEM ALL, MR. STARK?
AS MANY AS IT REQUIRES.

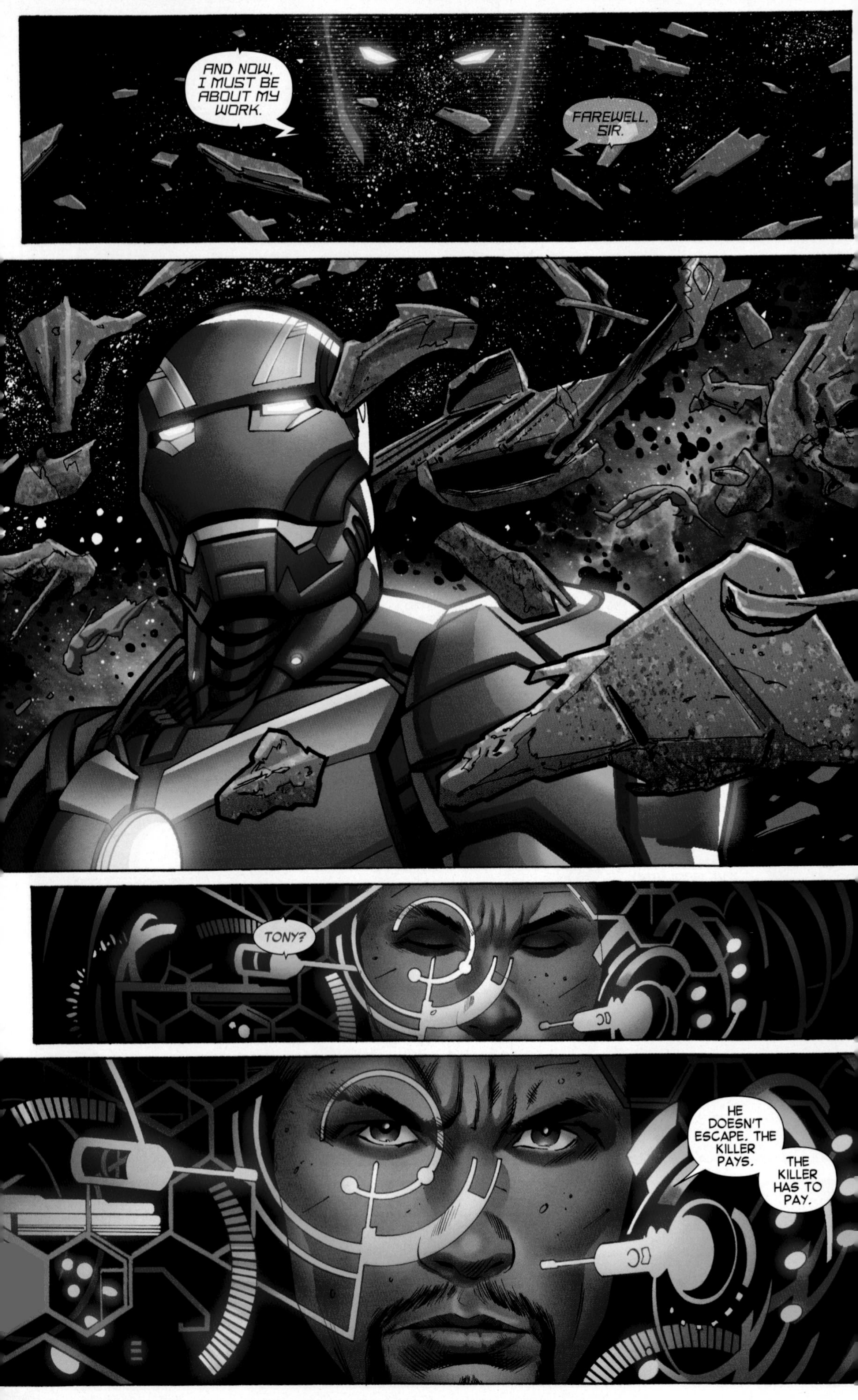
AND NOW, I MUST BE ABOUT MY WORK.
FAREWELL, SIR.
TONY?
HE DOESN'T ESCAPE. THE KILLER PAYS.
THE KILLER HAS TO PAY.

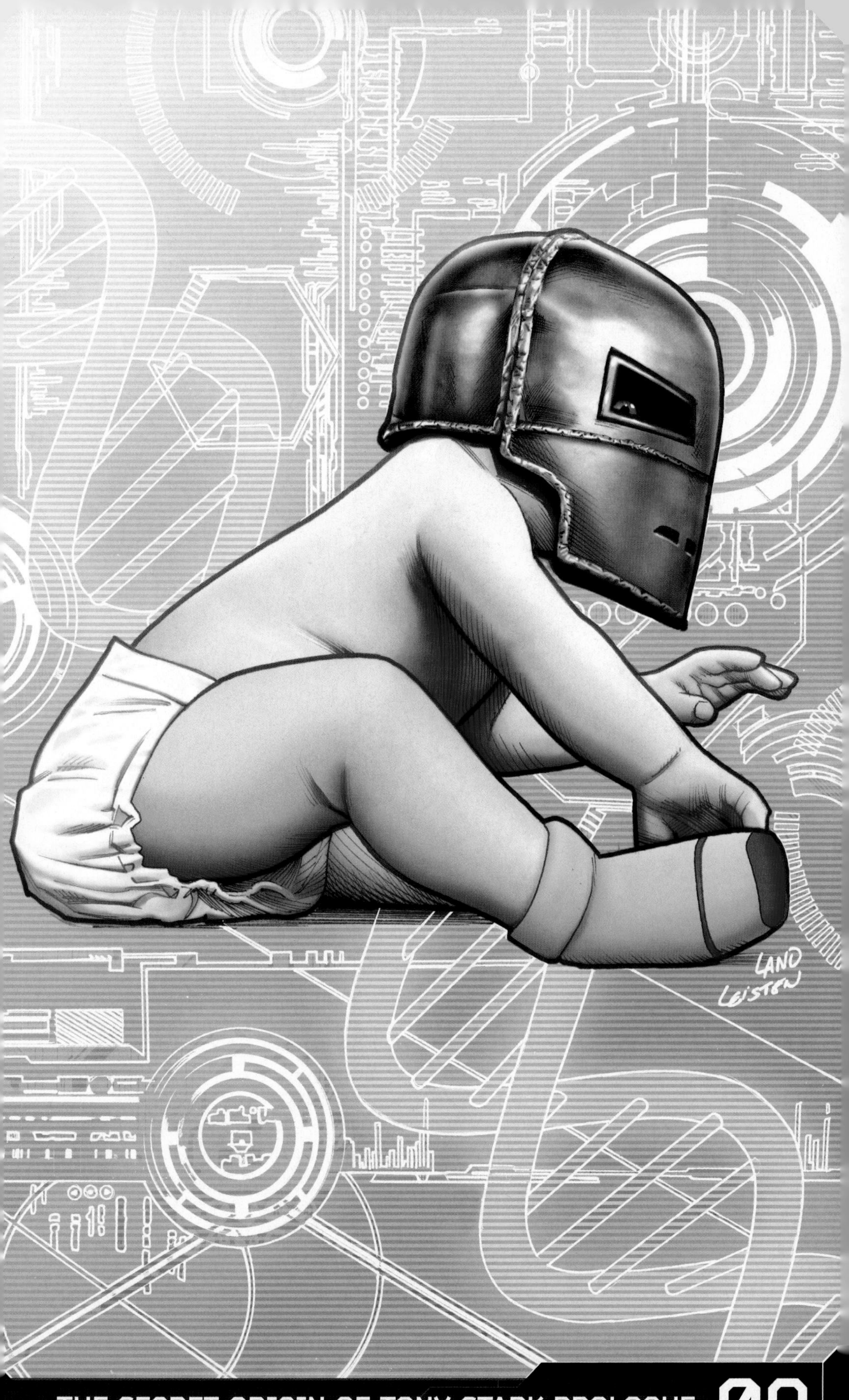
LAND
LEISTEN

THE SECRET ORIGIN OF TONY STARK PROLOGUE 09

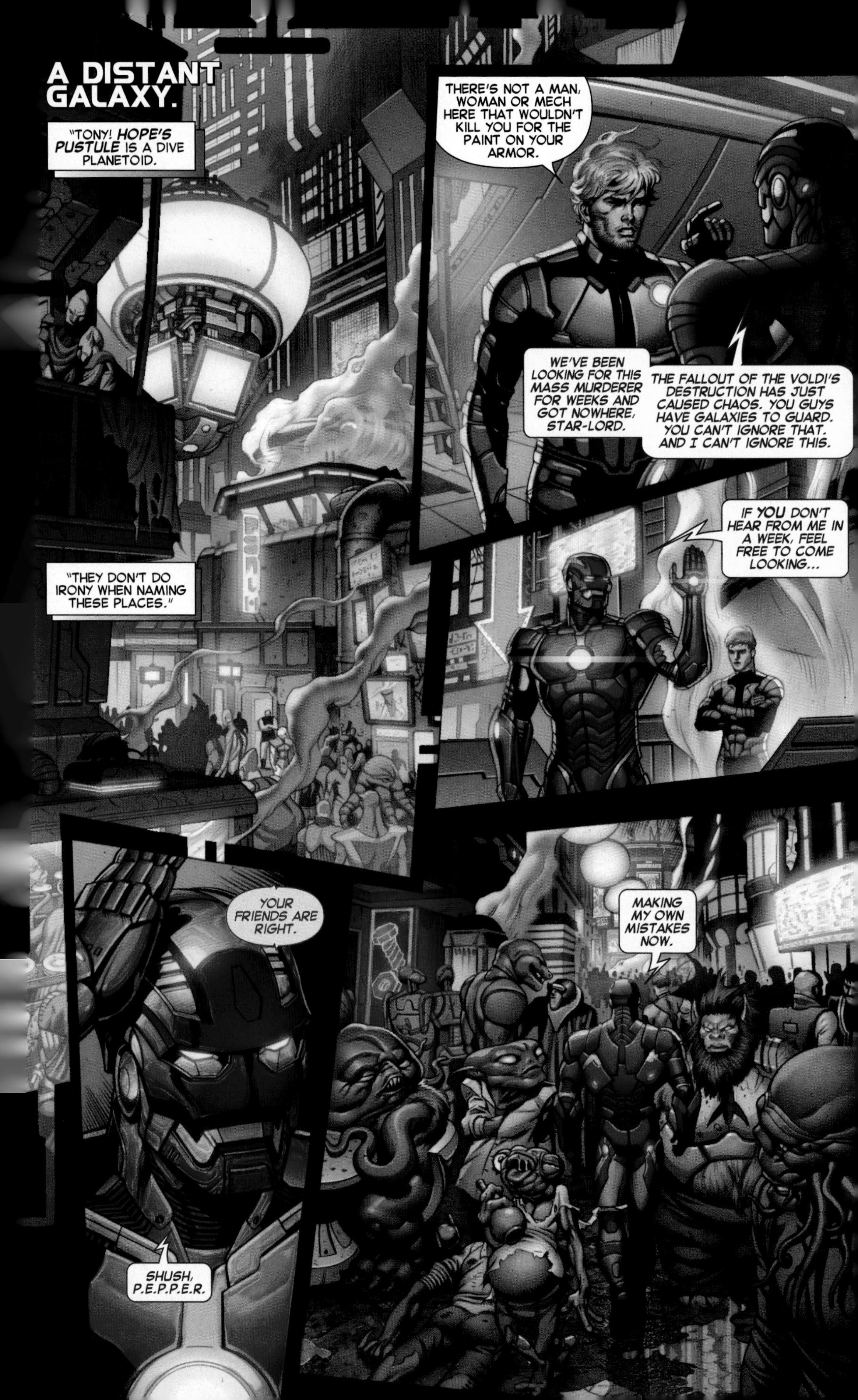

A DISTANT GALAXY.
"TONY! HOPE'S PUSTULE IS A DIVE PLANETOID.
"THEY DON'T DO IRONY WHEN NAMING THESE PLACES."
THERE'S NOT A MAN, WOMAN OR MECH HERE THAT WOULDN'T KILL YOU FOR THE PAINT ON YOUR ARMOR.
WE'VE BEEN LOOKING FOR THIS MASS MURDERER FOR WEEKS AND GOT NOWHERE, STAR-LORD.
THE FALLOUT OF THE VOLDI'S DESTRUCTION HAS JUST CAUSED CHAOS. YOU GUYS HAVE GALAXIES TO GUARD. YOU CAN'T IGNORE THAT. AND I CAN'T IGNORE THIS.
IF YOU DON'T HEAR FROM ME IN A WEEK, FEEL FREE TO COME LOOKING...
YOUR FRIENDS ARE RIGHT.
SHUSH, P.E.P.P.E.R.
MAKING MY OWN MISTAKES NOW.

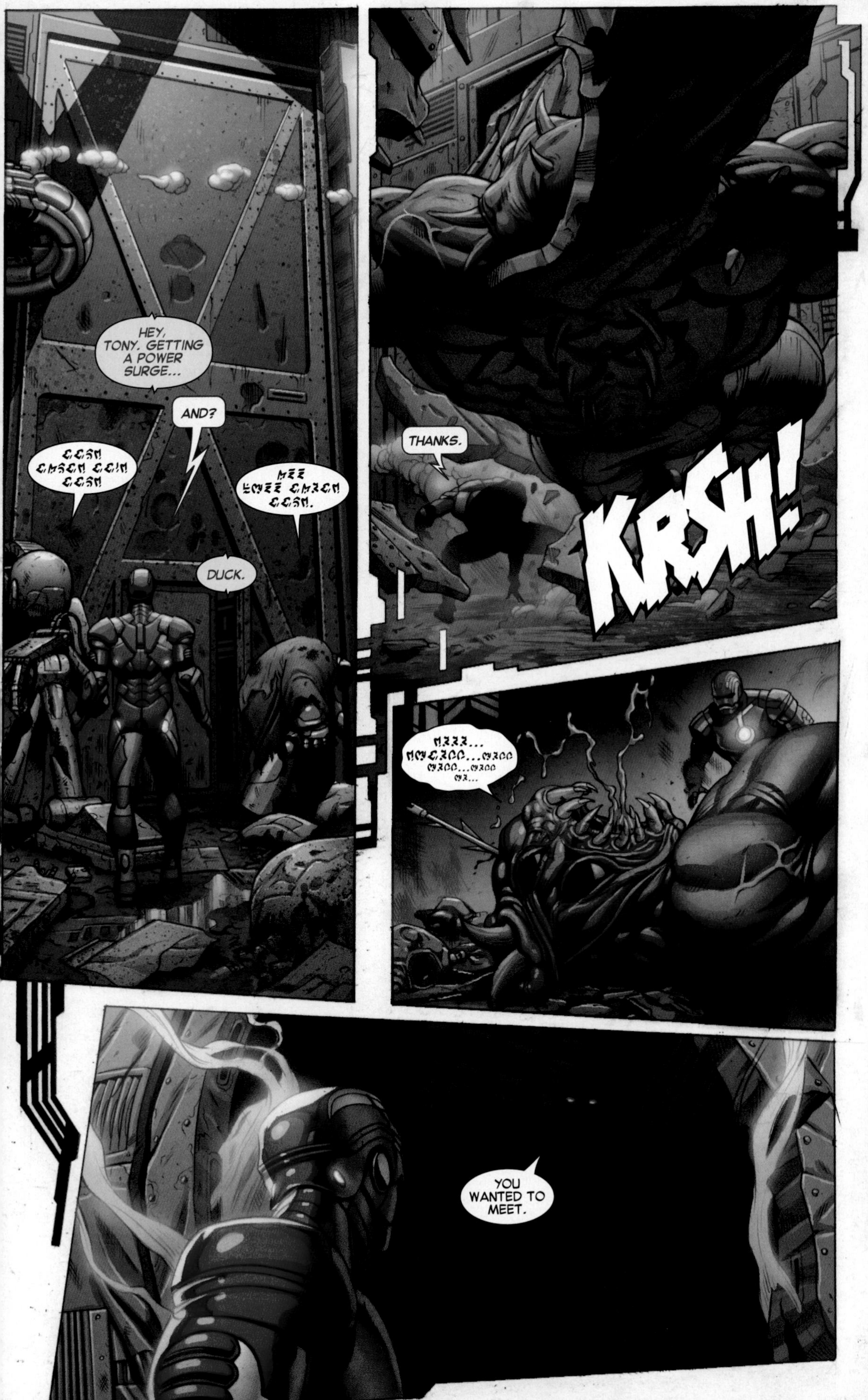
HEY, TONY. GETTING A POWER SURGE...
AND?
DUCK.
THANKS.
KRSH!
YOU WANTED TO MEET.

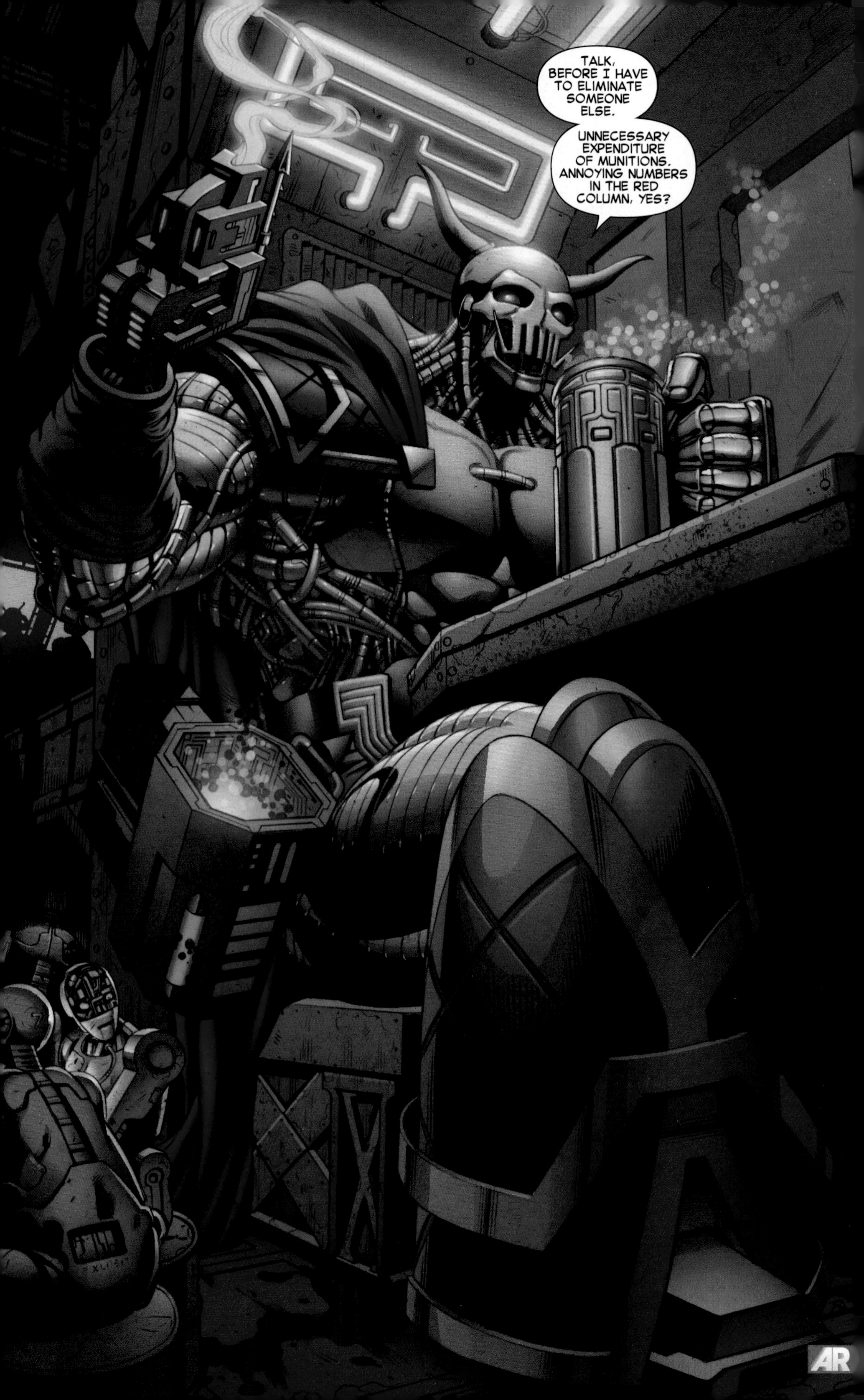
TALK, BEFORE I HAVE TO ELIMINATE SOMEONE ELSE.
UNNECESSARY EXPENDITURE OF MUNITIONS. ANNOYING NUMBERS IN THE RED COLUMN, YES?

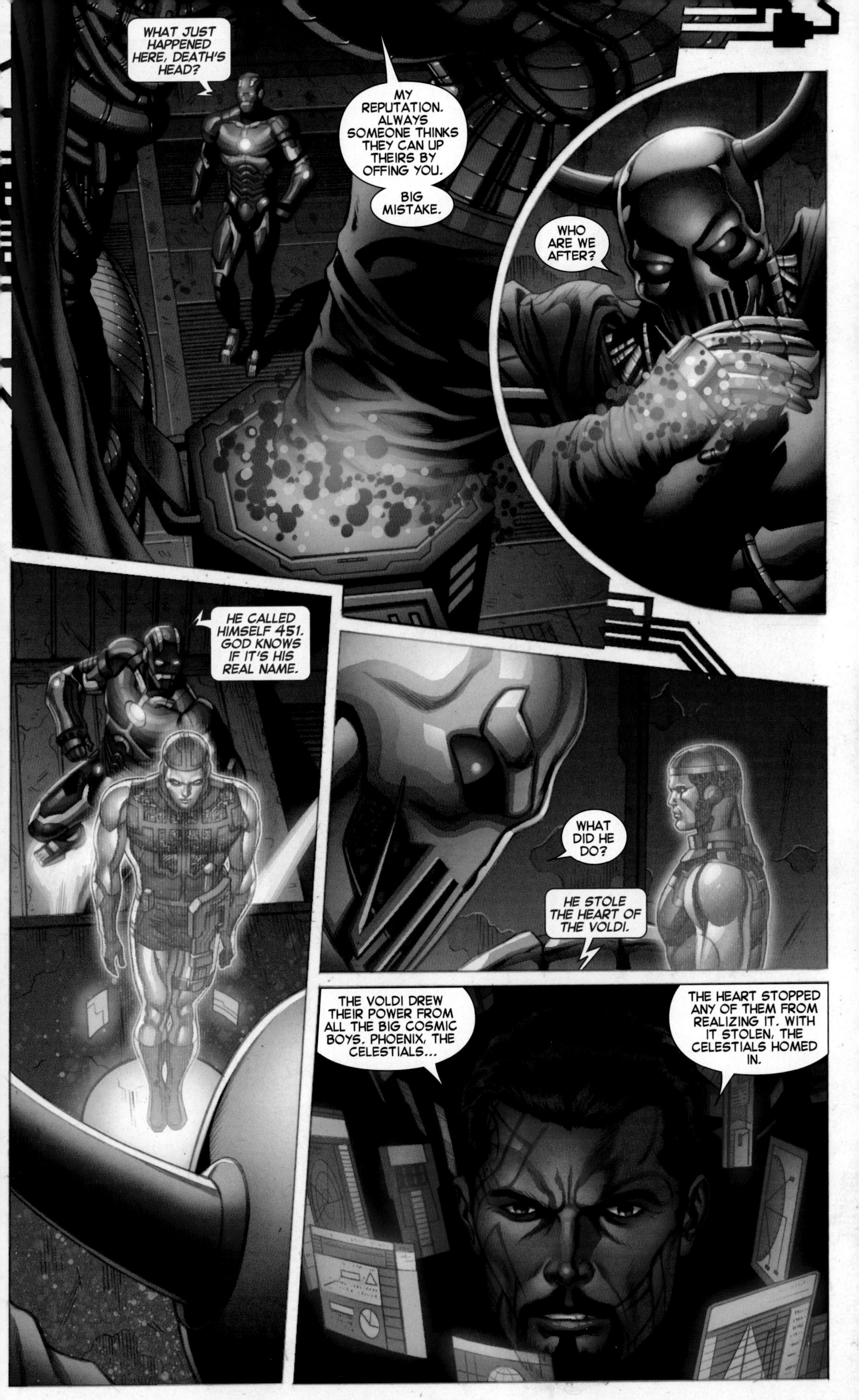
WHAT JUST HAPPENED HERE, DEATH'S HEAD?
MY REPUTATION. ALWAYS SOMEONE THINKS THEY CAN UP THEIRS BY OFFING YOU.
BIG MISTAKE.
WHO ARE WE AFTER?
HE CALLED HIMSELF 451. GOD KNOWS IF IT'S HIS REAL NAME.
WHAT DID HE DO?
HE STOLE THE HEART OF THE VOLDI.
THE VOLDI DREW THEIR POWER FROM ALL THE BIG COSMIC BOYS. PHOENIX, THE CELESTIALS...
THE HEART STOPPED ANY OF THEM FROM REALIZING IT. WITH IT STOLEN, THE CELESTIALS HOMED IN.

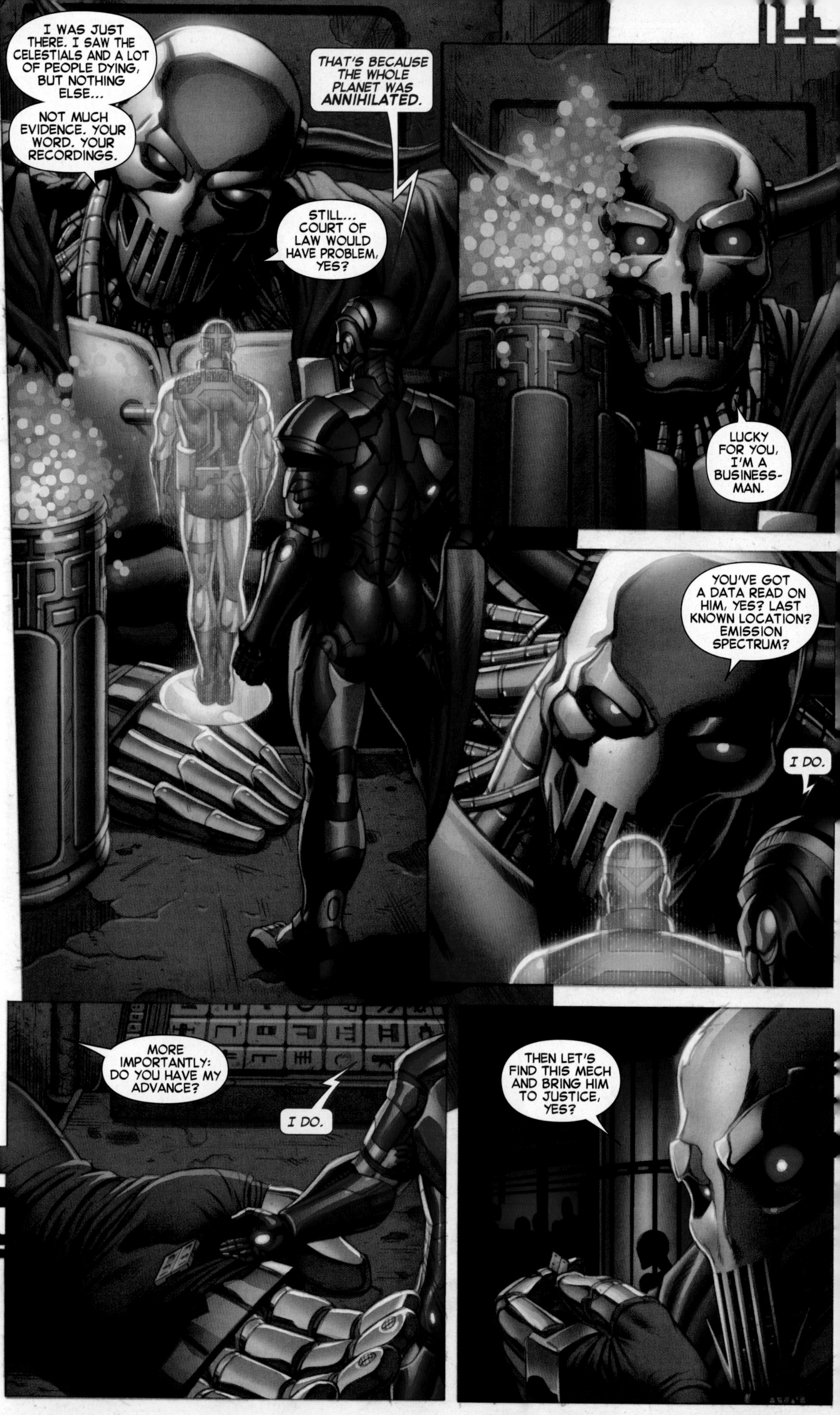
I WAS JUST THERE. I SAW THE CELESTIALS AND A LOT OF PEOPLE DYING, BUT NOTHING ELSE...
NOT MUCH EVIDENCE. YOUR WORD. YOUR RECORDINGS.
THAT'S BECAUSE THE WHOLE PLANET WAS ANNIHILATED.
STILL... COURT OF LAW WOULD HAVE PROBLEM, YES?
LUCKY FOR YOU, I'M A BUSINESS-MAN.
YOU'VE GOT A DATA READ ON HIM, YES? LAST KNOWN LOCATION? EMISSION SPECTRUM?
I DO.
MORE IMPORTANTLY: DO YOU HAVE MY ADVANCE?
I DO.
THEN LET'S FIND THIS MECH AND BRING HIM TO JUSTICE, YES?

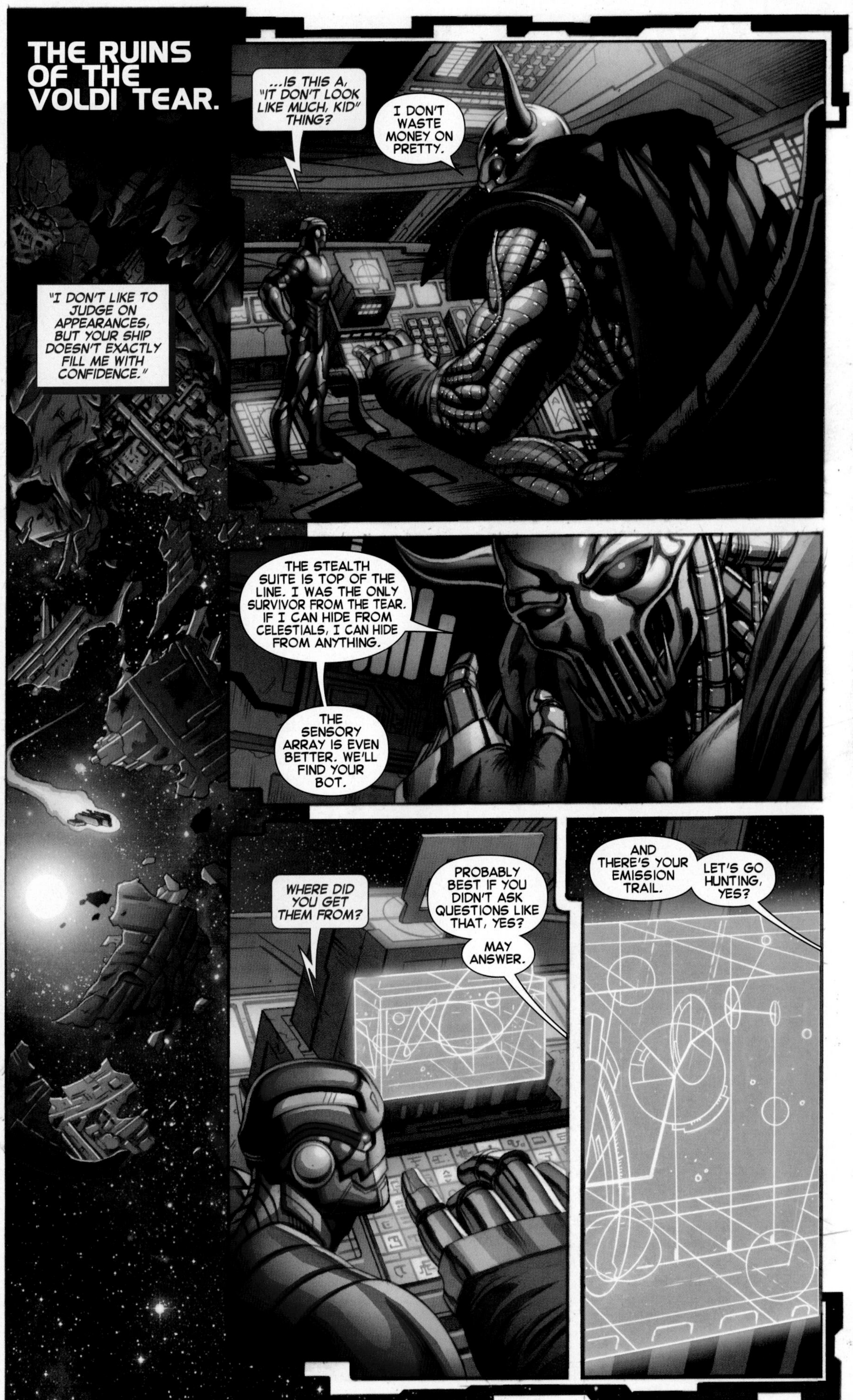
THE RUINS OF THE VOLDI TEAR.
...IS THIS A, "IT DON'T LOOK LIKE MUCH, KID" THING?
I DON'T WASTE MONEY ON PRETTY.
"I DON'T LIKE TO JUDGE ON APPEARANCES, BUT YOUR SHIP DOESN'T EXACTLY FILL ME WITH CONFIDENCE."
THE STEALTH SUITE IS TOP OF THE LINE. I WAS THE ONLY SURVIVOR FROM THE TEAR. IF I CAN HIDE FROM CELESTIALS, I CAN HIDE FROM ANYTHING.
THE SENSORY ARRAY IS EVEN BETTER. WE'LL FIND YOUR BOT.
WHERE DID YOU GET THEM FROM?
PROBABLY BEST IF YOU DIDN'T ASK QUESTIONS LIKE THAT, YES?
MAY ANSWER.
AND THERE'S YOUR EMISSION TRAIL.
LET'S GO HUNTING, YES?

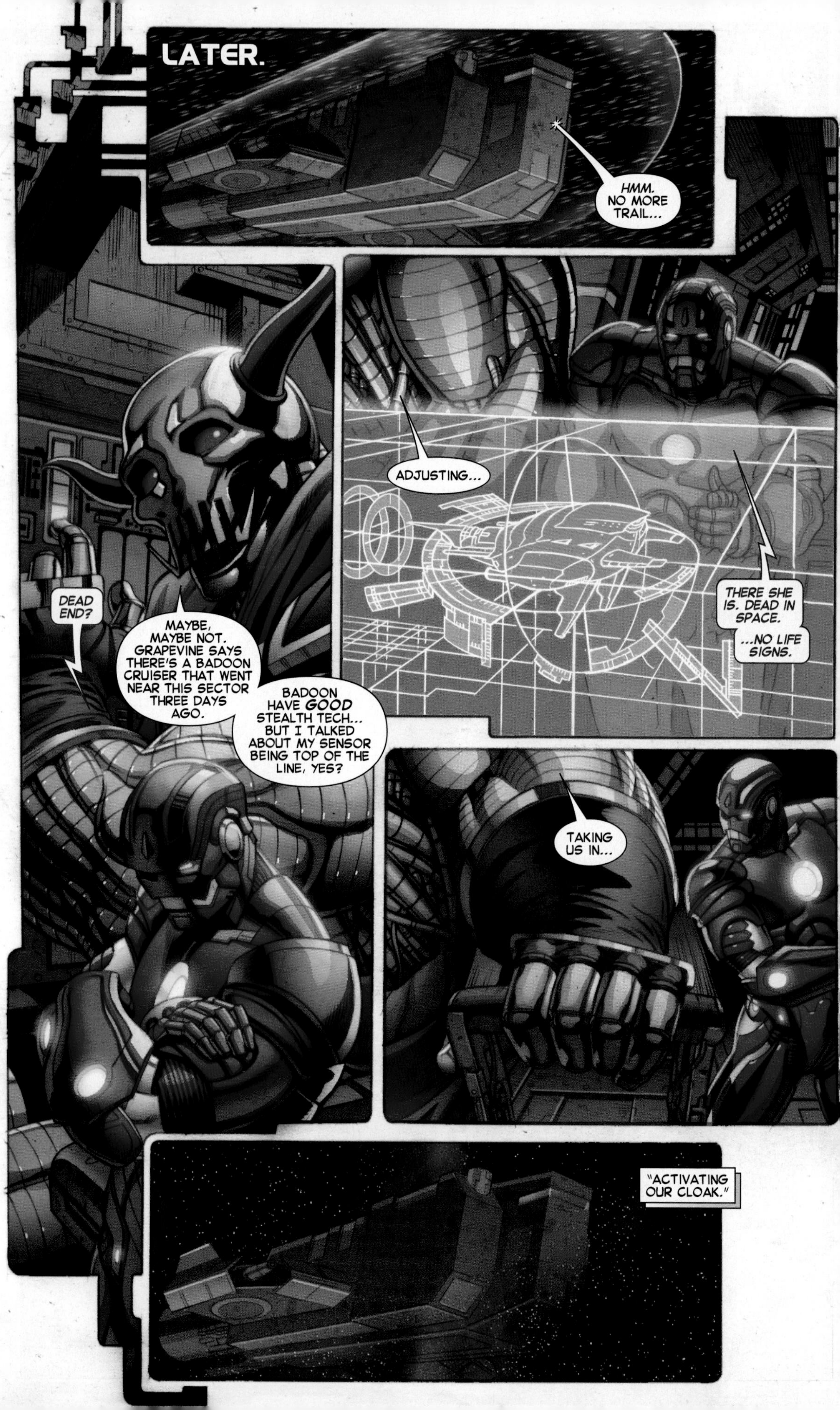
LATER.
HMM. NO MORE TRAIL...
DEAD END?
MAYBE, MAYBE NOT. GRAPEVINE SAYS THERE'S A BADOON CRUISER THAT WENT NEAR THIS SECTOR THREE DAYS AGO.
BADOON HAVE GOOD STEALTH TECH... BUT I TALKED ABOUT MY SENSOR BEING TOP OF THE LINE, YES?
ADJUSTING...
THERE SHE IS. DEAD IN SPACE.
...NO LIFE SIGNS.
TAKING US IN...
"ACTIVATING OUR CLOAK."

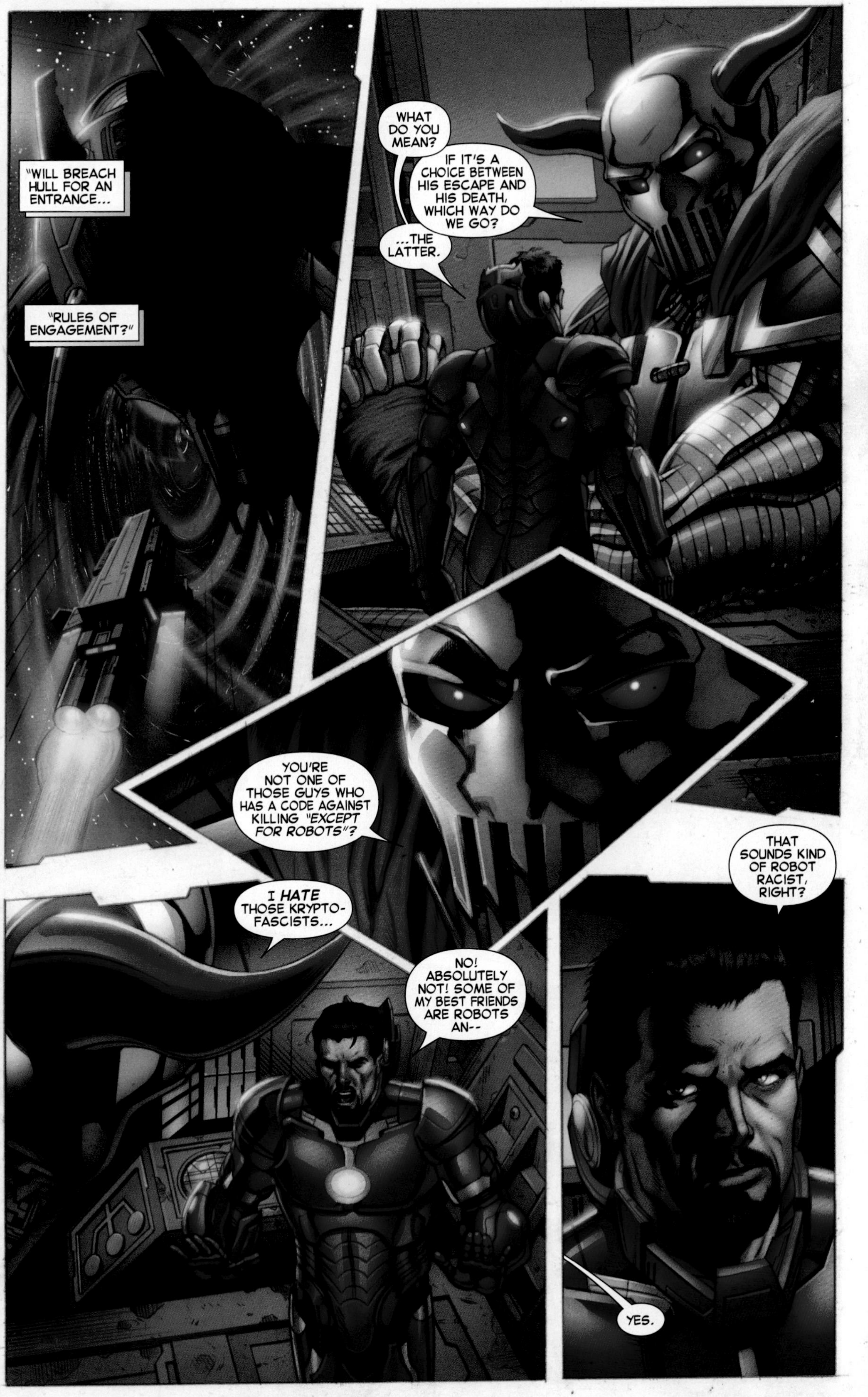
"WILL BREACH HULL FOR AN ENTRANCE...
"RULES OF ENGAGEMENT?"
WHAT DO YOU MEAN?
IF IT'S A CHOICE BETWEEN HIS ESCAPE AND HIS DEATH, WHICH WAY DO WE GO?
...THE LATTER.
YOU'RE NOT ONE OF THOSE GUYS WHO HAS A CODE AGAINST KILLING *"EXCEPT FOR ROBOTS"*?
I *HATE* THOSE KRYPTO-FASCISTS...
NO! ABSOLUTELY NOT! SOME OF MY BEST FRIENDS ARE ROBOTS AN--
THAT SOUNDS KIND OF ROBOT RACIST, RIGHT?
YES.

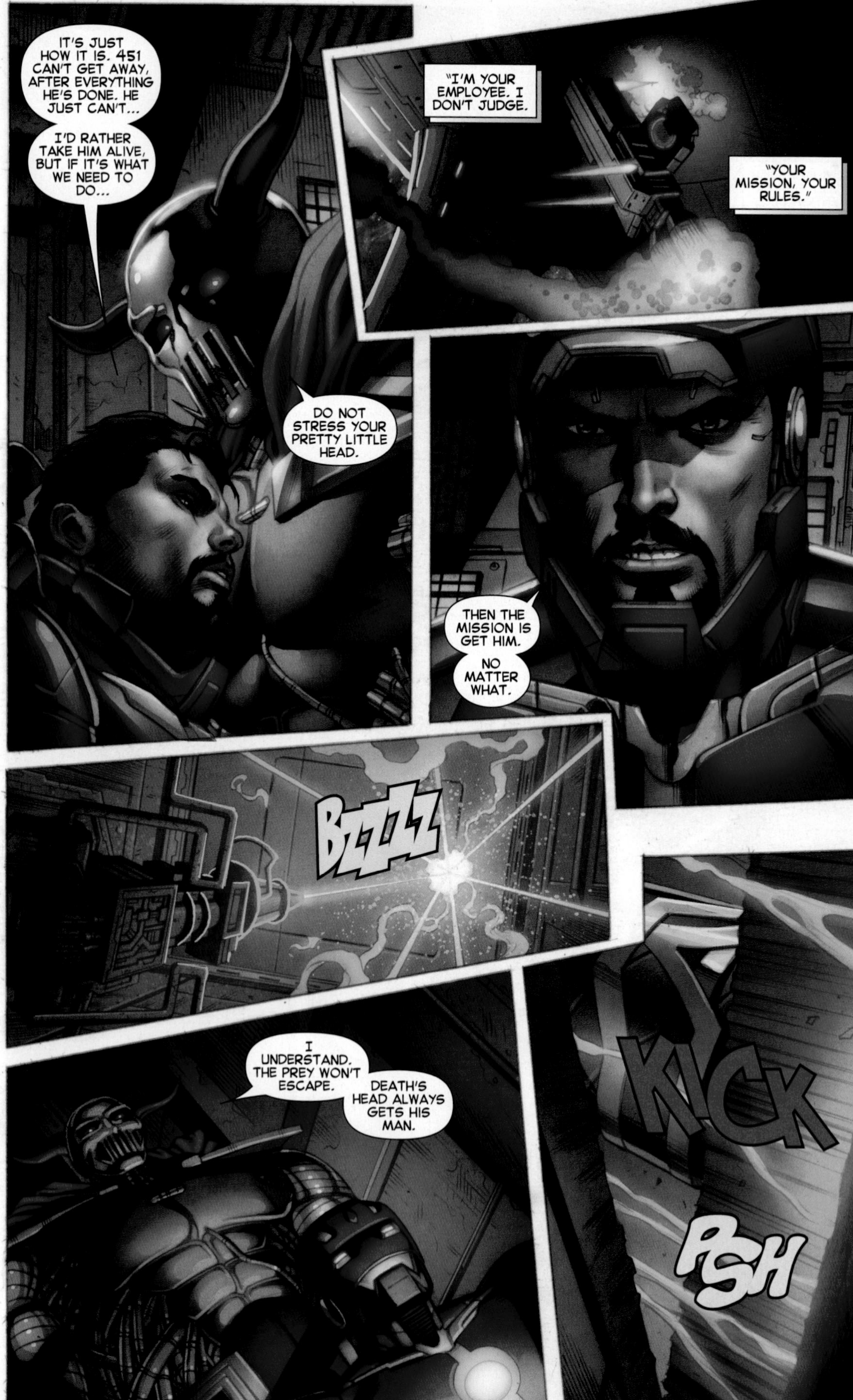
IT'S JUST HOW IT IS. 451 CAN'T GET AWAY, AFTER EVERYTHING HE'S DONE. HE JUST CAN'T...
I'D RATHER TAKE HIM ALIVE, BUT IF IT'S WHAT WE NEED TO DO...
"I'M YOUR EMPLOYEE. I DON'T JUDGE.
"YOUR MISSION, YOUR RULES."
DO NOT STRESS YOUR PRETTY LITTLE HEAD.
THEN THE MISSION IS GET HIM.
NO MATTER WHAT.
BZZZZ
I UNDERSTAND. THE PREY WON'T ESCAPE.
DEATH'S HEAD ALWAYS GETS HIS MAN.
KICK
PSH

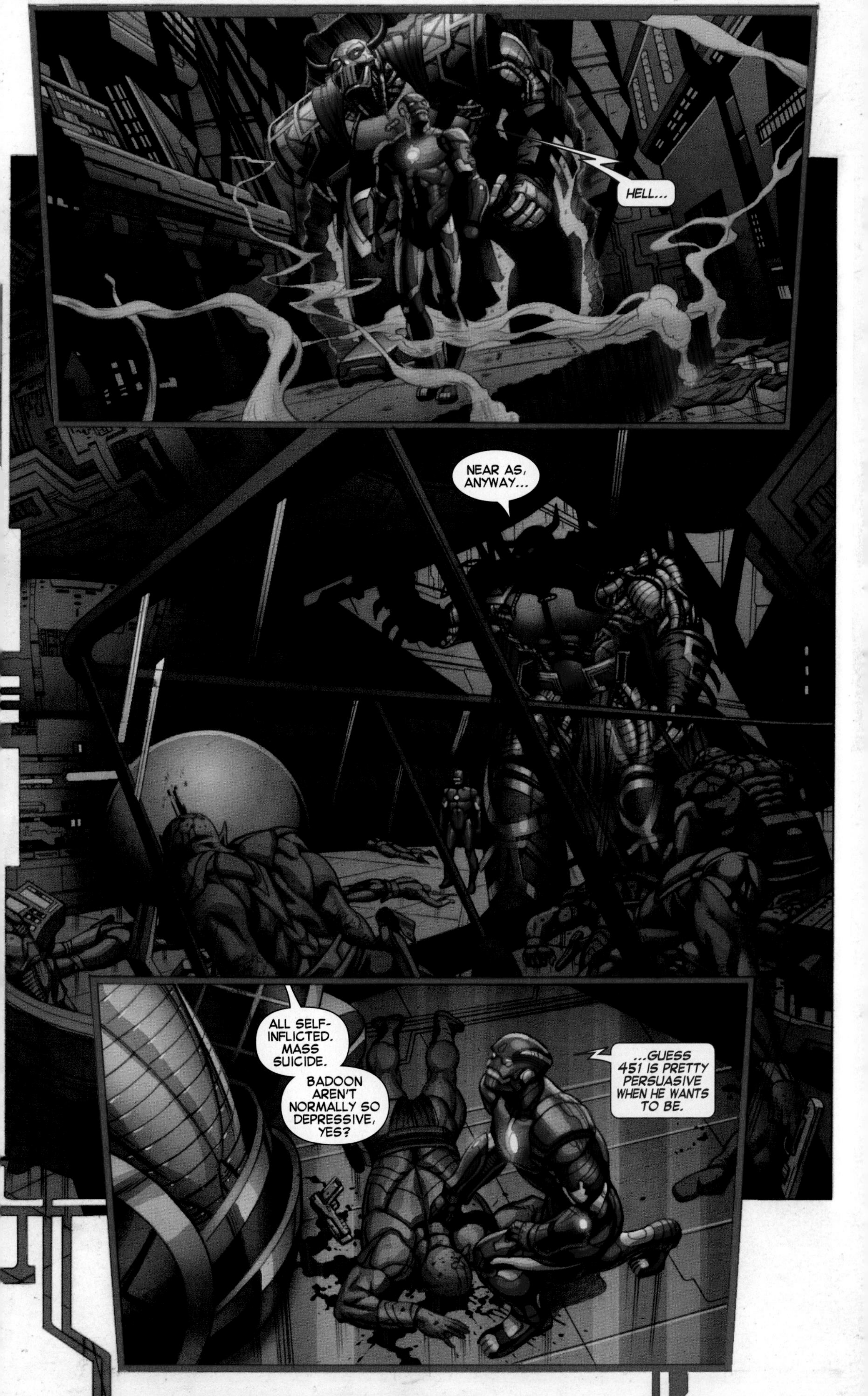
HELL...
NEAR AS, ANYWAY...
ALL SELF-INFLICTED. MASS SUICIDE.
BADOON AREN'T NORMALLY SO DEPRESSIVE, YES?
...GUESS 451 IS PRETTY PERSUASIVE WHEN HE WANTS TO BE.

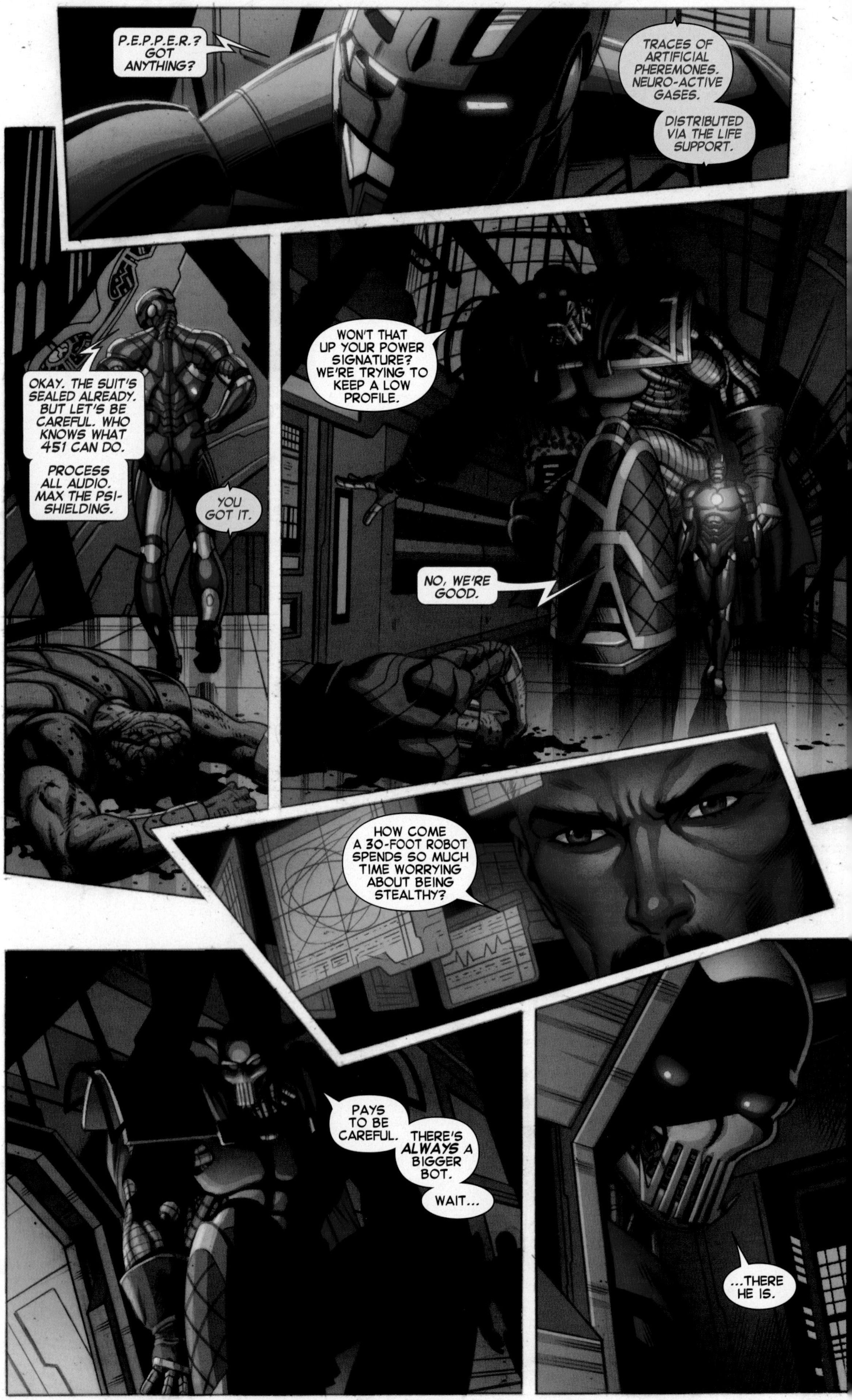
P.E.P.P.E.R.? GOT ANYTHING?
TRACES OF ARTIFICIAL PHEREMONES. NEURO-ACTIVE GASES.
DISTRIBUTED VIA THE LIFE SUPPORT.
OKAY. THE SUIT'S SEALED ALREADY. BUT LET'S BE CAREFUL. WHO KNOWS WHAT 451 CAN DO.
PROCESS ALL AUDIO. MAX THE PSI-SHIELDING.
YOU GOT IT.
WON'T THAT UP YOUR POWER SIGNATURE? WE'RE TRYING TO KEEP A LOW PROFILE.
NO, WE'RE GOOD.
HOW COME A 30-FOOT ROBOT SPENDS SO MUCH TIME WORRYING ABOUT BEING STEALTHY?
PAYS TO BE CAREFUL.
THERE'S *ALWAYS* A BIGGER BOT.
WAIT...
...THERE HE IS.

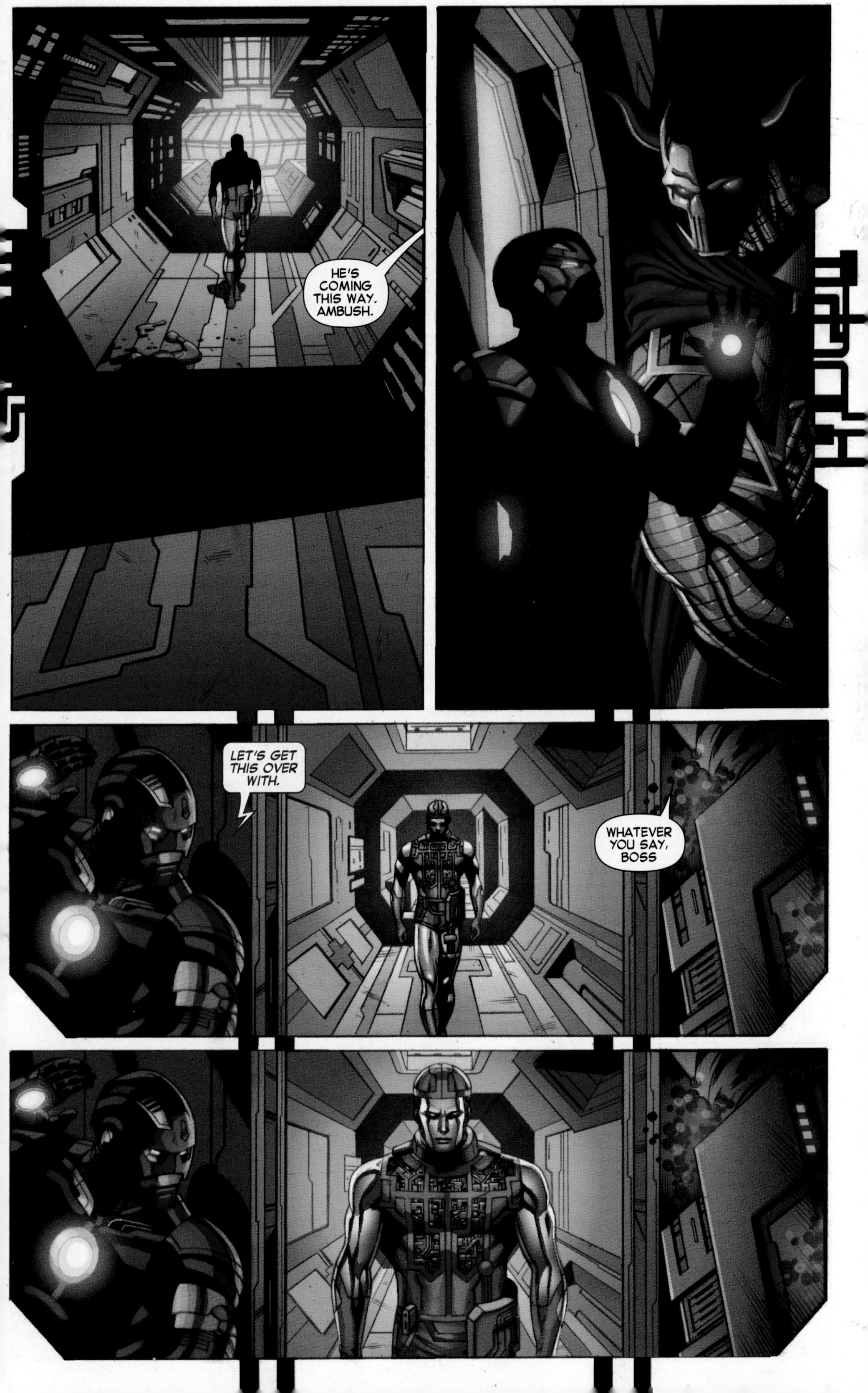
HE'S COMING THIS WAY. AMBUSH.
LET'S GET THIS OVER WITH.
WHATEVER YOU SAY, BOSS

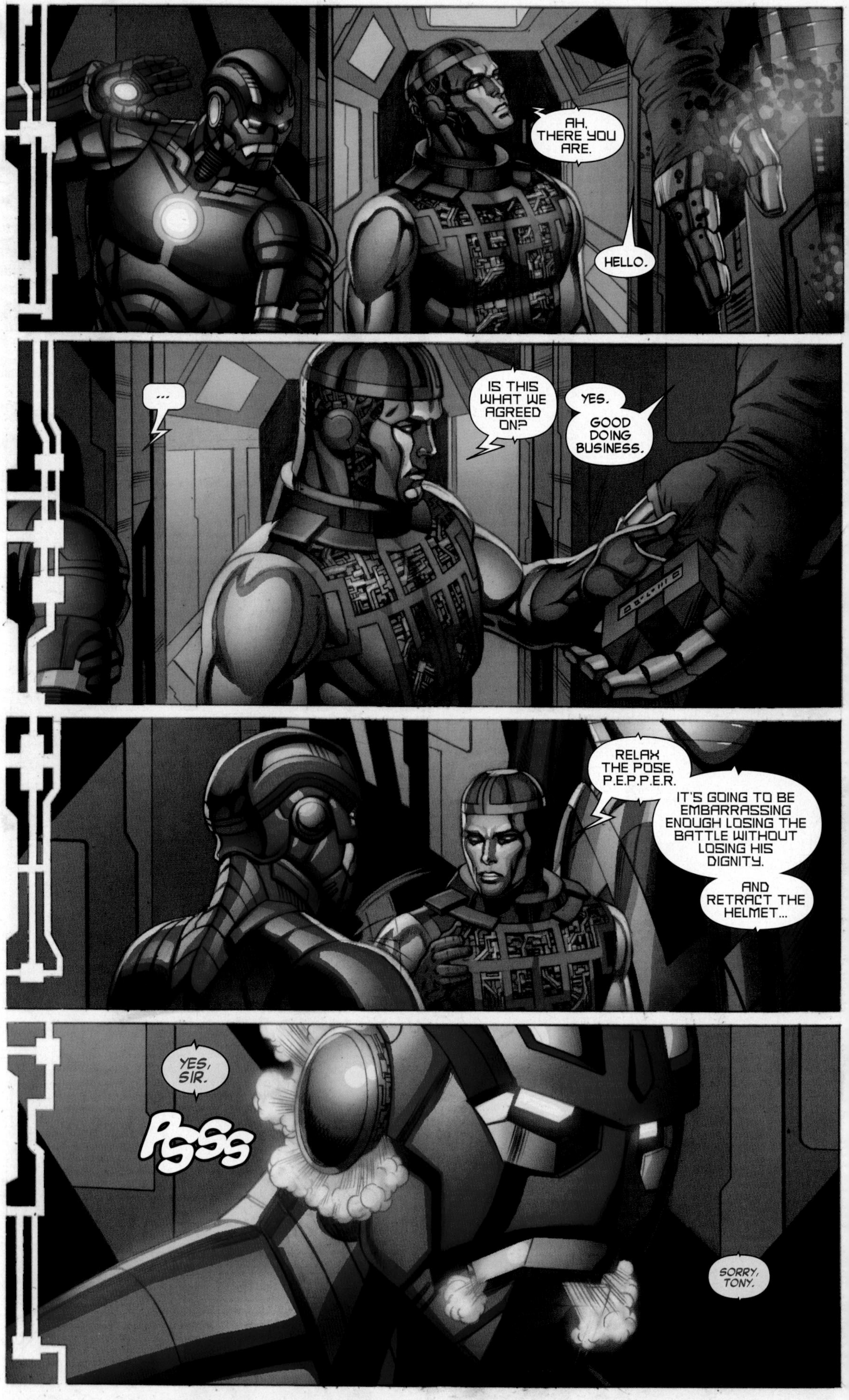
AH, THERE YOU ARE.
HELLO.
...
IS THIS WHAT WE AGREED ON?
YES.
GOOD DOING BUSINESS.
RELAX THE POSE, P.E.P.P.E.R.
IT'S GOING TO BE EMBARRASSING ENOUGH LOSING THE BATTLE WITHOUT LOSING HIS DIGNITY.
AND RETRACT THE HELMET...
YES, SIR.
PSSS
SORRY, TONY.

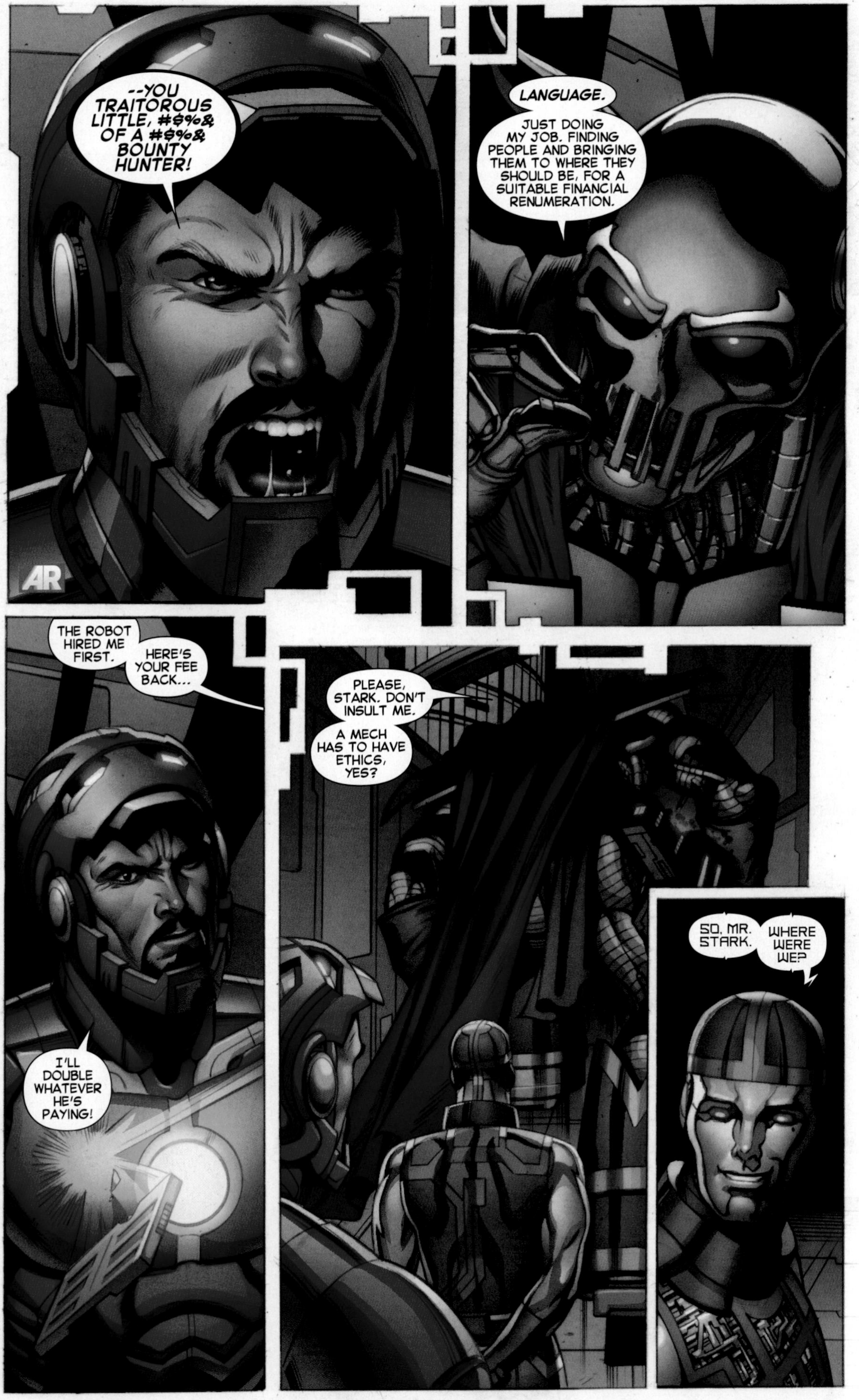
--YOU TRAITOROUS LITTLE, #$%& OF A #$%& BOUNTY HUNTER!
LANGUAGE.
JUST DOING MY JOB. FINDING PEOPLE AND BRINGING THEM TO WHERE THEY SHOULD BE, FOR A SUITABLE FINANCIAL RENUMERATION.
THE ROBOT HIRED ME FIRST.
HERE'S YOUR FEE BACK...
I'LL DOUBLE WHATEVER HE'S PAYING!
PLEASE, STARK. DON'T INSULT ME.
A MECH HAS TO HAVE ETHICS, YES?
SO, MR. STARK.
WHERE WERE WE?

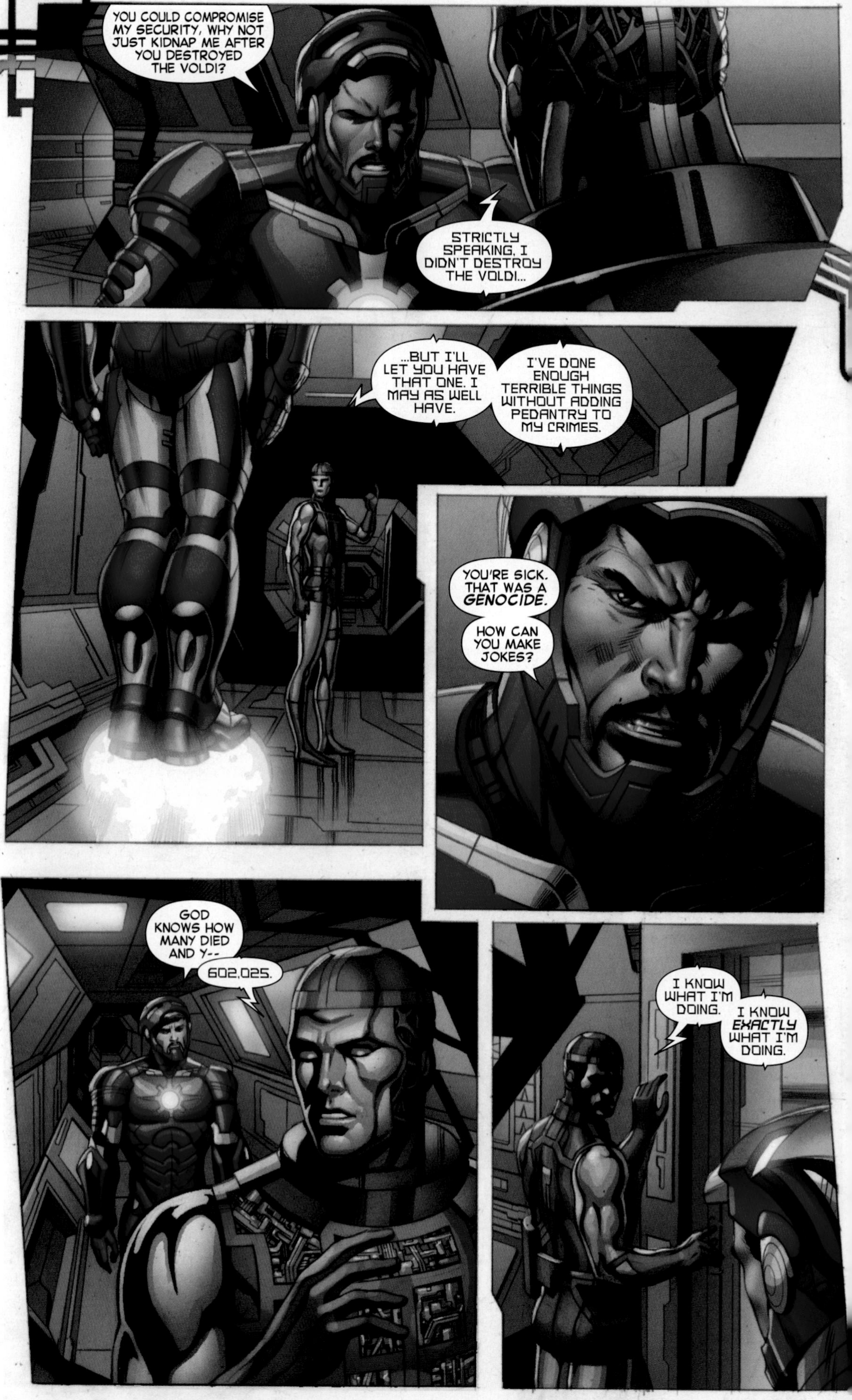
YOU COULD COMPROMISE MY SECURITY, WHY NOT JUST KIDNAP ME AFTER YOU DESTROYED THE VOLDI?
STRICTLY SPEAKING, I DIDN'T DESTROY THE VOLDI...
...BUT I'LL LET YOU HAVE THAT ONE. I MAY AS WELL HAVE.
I'VE DONE ENOUGH TERRIBLE THINGS WITHOUT ADDING PEDANTRY TO MY CRIMES.
YOU'RE SICK. THAT WAS A GENOCIDE.
HOW CAN YOU MAKE JOKES?
GOD KNOWS HOW MANY DIED AND Y--
602,025.
I KNOW WHAT I'M DOING.
I KNOW EXACTLY WHAT I'M DOING.

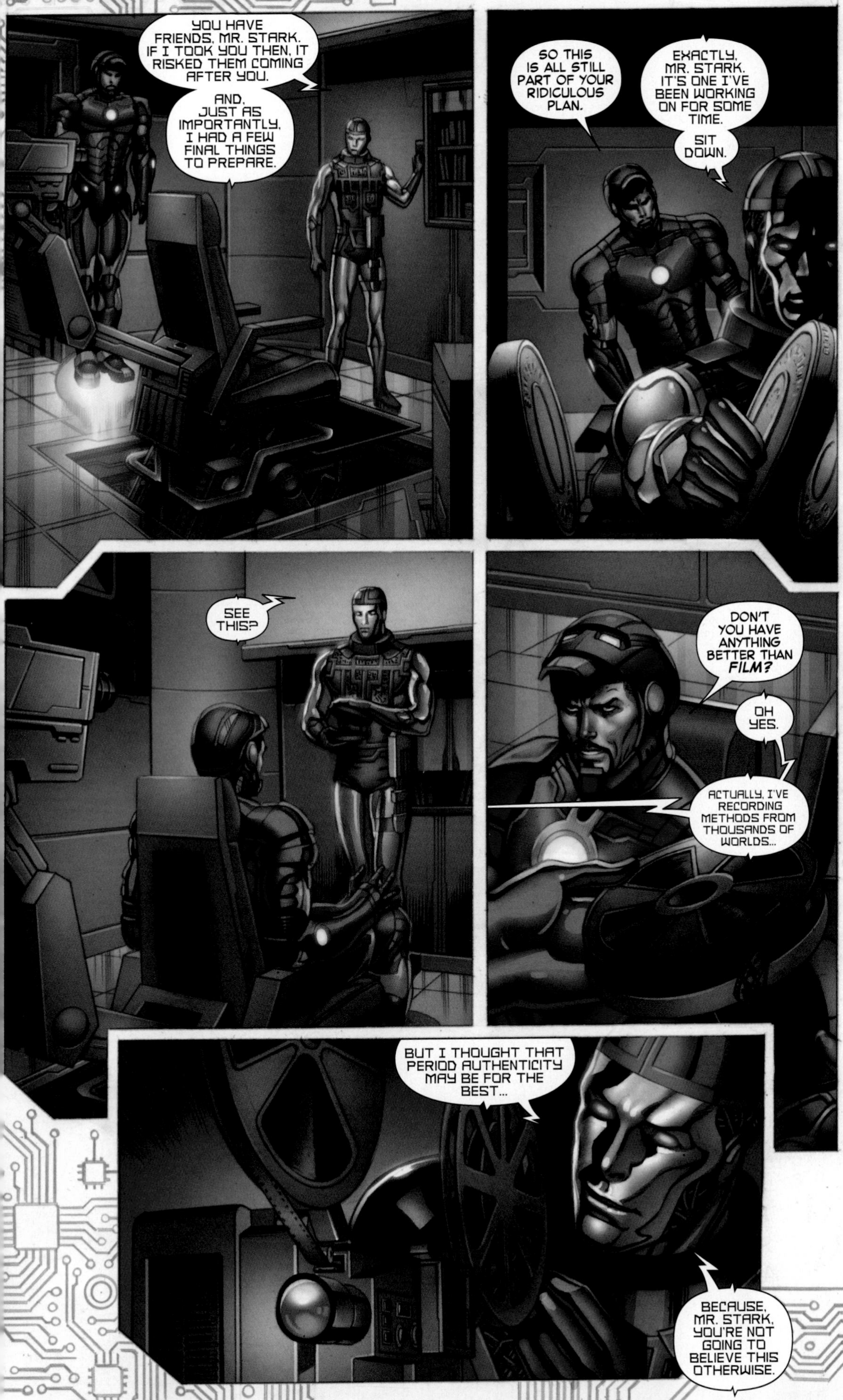
YOU HAVE FRIENDS, MR. STARK. IF I TOOK YOU THEN, IT RISKED THEM COMING AFTER YOU.
AND, JUST AS IMPORTANTLY, I HAD A FEW FINAL THINGS TO PREPARE.
SO THIS IS ALL STILL PART OF YOUR RIDICULOUS PLAN.
EXACTLY, MR. STARK. IT'S ONE I'VE BEEN WORKING ON FOR SOME TIME.
SIT DOWN.
SEE THIS?
DON'T YOU HAVE ANYTHING BETTER THAN *FILM?*
OH YES.
ACTUALLY, I'VE RECORDING METHODS FROM THOUSANDS OF WORLDS...
BUT I THOUGHT THAT PERIOD AUTHENTICITY MAY BE FOR THE BEST...
BECAUSE, MR. STARK, YOU'RE NOT GOING TO BELIEVE THIS OTHERWISE.

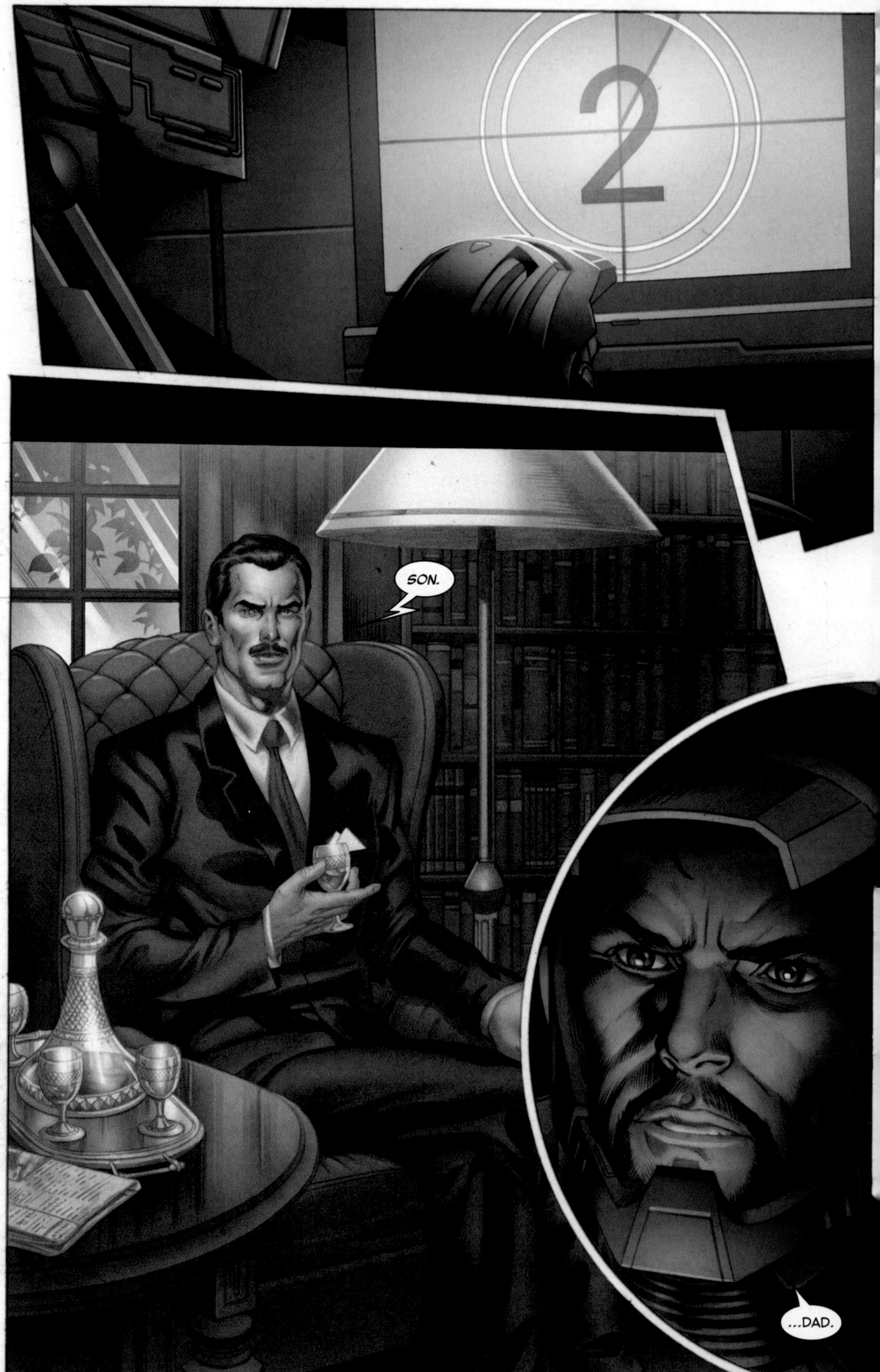
SON.
...DAD.

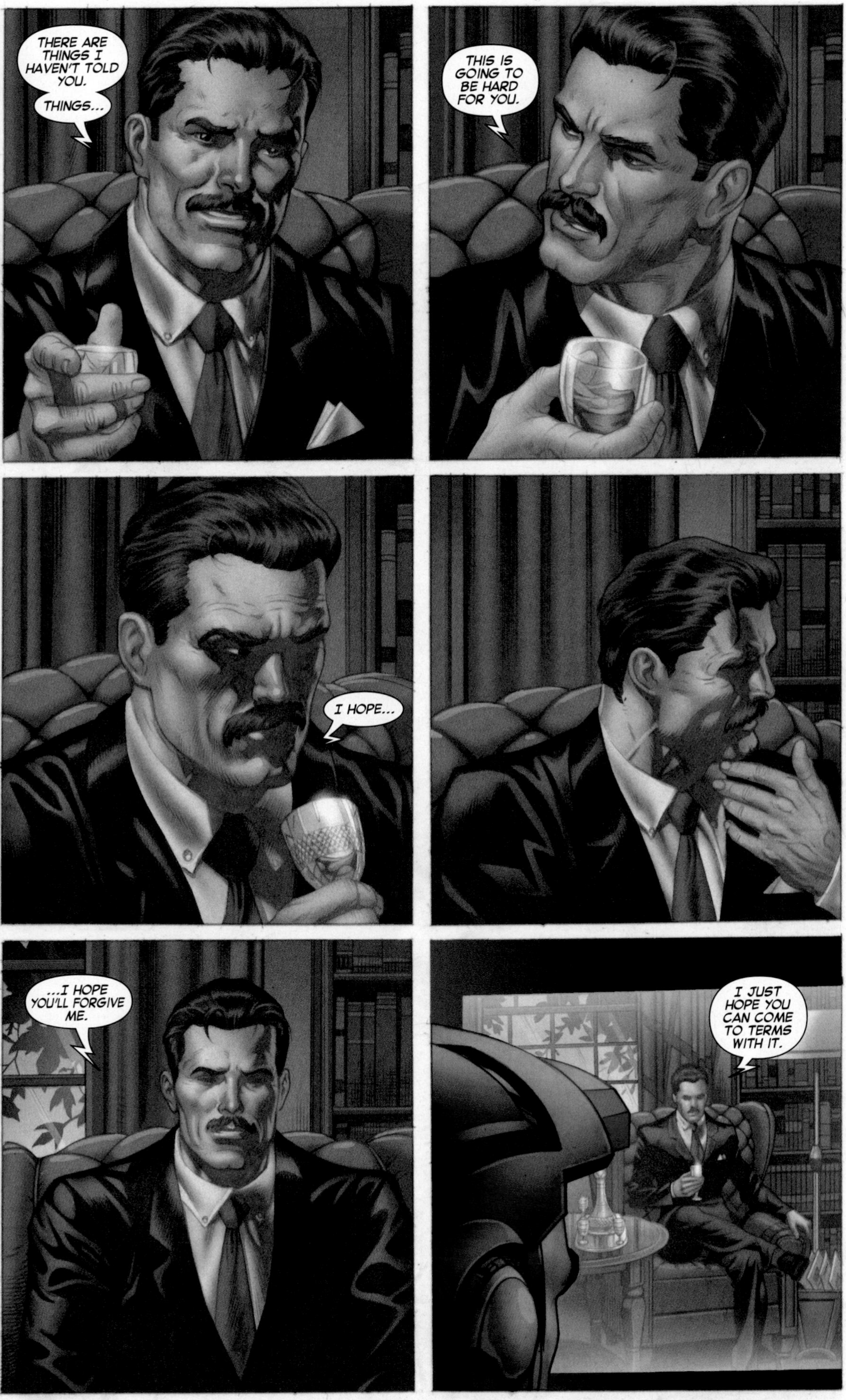
THERE ARE THINGS I HAVEN'T TOLD YOU.
THINGS...
THIS IS GOING TO BE HARD FOR YOU.
I HOPE...
...I HOPE YOU'LL FORGIVE ME.
I JUST HOPE YOU CAN COME TO TERMS WITH IT.

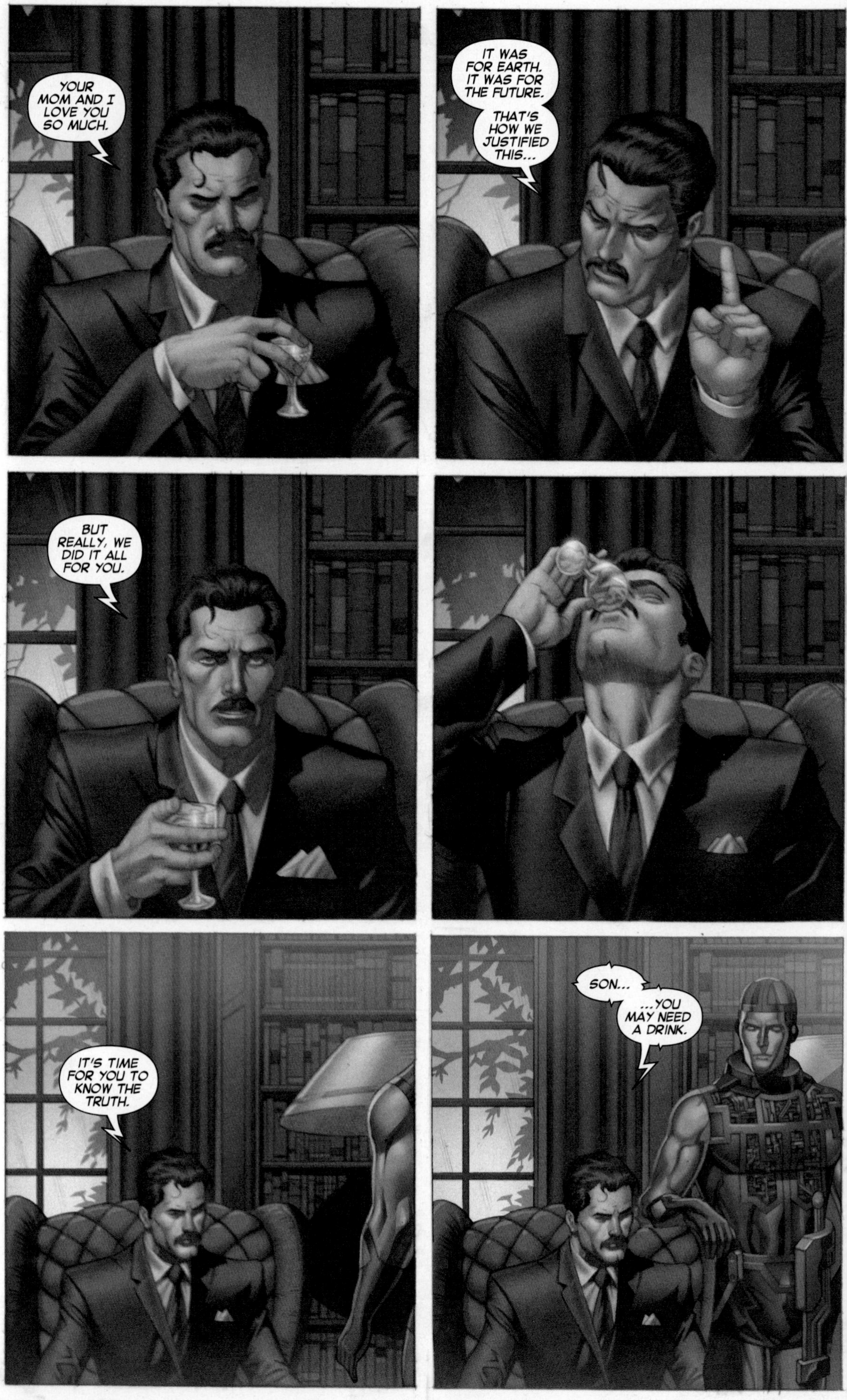
YOUR MOM AND I LOVE YOU SO MUCH.
IT WAS FOR EARTH. IT WAS FOR THE FUTURE.
THAT'S HOW WE JUSTIFIED THIS...
BUT REALLY, WE DID IT ALL FOR YOU.
IT'S TIME FOR YOU TO KNOW THE TRUTH.
SON...
...YOU MAY NEED A DRINK.

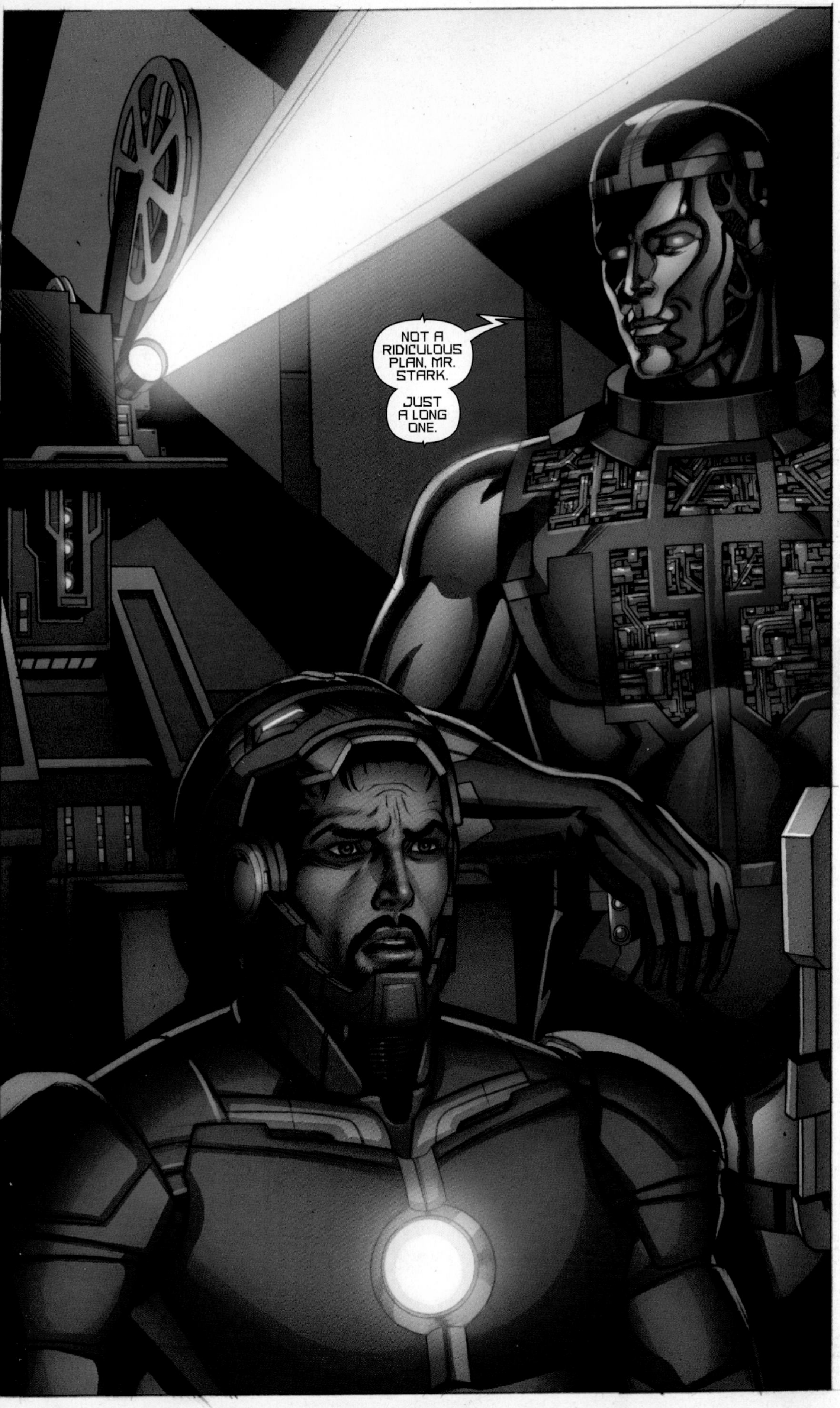
NOT A RIDICULOUS PLAN, MR. STARK.
JUST A LONG ONE.

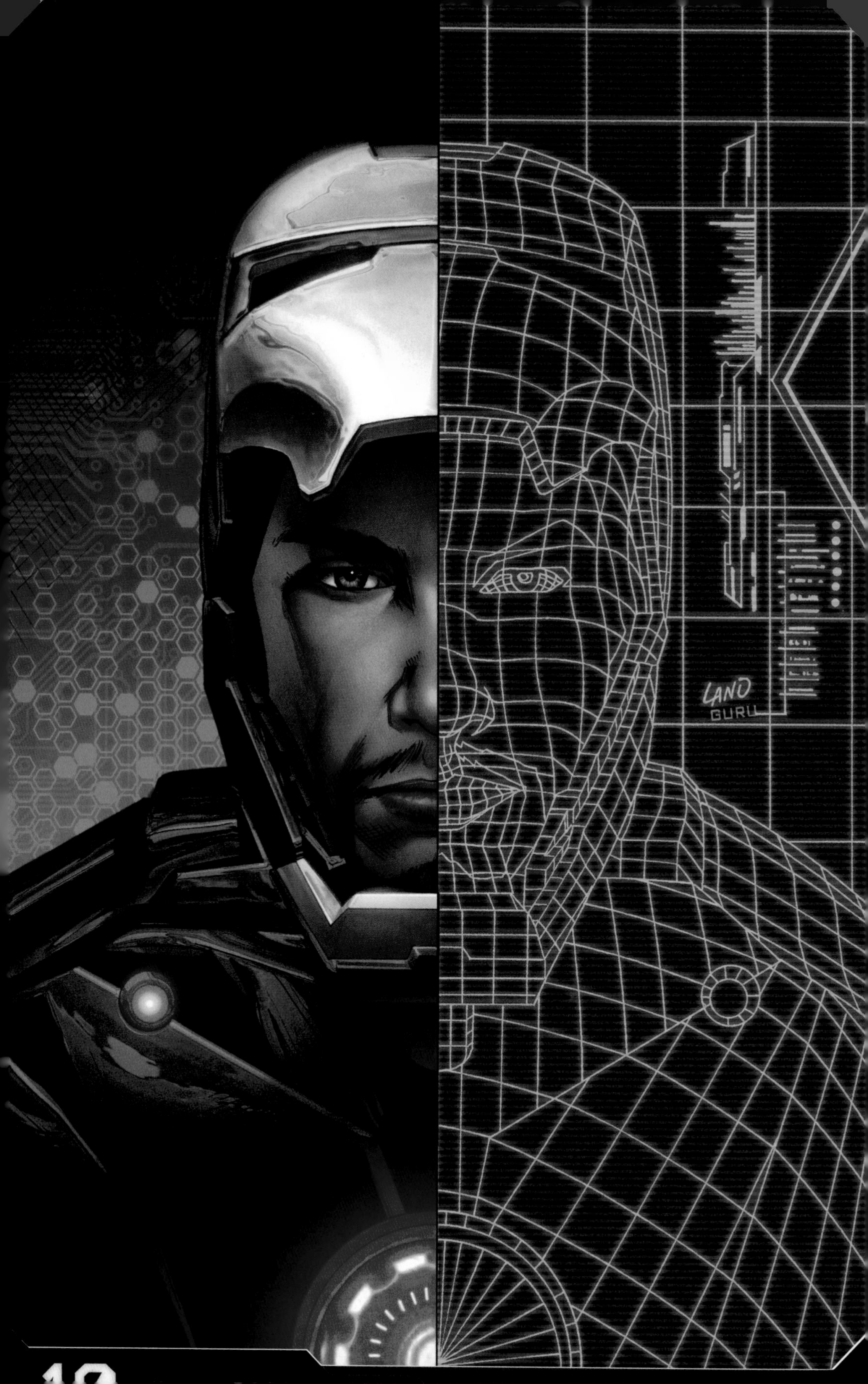

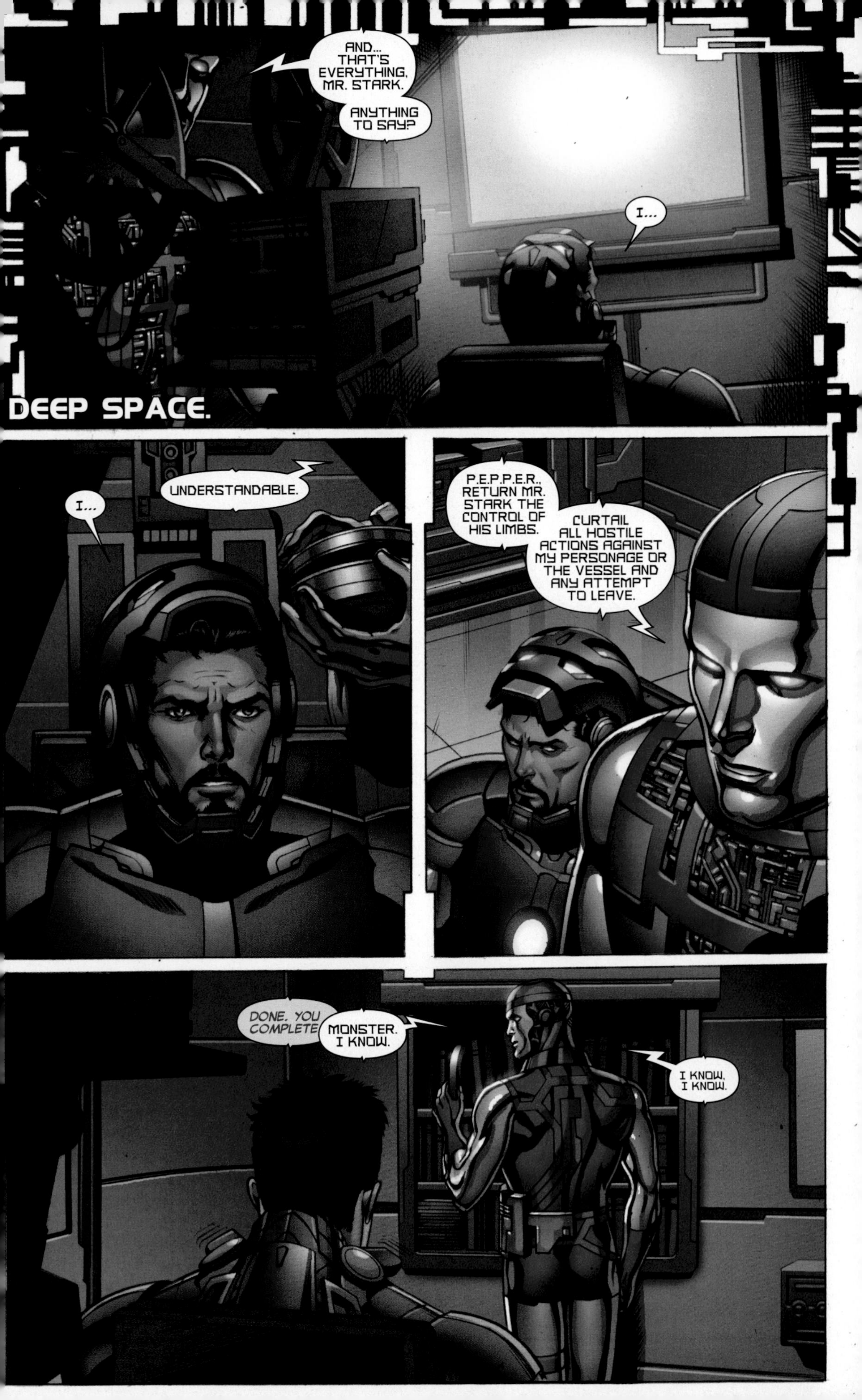
AND... THAT'S EVERYTHING, MR. STARK.
ANYTHING TO SAY?
I...
DEEP SPACE.
I...
UNDERSTANDABLE.
P.E.P.P.E.R., RETURN MR. STARK THE CONTROL OF HIS LIMBS.
CURTAIL ALL HOSTILE ACTIONS AGAINST MY PERSONAGE OR THE VESSEL AND ANY ATTEMPT TO LEAVE.
DONE. YOU COMPLETE
MONSTER. I KNOW.
I KNOW. I KNOW.

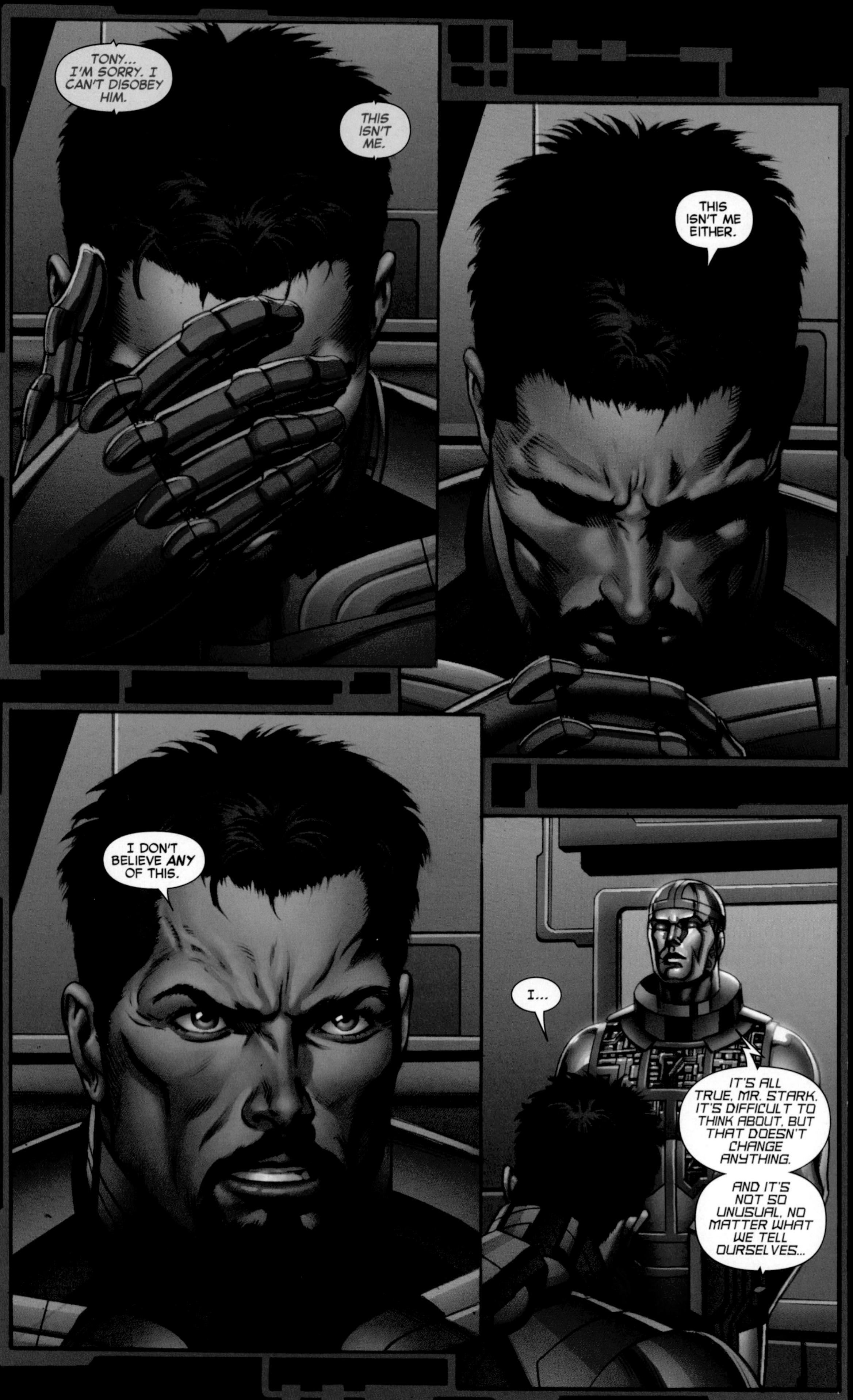
TONY... I'M SORRY. I CAN'T DISOBEY HIM.
THIS ISN'T ME.
THIS ISN'T ME EITHER.
I DON'T BELIEVE ANY OF THIS.
I...
IT'S ALL TRUE, MR. STARK. IT'S DIFFICULT TO THINK ABOUT, BUT THAT DOESN'T CHANGE ANYTHING.
AND IT'S NOT SO UNUSUAL, NO MATTER WHAT WE TELL OURSELVES...

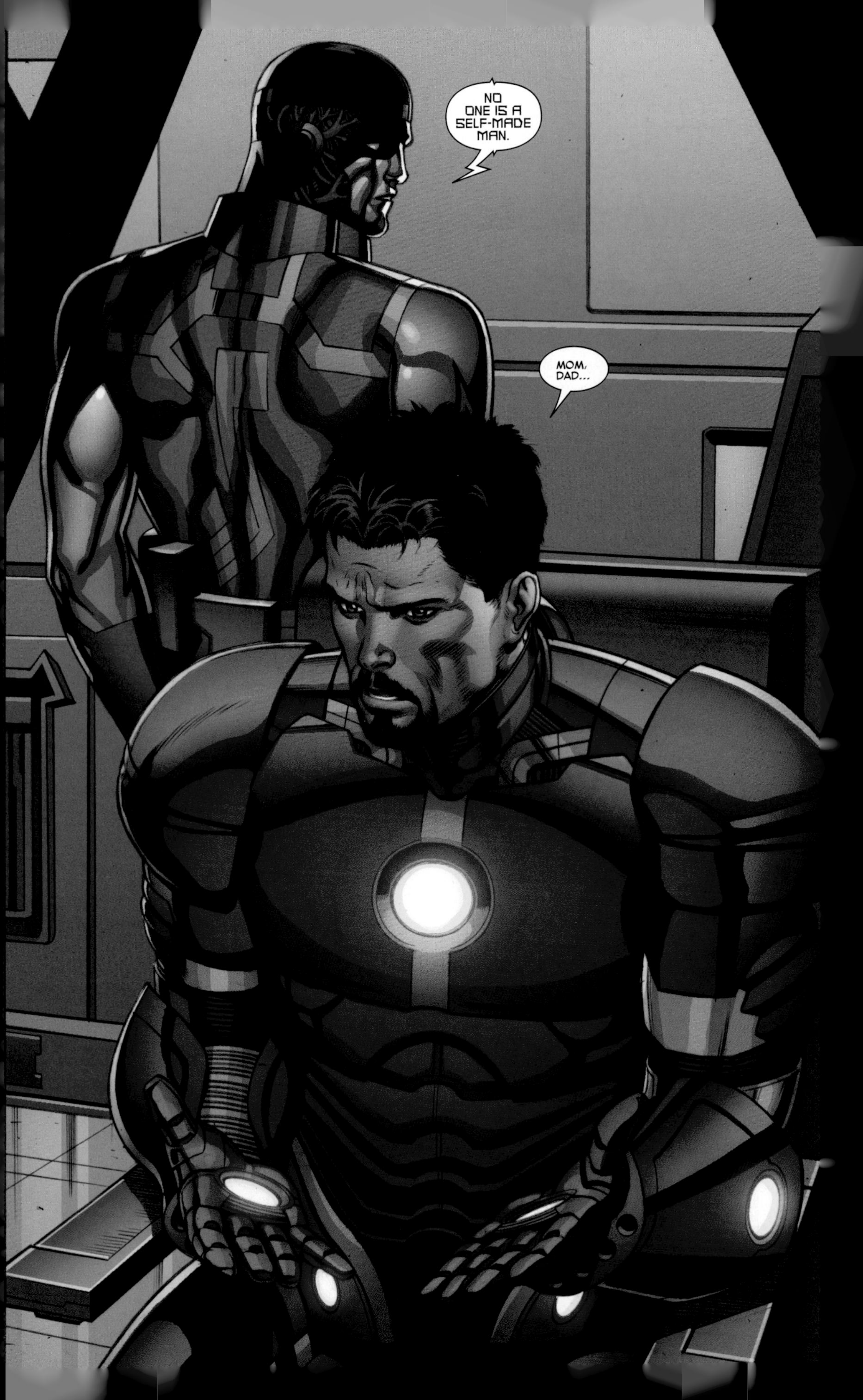
NO ONE IS A SELF-MADE MAN.
MOM, DAD...

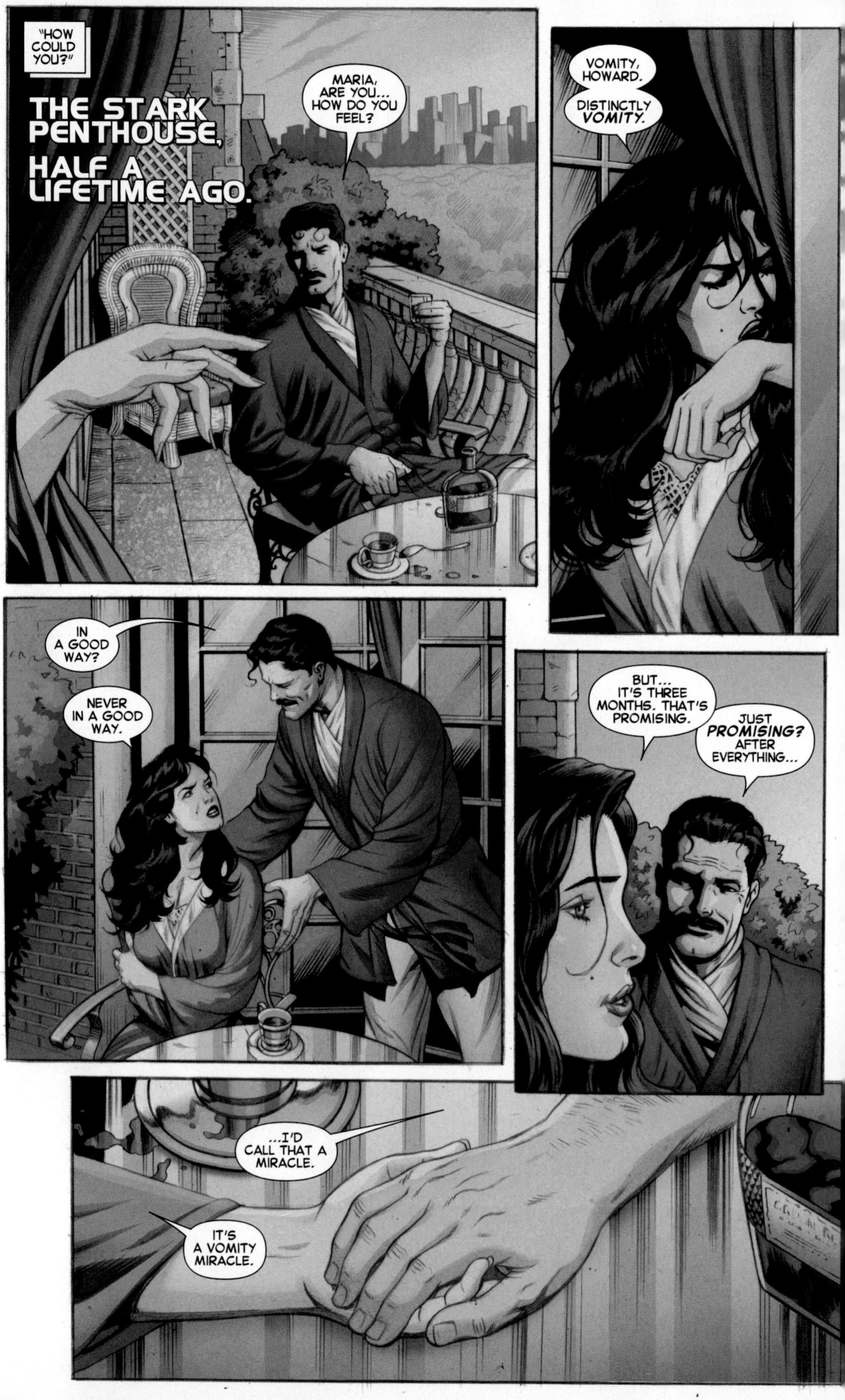
"HOW COULD YOU?"
THE STARK PENTHOUSE,
HALF A LIFETIME AGO.
MARIA, ARE YOU... HOW DO YOU FEEL?
VOMITY, HOWARD.
DISTINCTLY *VOMITY*.
IN A GOOD WAY?
NEVER IN A GOOD WAY.
BUT... IT'S THREE MONTHS. THAT'S PROMISING.
JUST *PROMISING?* AFTER EVERYTHING...
...I'D CALL THAT A MIRACLE.
IT'S A VOMITY MIRACLE.

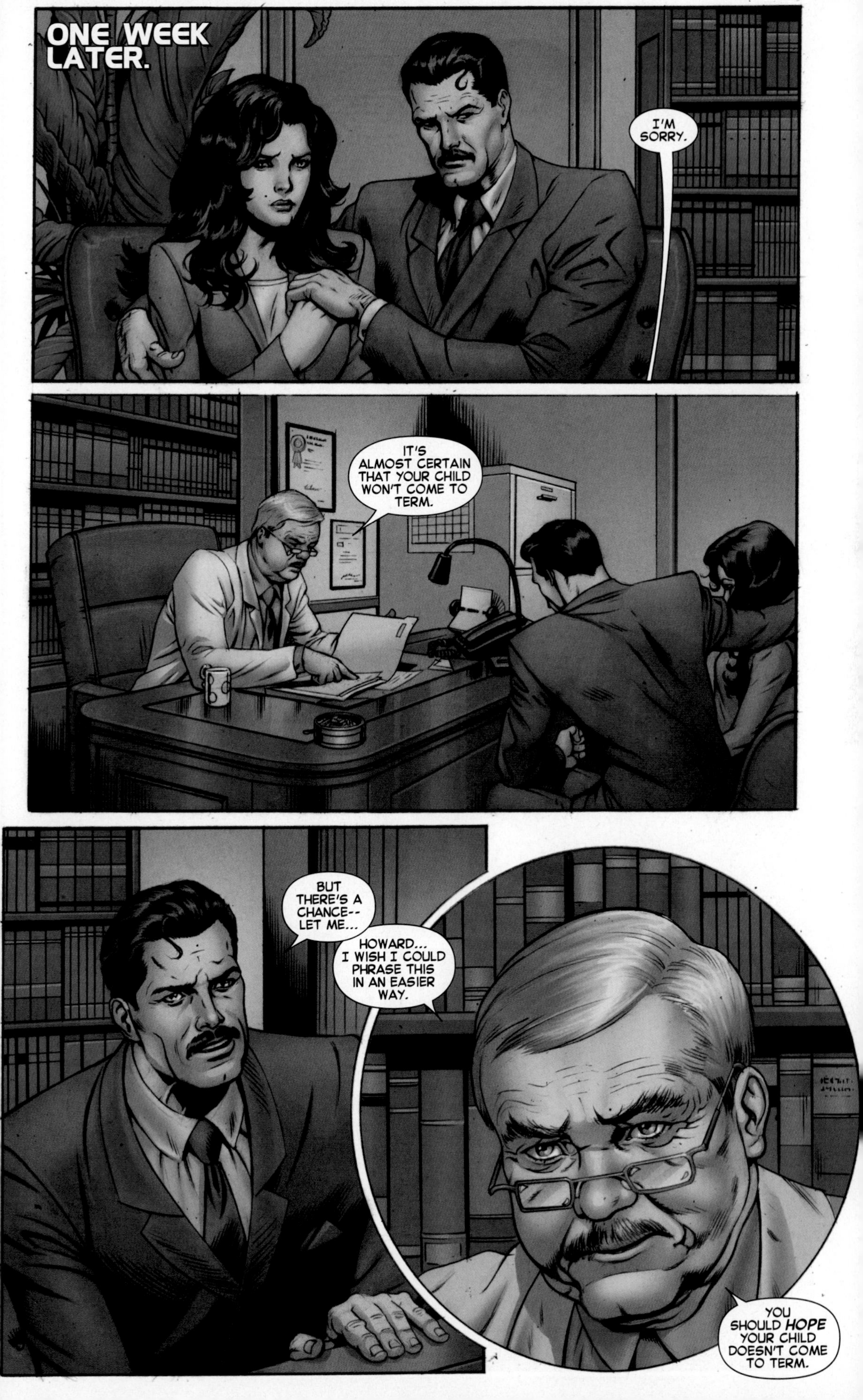
ONE WEEK LATER.
I'M SORRY.
IT'S ALMOST CERTAIN THAT YOUR CHILD WON'T COME TO TERM.
BUT THERE'S A CHANCE-- LET ME...
HOWARD... I WISH I COULD PHRASE THIS IN AN EASIER WAY.
YOU SHOULD *HOPE* YOUR CHILD DOESN'T COME TO TERM.

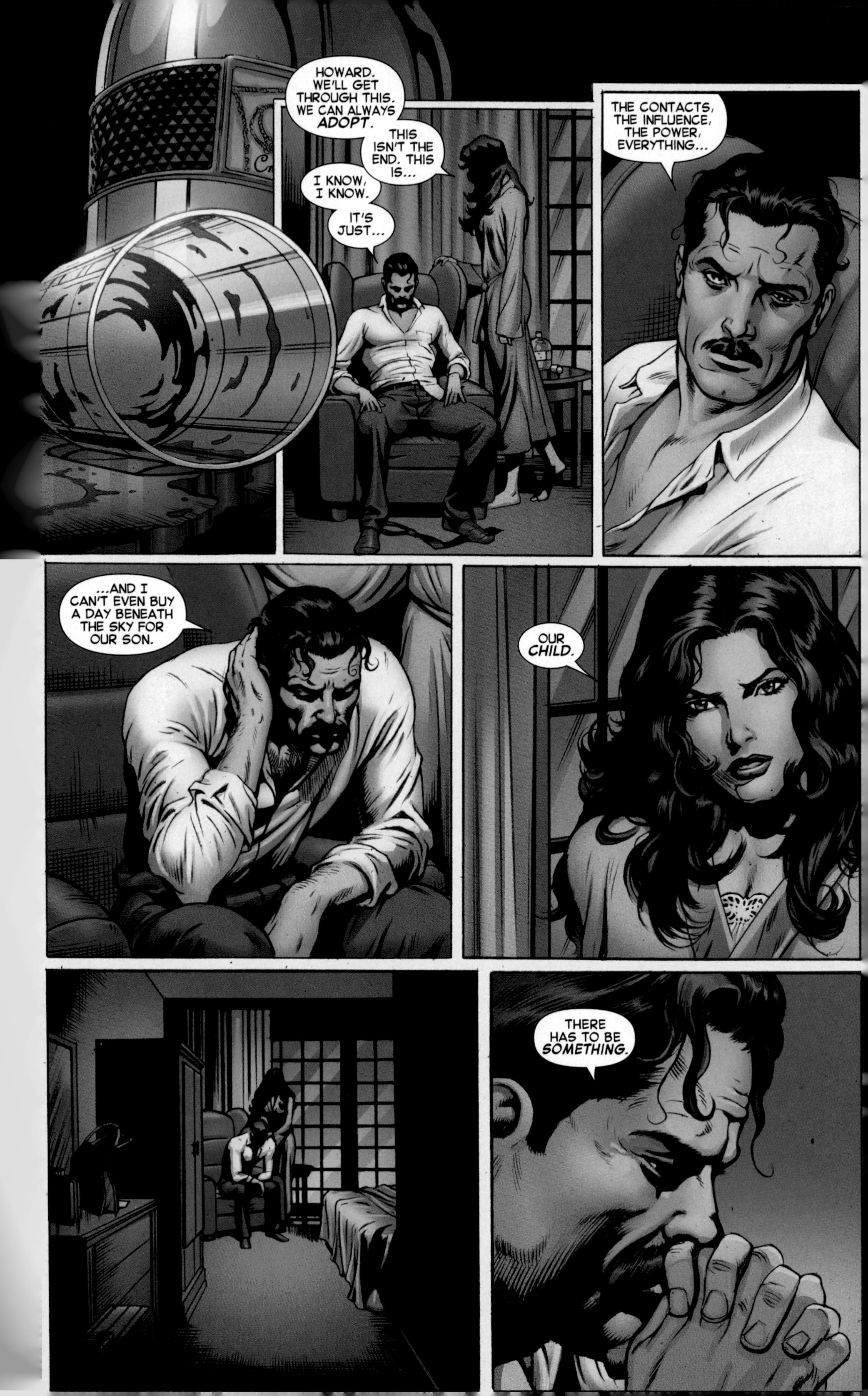
HOWARD. WE'LL GET THROUGH THIS. WE CAN ALWAYS *ADOPT*.
THIS ISN'T THE END. THIS IS...
I KNOW, I KNOW.
IT'S JUST...
THE CONTACTS, THE INFLUENCE, THE POWER, EVERYTHING...
...AND I CAN'T EVEN BUY A DAY BENEATH THE SKY FOR OUR SON.
OUR *CHILD*.
THERE HAS TO BE *SOMETHING*.

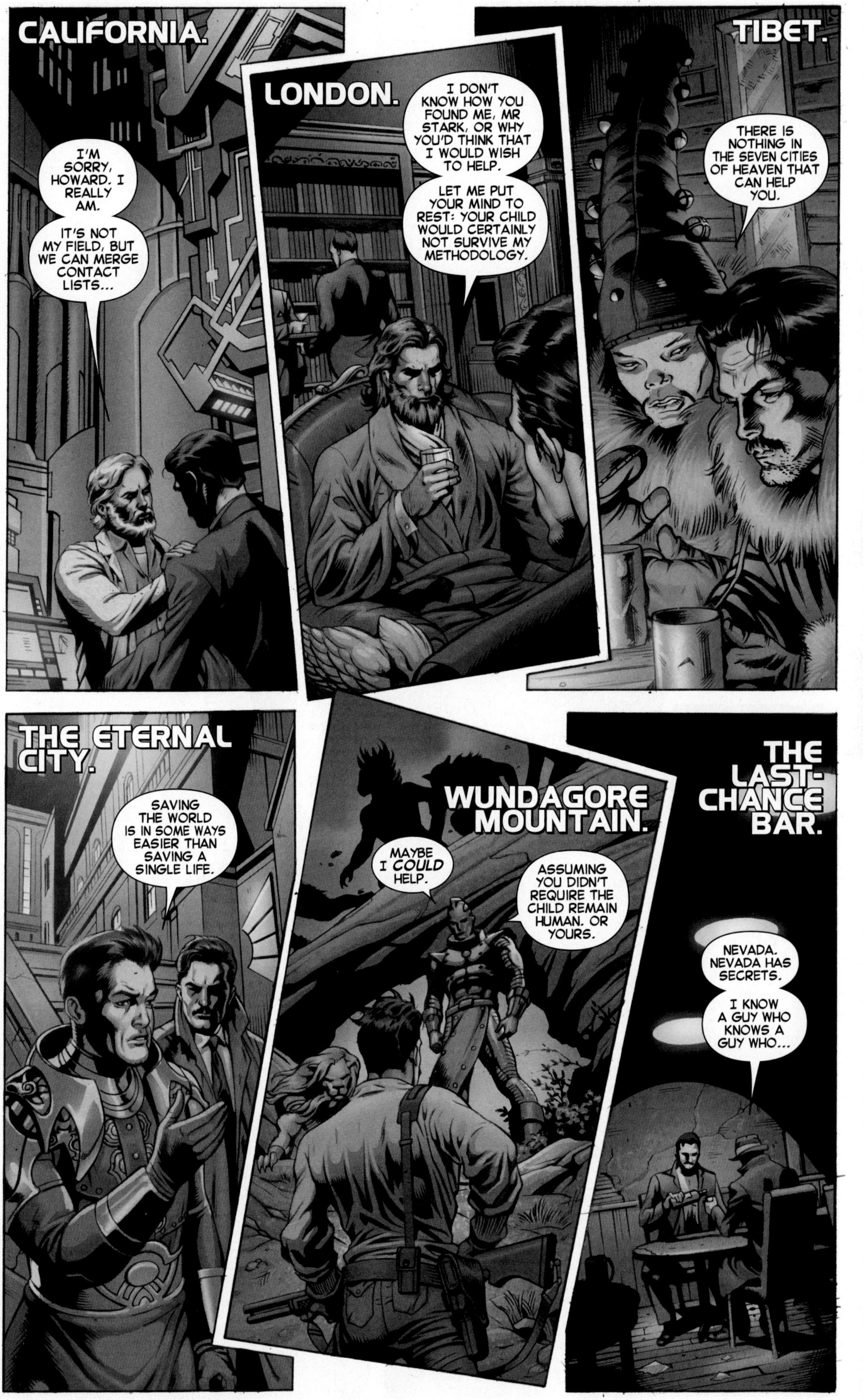
CALIFORNIA.
I'M SORRY, HOWARD. I REALLY AM.
IT'S NOT MY FIELD, BUT WE CAN MERGE CONTACT LISTS...
LONDON.
I DON'T KNOW HOW YOU FOUND ME, MR STARK, OR WHY YOU'D THINK THAT I WOULD WISH TO HELP.
LET ME PUT YOUR MIND TO REST: YOUR CHILD WOULD CERTAINLY NOT SURVIVE MY METHODOLOGY.
TIBET.
THERE IS NOTHING IN THE SEVEN CITIES OF HEAVEN THAT CAN HELP YOU.
THE ETERNAL CITY.
SAVING THE WORLD IS IN SOME WAYS EASIER THAN SAVING A SINGLE LIFE.
WUNDAGORE MOUNTAIN.
MAYBE I *COULD* HELP.
ASSUMING YOU DIDN'T REQUIRE THE CHILD REMAIN HUMAN. OR YOURS.
THE LAST-CHANCE BAR.
NEVADA. NEVADA HAS SECRETS.
I KNOW A GUY WHO KNOWS A GUY WHO...

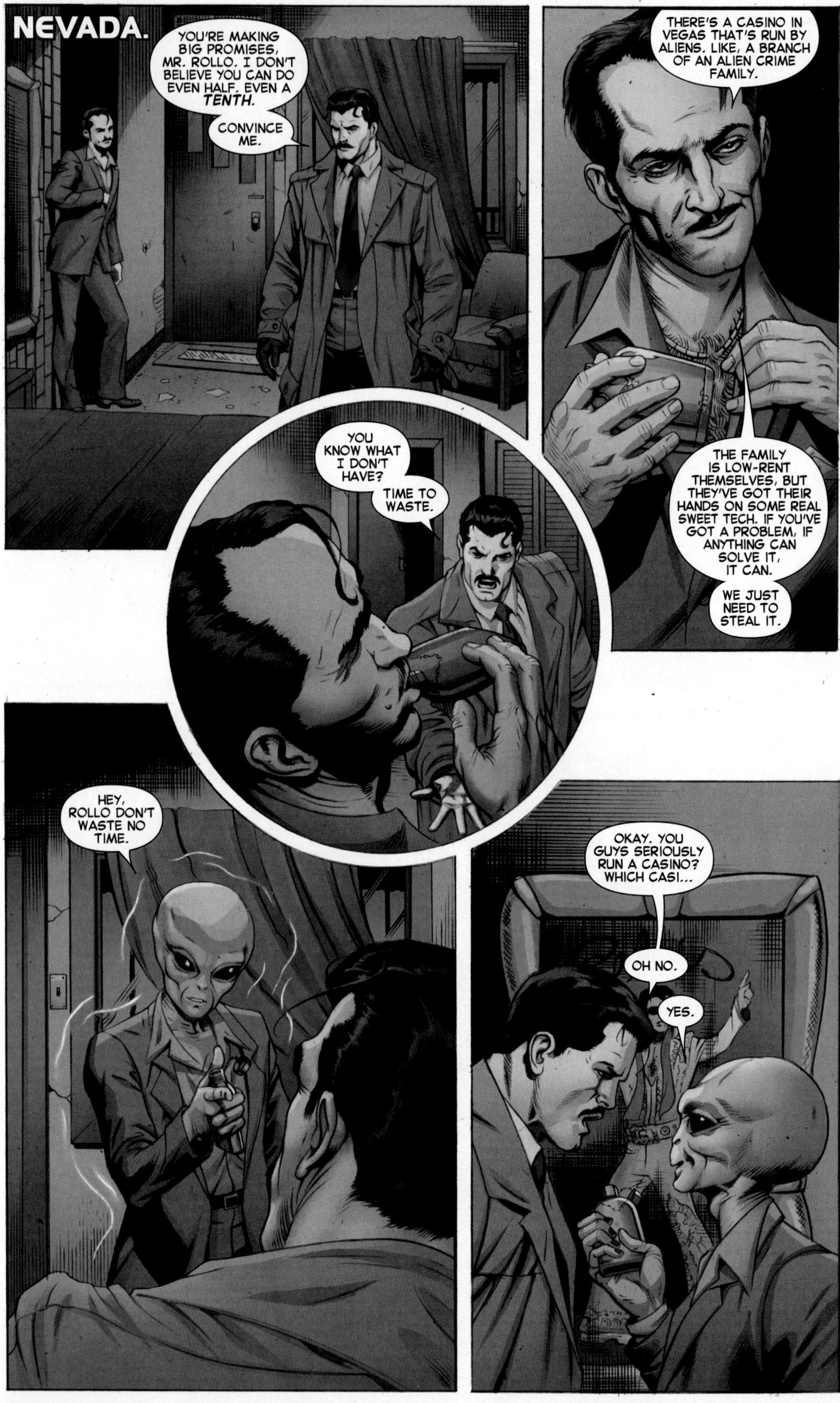
NEVADA.
YOU'RE MAKING BIG PROMISES, MR. ROLLO. I DON'T BELIEVE YOU CAN DO EVEN HALF. EVEN A TENTH.
CONVINCE ME.
THERE'S A CASINO IN VEGAS THAT'S RUN BY ALIENS. LIKE, A BRANCH OF AN ALIEN CRIME FAMILY.
YOU KNOW WHAT I DON'T HAVE?
TIME TO WASTE.
THE FAMILY IS LOW-RENT THEMSELVES, BUT THEY'VE GOT THEIR HANDS ON SOME REAL SWEET TECH. IF YOU'VE GOT A PROBLEM, IF ANYTHING CAN SOLVE IT, IT CAN.
WE JUST NEED TO STEAL IT.
HEY, ROLLO DON'T WASTE NO TIME.
OKAY. YOU GUYS SERIOUSLY RUN A CASINO? WHICH CASI...
OH NO.
YES.

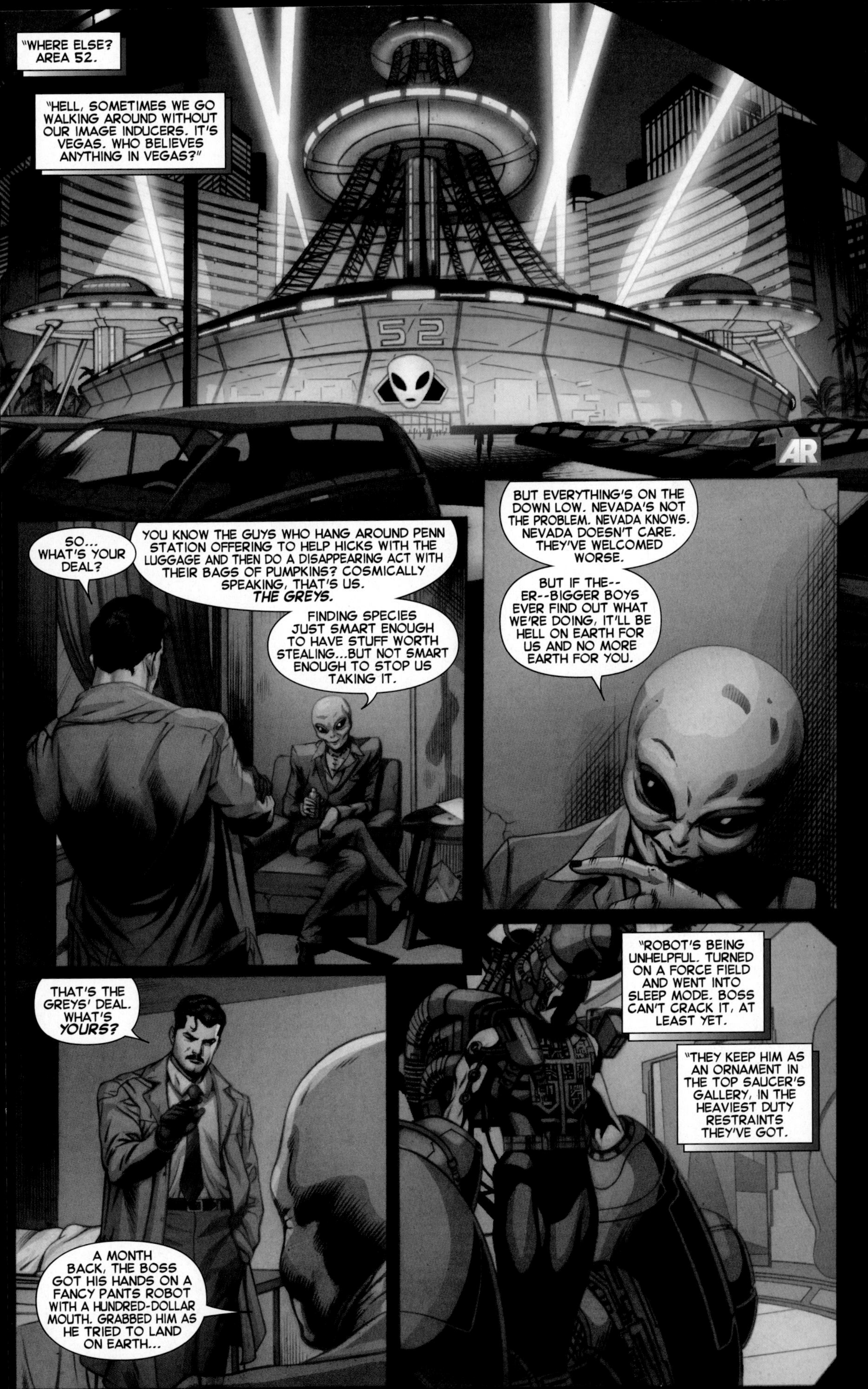
"WHERE ELSE? AREA 52.
"HELL, SOMETIMES WE GO WALKING AROUND WITHOUT OUR IMAGE INDUCERS. IT'S VEGAS. WHO BELIEVES ANYTHING IN VEGAS?"
52
AR
SO... WHAT'S YOUR DEAL?
YOU KNOW THE GUYS WHO HANG AROUND PENN STATION OFFERING TO HELP HICKS WITH THE LUGGAGE AND THEN DO A DISAPPEARING ACT WITH THEIR BAGS OF PUMPKINS? COSMICALLY SPEAKING, THAT'S US. *THE GREYS.*
FINDING SPECIES JUST SMART ENOUGH TO HAVE STUFF WORTH STEALING...BUT NOT SMART ENOUGH TO STOP US TAKING IT.
BUT EVERYTHING'S ON THE DOWN LOW. NEVADA'S NOT THE PROBLEM. NEVADA KNOWS. NEVADA DOESN'T CARE. THEY'VE WELCOMED WORSE.
BUT IF THE-- ER--BIGGER BOYS EVER FIND OUT WHAT WE'RE DOING, IT'LL BE HELL ON EARTH FOR US AND NO MORE EARTH FOR YOU.
THAT'S THE GREYS' DEAL. WHAT'S *YOURS?*
A MONTH BACK, THE BOSS GOT HIS HANDS ON A FANCY PANTS ROBOT WITH A HUNDRED-DOLLAR MOUTH. GRABBED HIM AS HE TRIED TO LAND ON EARTH...
"ROBOT'S BEING UNHELPFUL. TURNED ON A FORCE FIELD AND WENT INTO SLEEP MODE. BOSS CAN'T CRACK IT, AT LEAST YET.
"THEY KEEP HIM AS AN ORNAMENT IN THE TOP SAUCER'S GALLERY, IN THE HEAVIEST DUTY RESTRAINTS THEY'VE GOT.

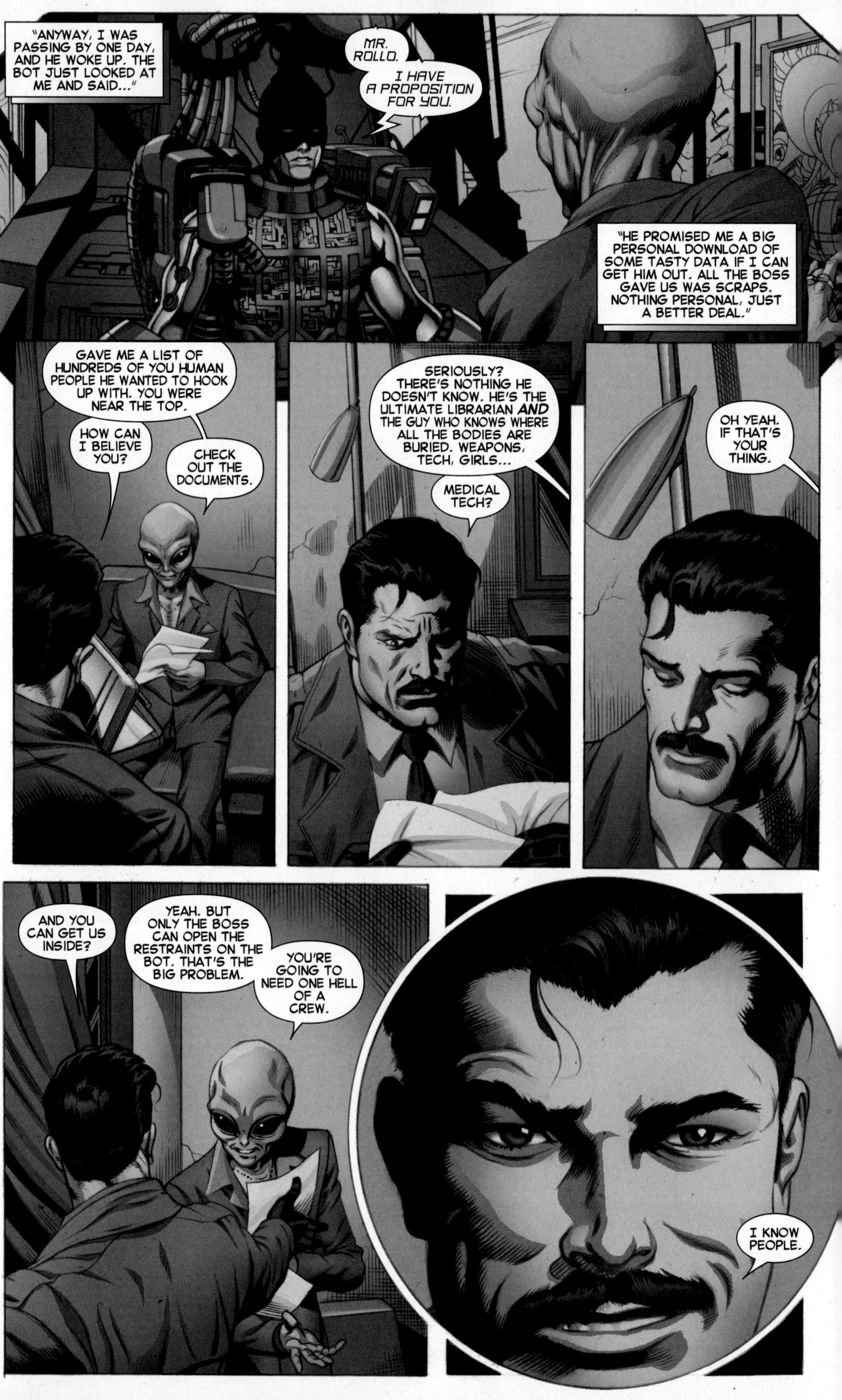
"ANYWAY, I WAS PASSING BY ONE DAY, AND HE WOKE UP. THE BOT JUST LOOKED AT ME AND SAID..."
MR. ROLLO.
I HAVE A PROPOSITION FOR YOU.
"HE PROMISED ME A BIG PERSONAL DOWNLOAD OF SOME TASTY DATA IF I CAN GET HIM OUT. ALL THE BOSS GAVE US WAS SCRAPS. NOTHING PERSONAL, JUST A BETTER DEAL."
GAVE ME A LIST OF HUNDREDS OF YOU HUMAN PEOPLE HE WANTED TO HOOK UP WITH. YOU WERE NEAR THE TOP.
HOW CAN I BELIEVE YOU?
CHECK OUT THE DOCUMENTS.
SERIOUSLY? THERE'S NOTHING HE DOESN'T KNOW. HE'S THE ULTIMATE LIBRARIAN AND THE GUY WHO KNOWS WHERE ALL THE BODIES ARE BURIED. WEAPONS, TECH, GIRLS...
MEDICAL TECH?
OH YEAH. IF THAT'S YOUR THING.
AND YOU CAN GET US INSIDE?
YEAH. BUT ONLY THE BOSS CAN OPEN THE RESTRAINTS ON THE BOT. THAT'S THE BIG PROBLEM.
YOU'RE GOING TO NEED ONE HELL OF A CREW.
I KNOW PEOPLE.

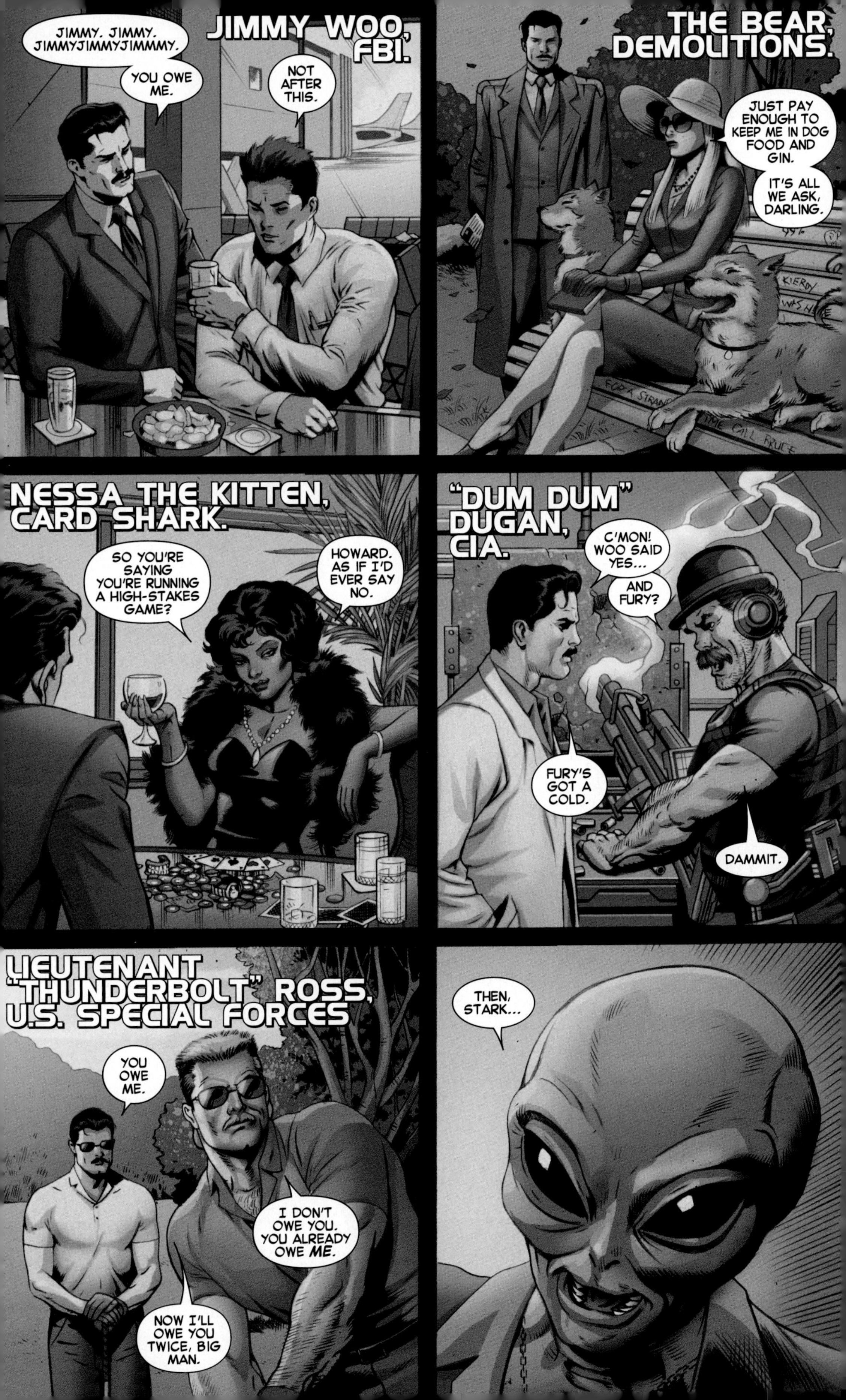
JIMMY WOO, FBI.
JIMMY. JIMMY. JIMMYJIMMYJIMMMY.
YOU OWE ME.
NOT AFTER THIS.
THE BEAR, DEMOLITIONS.
JUST PAY ENOUGH TO KEEP ME IN DOG FOOD AND GIN.
IT'S ALL WE ASK, DARLING.
NESSA THE KITTEN, CARD SHARK.
SO YOU'RE SAYING YOU'RE RUNNING A HIGH-STAKES GAME?
HOWARD. AS IF I'D EVER SAY NO.
"DUM DUM" DUGAN, CIA.
C'MON! WOO SAID YES...
AND FURY?
FURY'S GOT A COLD.
DAMMIT.
LIEUTENANT "THUNDERBOLT" ROSS, U.S. SPECIAL FORCES
YOU OWE ME.
I DON'T OWE YOU. YOU ALREADY OWE *ME*.
NOW I'LL OWE YOU TWICE, BIG MAN.
THEN, STARK...

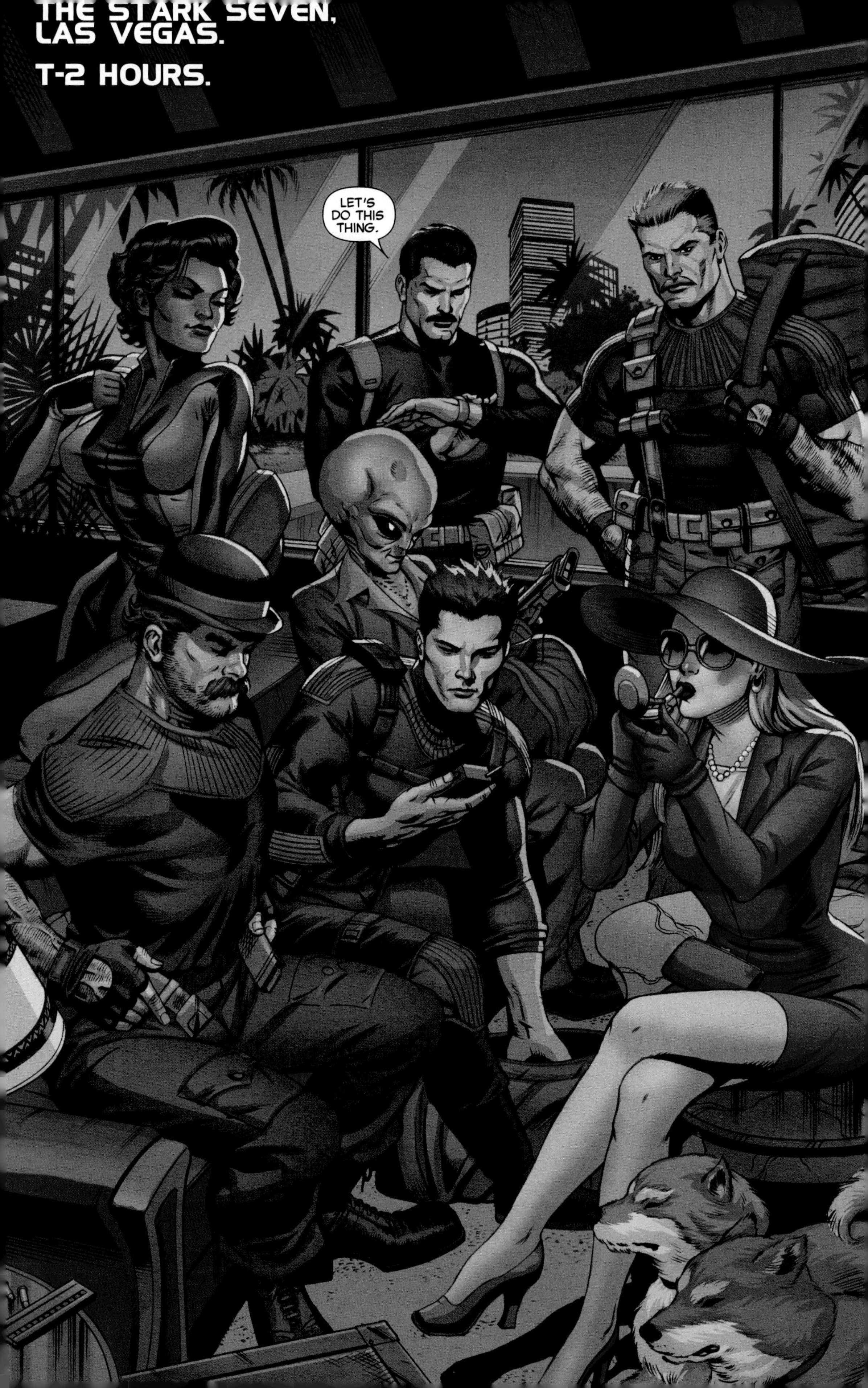
THE STARK SEVEN, LAS VEGAS.
T-2 HOURS.
LET'S DO THIS THING.

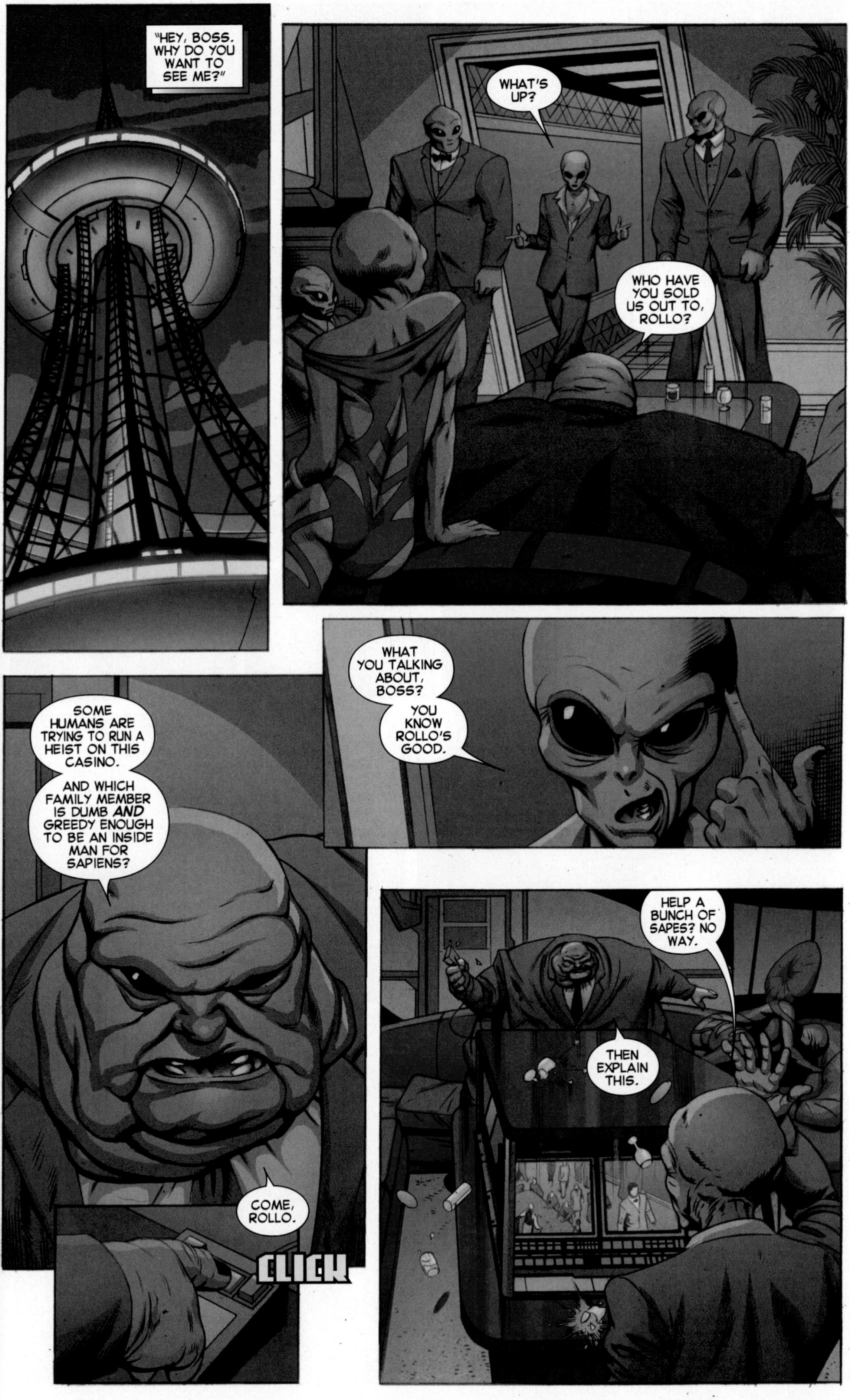
"HEY, BOSS. WHY DO YOU WANT TO SEE ME?"
WHAT'S UP?
WHO HAVE YOU SOLD US OUT TO, ROLLO?
WHAT YOU TALKING ABOUT, BOSS?
YOU KNOW ROLLO'S GOOD.
SOME HUMANS ARE TRYING TO RUN A HEIST ON THIS CASINO.
AND WHICH FAMILY MEMBER IS DUMB AND GREEDY ENOUGH TO BE AN INSIDE MAN FOR SAPIENS?
COME, ROLLO.
CLICK
HELP A BUNCH OF SAPES? NO WAY.
THEN EXPLAIN THIS.

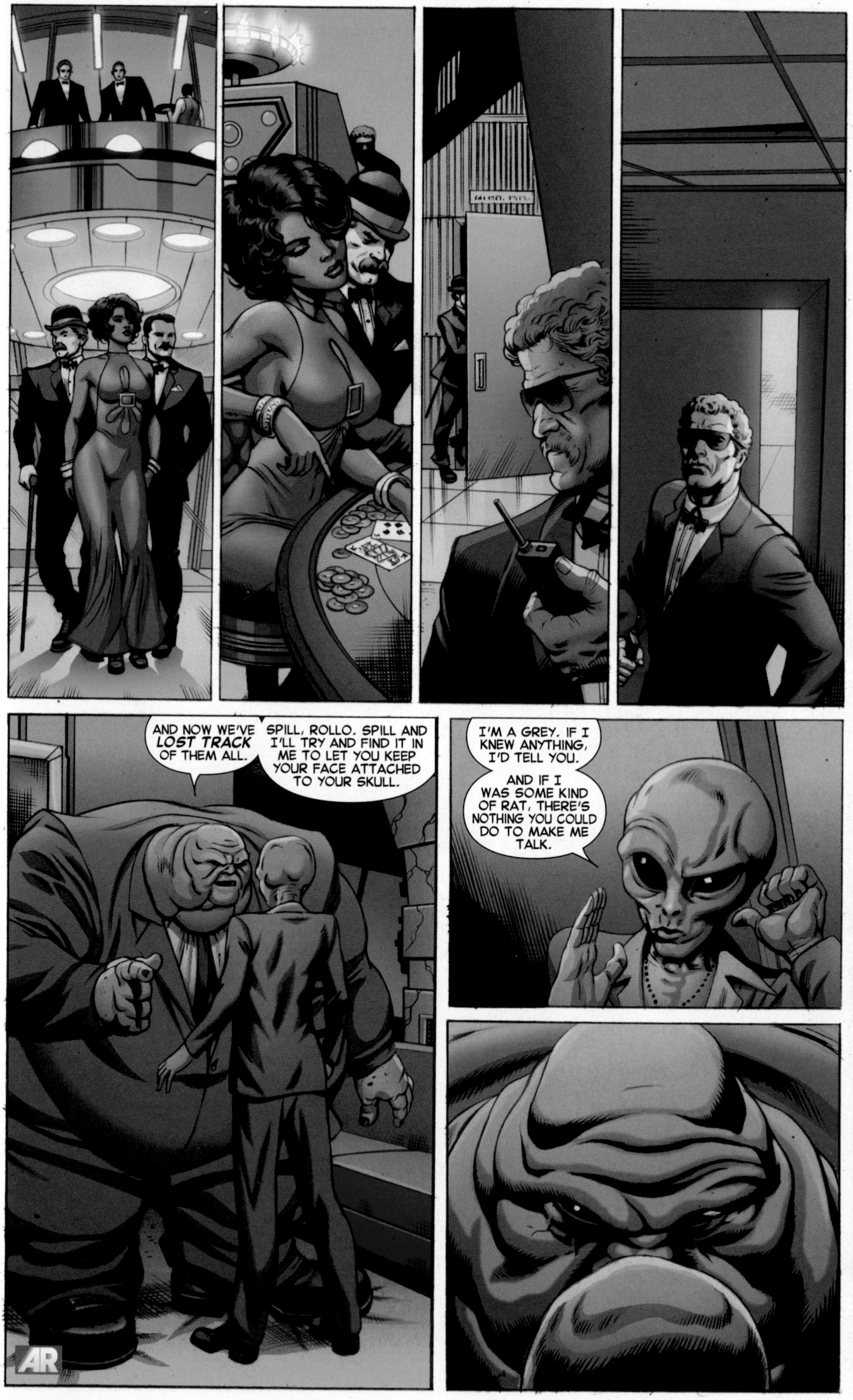
AND NOW WE'VE LOST TRACK OF THEM ALL.
SPILL, ROLLO. SPILL AND I'LL TRY AND FIND IT IN ME TO LET YOU KEEP YOUR FACE ATTACHED TO YOUR SKULL.
I'M A GREY. IF I KNEW ANYTHING, I'D TELL YOU.
AND IF I WAS SOME KIND OF RAT, THERE'S NOTHING YOU COULD DO TO MAKE ME TALK.

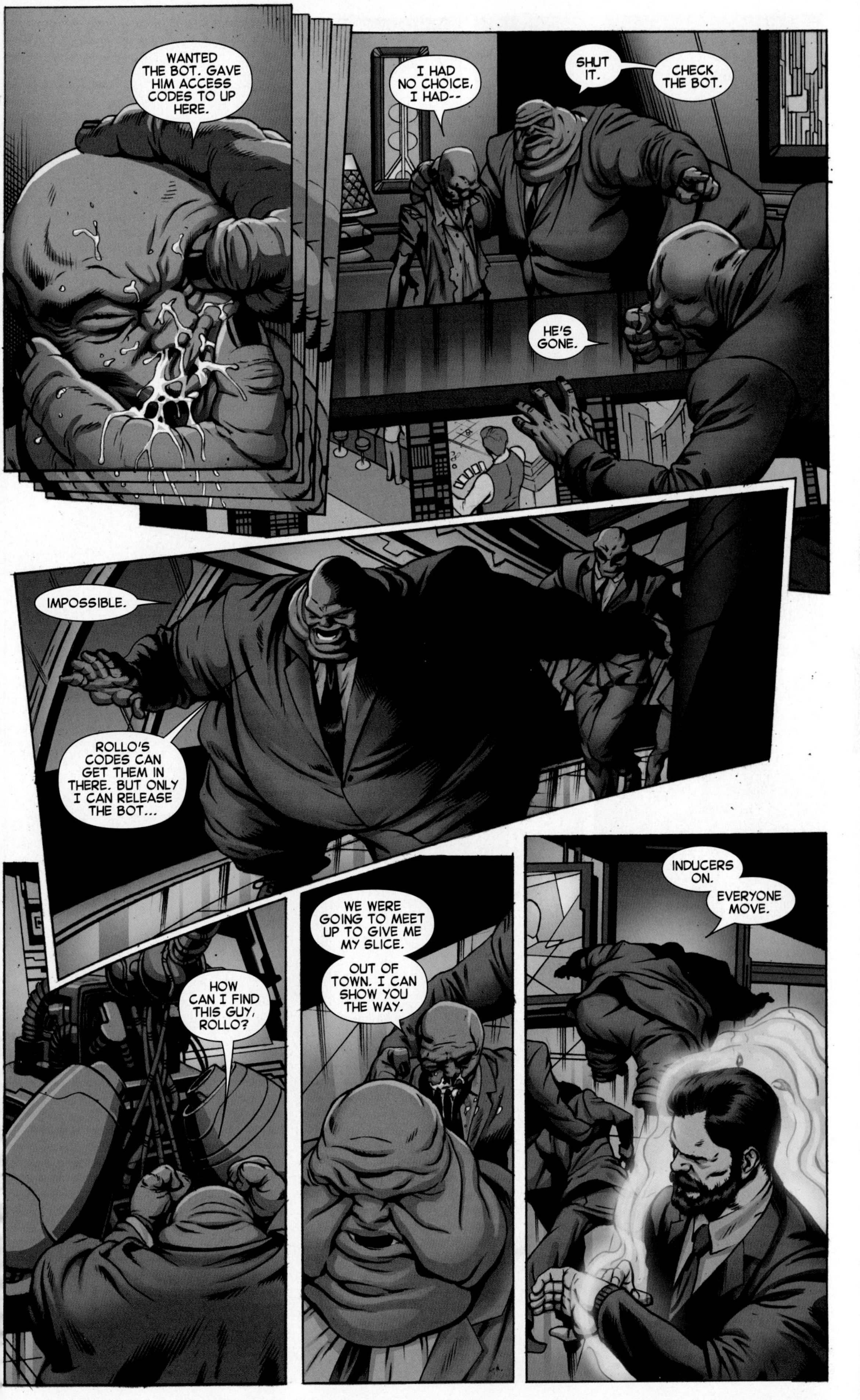
WANTED THE BOT. GAVE HIM ACCESS CODES TO UP HERE.
I HAD NO CHOICE, I HAD--
SHUT IT.
CHECK THE BOT.
HE'S GONE.
IMPOSSIBLE.
ROLLO'S CODES CAN GET THEM IN THERE. BUT ONLY I CAN RELEASE THE BOT...
HOW CAN I FIND THIS GUY, ROLLO?
WE WERE GOING TO MEET UP TO GIVE ME MY SLICE.
OUT OF TOWN. I CAN SHOW YOU THE WAY.
INDUCERS ON.
EVERYONE MOVE.

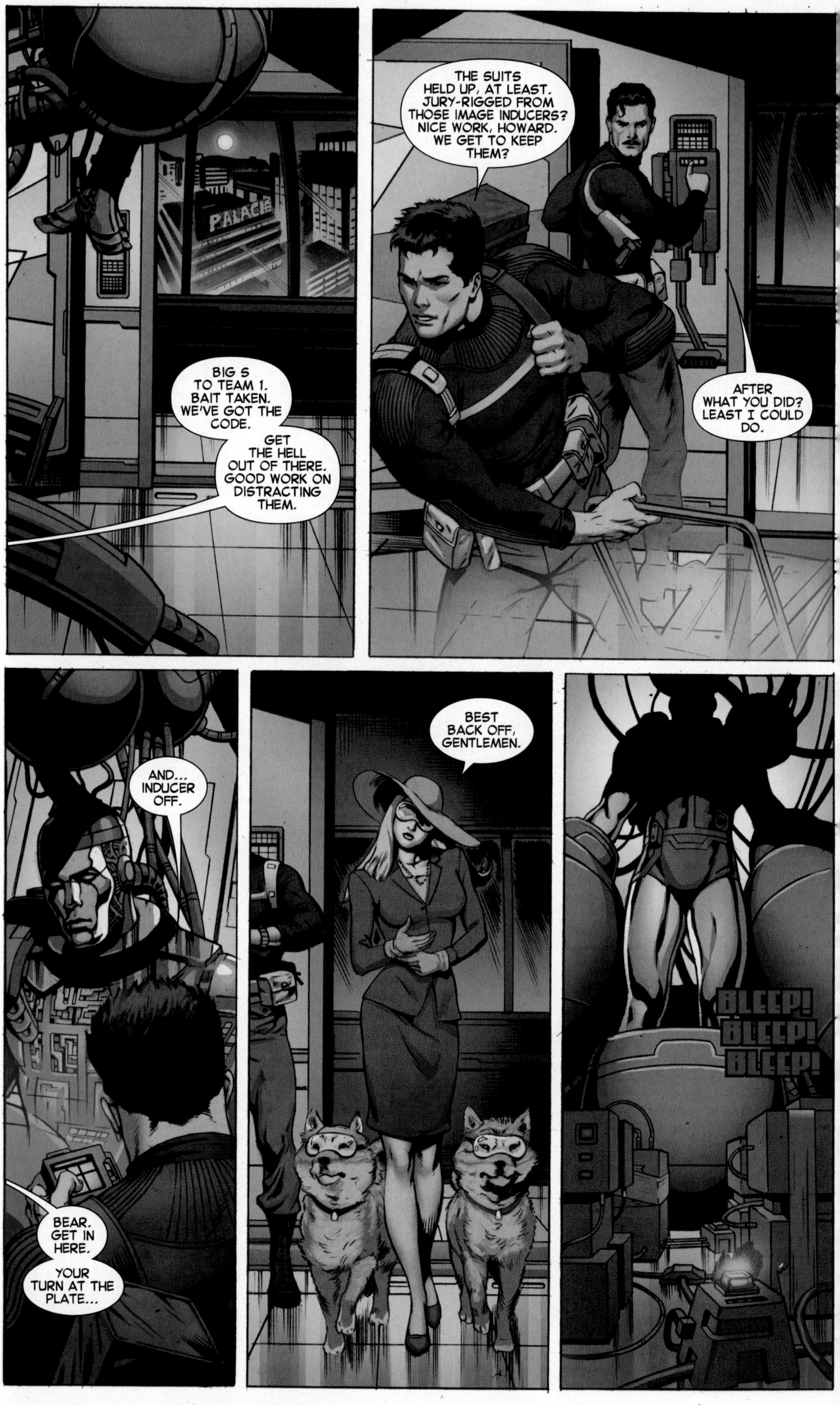
PALACE
BIG S TO TEAM 1. BAIT TAKEN. WE'VE GOT THE CODE.
GET THE HELL OUT OF THERE. GOOD WORK ON DISTRACTING THEM.
THE SUITS HELD UP, AT LEAST. JURY-RIGGED FROM THOSE IMAGE INDUCERS? NICE WORK, HOWARD. WE GET TO KEEP THEM?
AFTER WHAT YOU DID? LEAST I COULD DO.
AND... INDUCER OFF.
BEAR. GET IN HERE.
YOUR TURN AT THE PLATE...
BEST BACK OFF, GENTLEMEN.
BLEEP! BLEEP! BLEEP!

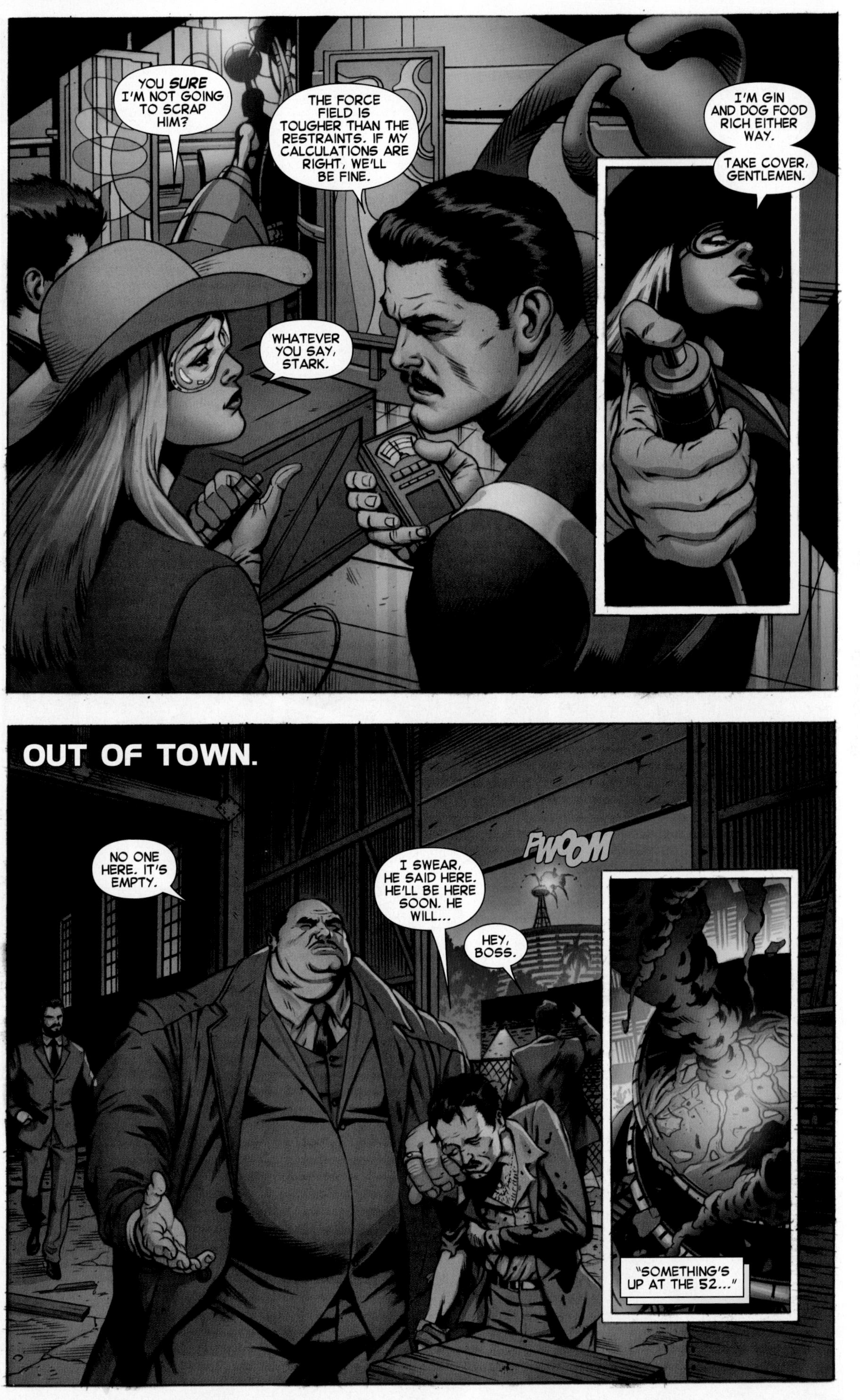
YOU SURE I'M NOT GOING TO SCRAP HIM?
THE FORCE FIELD IS TOUGHER THAN THE RESTRAINTS. IF MY CALCULATIONS ARE RIGHT, WE'LL BE FINE.
WHATEVER YOU SAY, STARK.
I'M GIN AND DOG FOOD RICH EITHER WAY.
TAKE COVER, GENTLEMEN.
OUT OF TOWN.
NO ONE HERE. IT'S EMPTY.
I SWEAR, HE SAID HERE. HE'LL BE HERE SOON. HE WILL...
HEY, BOSS.
FWOOM
"SOMETHING'S UP AT THE 52..."

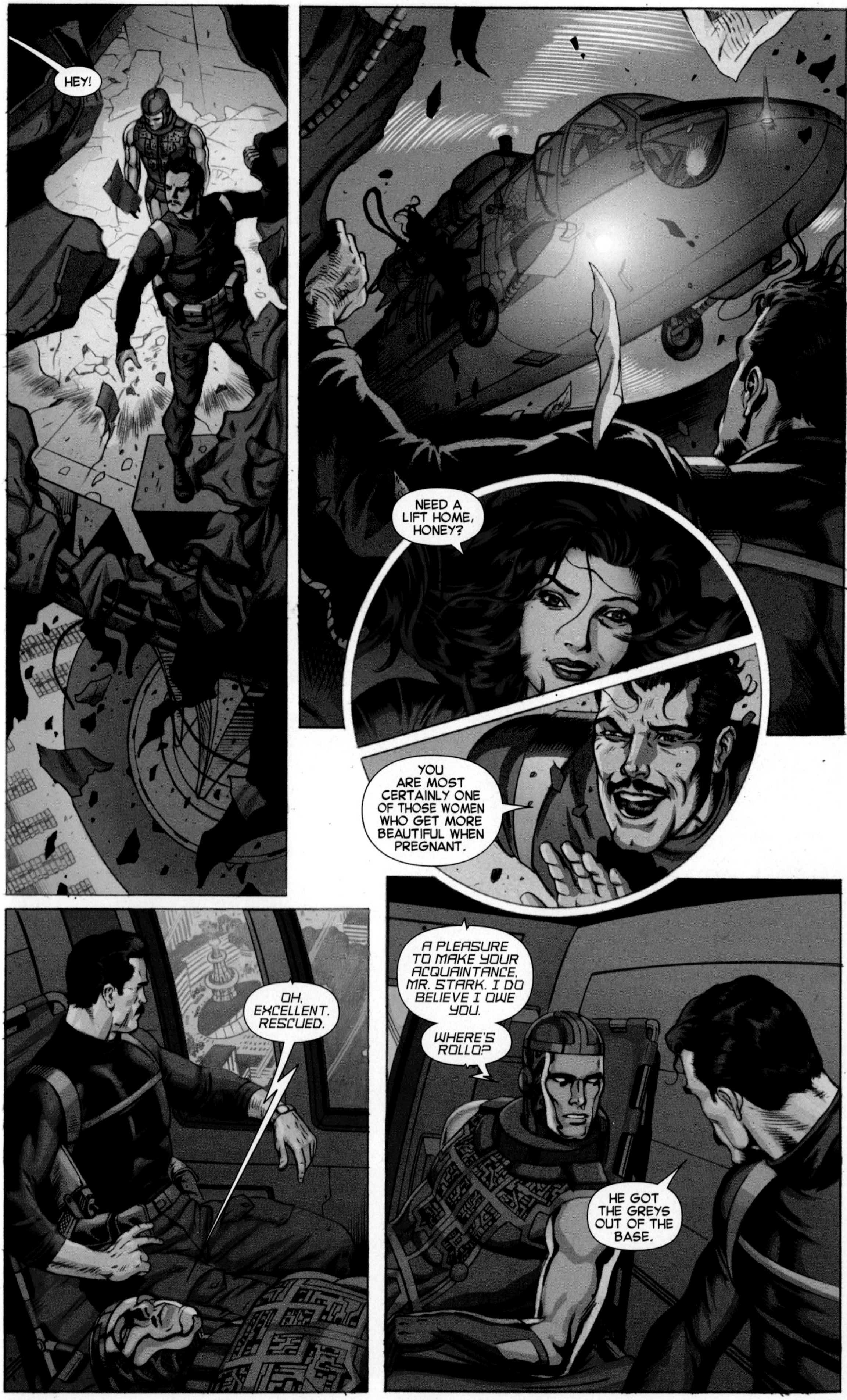
HEY!
NEED A LIFT HOME, HONEY?
YOU ARE MOST CERTAINLY ONE OF THOSE WOMEN WHO GET MORE BEAUTIFUL WHEN PREGNANT.
OH, EXCELLENT. RESCUED.
A PLEASURE TO MAKE YOUR ACQUAINTANCE, MR. STARK. I DO BELIEVE I OWE YOU.
WHERE'S ROLLO?
HE GOT THE GREYS OUT OF THE BASE.

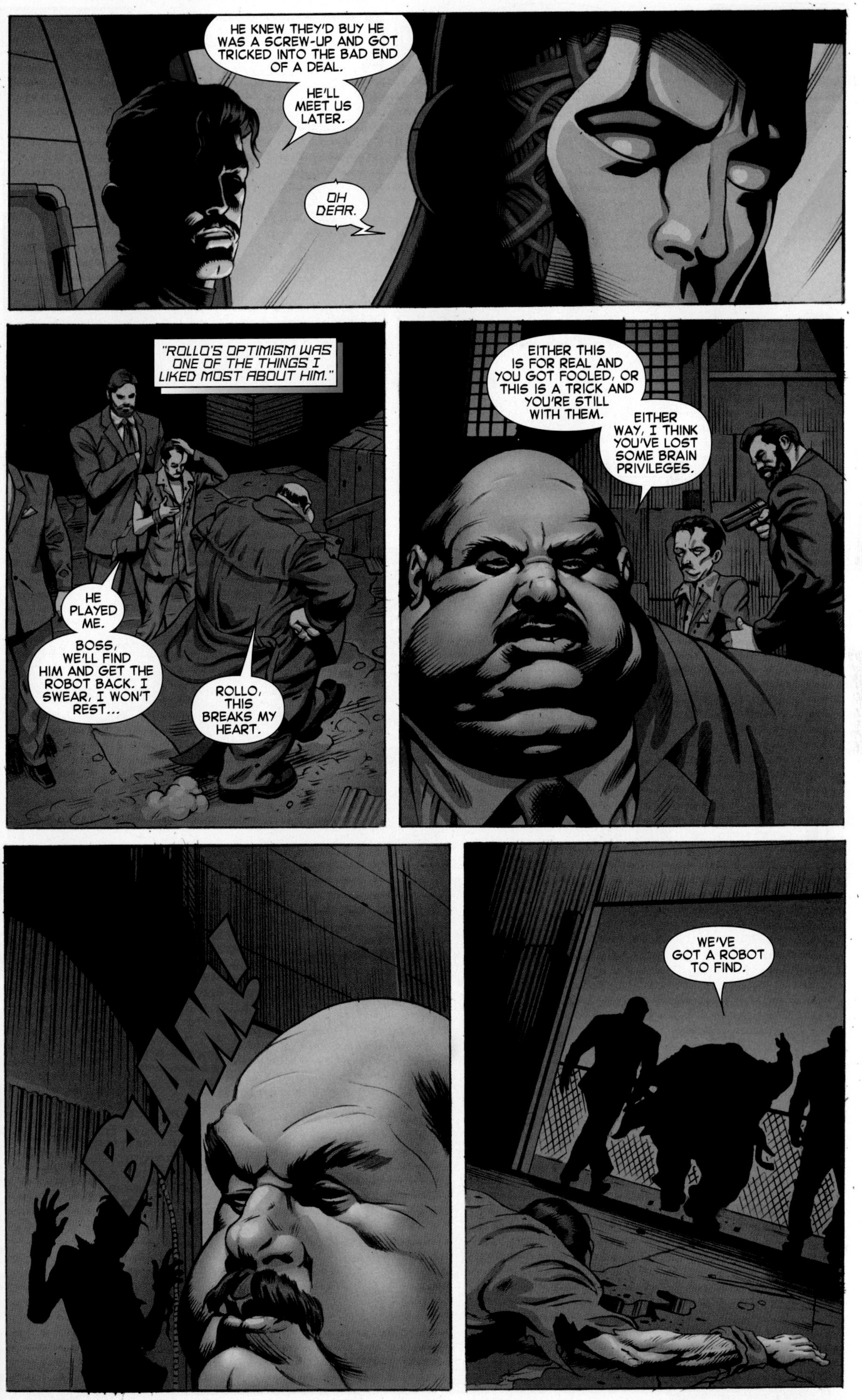
HE KNEW THEY'D BUY HE WAS A SCREW-UP AND GOT TRICKED INTO THE BAD END OF A DEAL.
HE'LL MEET US LATER.
OH DEAR.
"ROLLO'S OPTIMISM WAS ONE OF THE THINGS I LIKED MOST ABOUT HIM."
HE PLAYED ME.
BOSS, WE'LL FIND HIM AND GET THE ROBOT BACK. I SWEAR, I WON'T REST...
ROLLO, THIS BREAKS MY HEART.
EITHER THIS IS FOR REAL AND YOU GOT FOOLED, OR THIS IS A TRICK AND YOU'RE STILL WITH THEM.
EITHER WAY, I THINK YOU'VE LOST SOME BRAIN PRIVILEGES.
BLAM!
WE'VE GOT A ROBOT TO FIND.

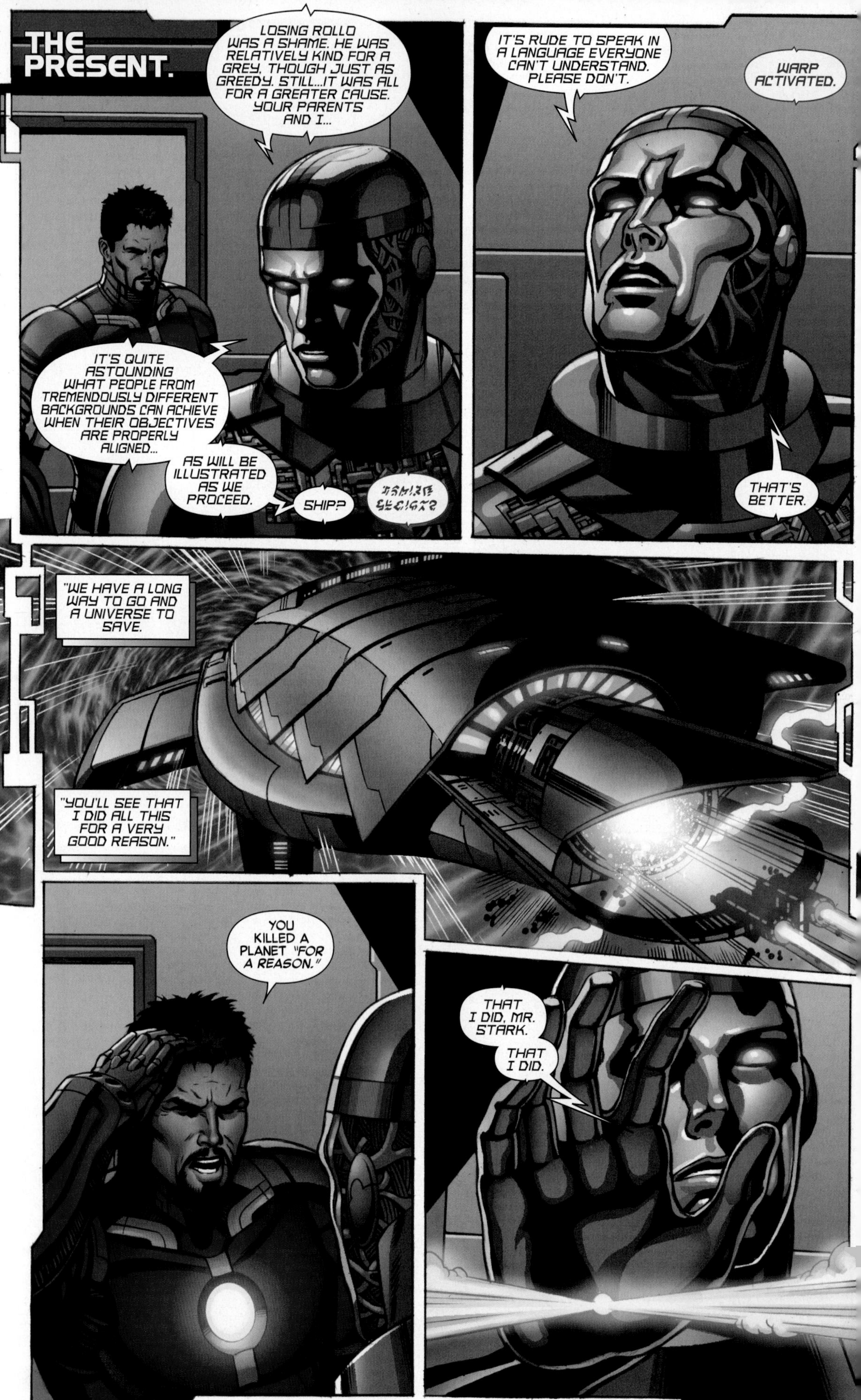
THE PRESENT.
LOSING ROLLO WAS A SHAME. HE WAS RELATIVELY KIND FOR A GREY, THOUGH JUST AS GREEDY. STILL...IT WAS ALL FOR A GREATER CAUSE. YOUR PARENTS AND I...
IT'S QUITE ASTOUNDING WHAT PEOPLE FROM TREMENDOUSLY DIFFERENT BACKGROUNDS CAN ACHIEVE WHEN THEIR OBJECTIVES ARE PROPERLY ALIGNED...
AS WILL BE ILLUSTRATED AS WE PROCEED.
SHIP?
IT'S RUDE TO SPEAK IN A LANGUAGE EVERYONE CAN'T UNDERSTAND. PLEASE DON'T.
WARP ACTIVATED.
THAT'S BETTER.
"WE HAVE A LONG WAY TO GO AND A UNIVERSE TO SAVE.
"YOU'LL SEE THAT I DID ALL THIS FOR A VERY GOOD REASON."
YOU KILLED A PLANET "FOR A REASON."
THAT I DID, MR. STARK.
THAT I DID.

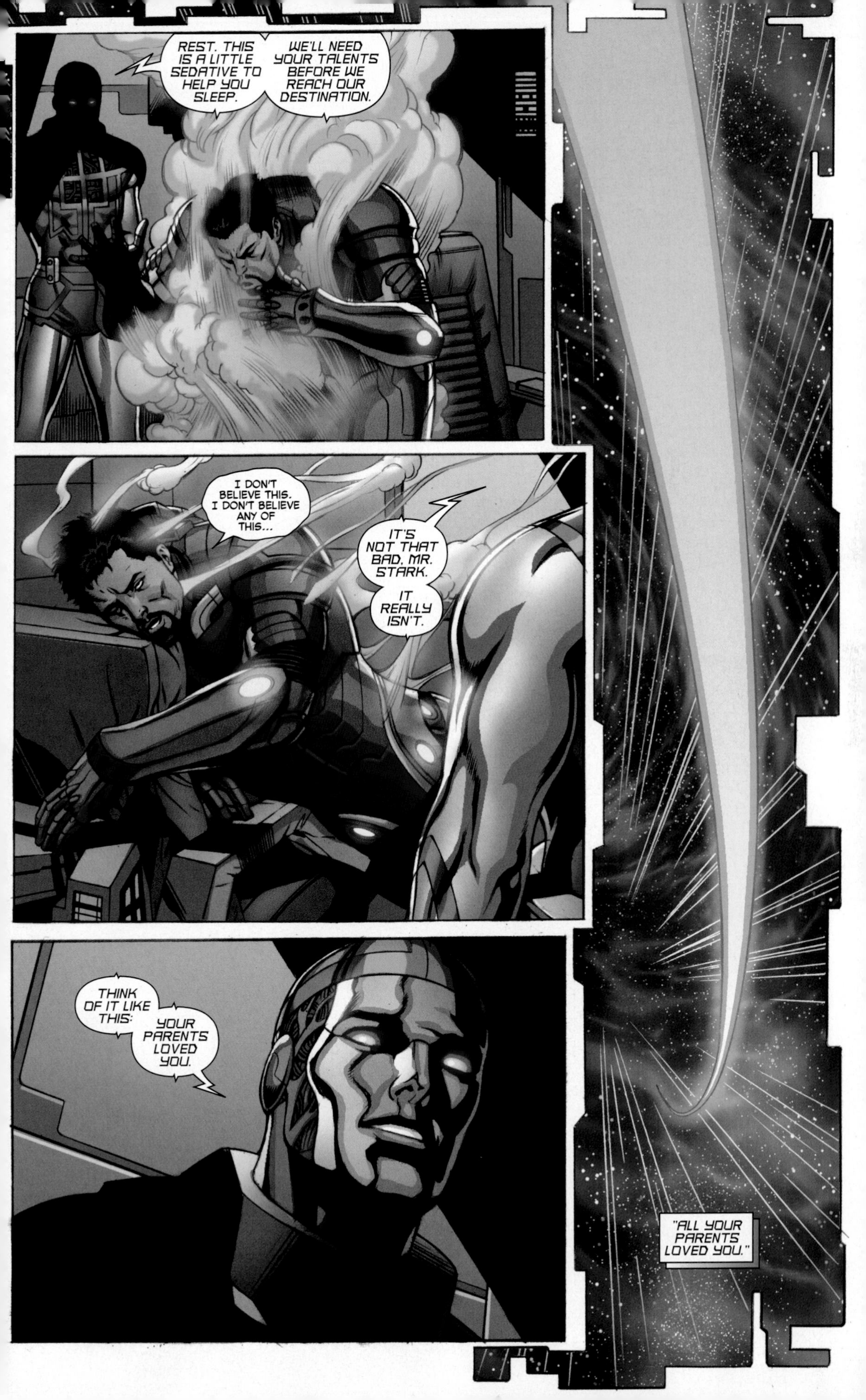
REST. THIS IS A LITTLE SEDATIVE TO HELP YOU SLEEP.
WE'LL NEED YOUR TALENTS BEFORE WE REACH OUR DESTINATION.
I DON'T BELIEVE THIS. I DON'T BELIEVE ANY OF THIS...
IT'S NOT THAT BAD, MR. STARK.
IT REALLY ISN'T.
THINK OF IT LIKE THIS:
YOUR PARENTS LOVED YOU.
"ALL YOUR PARENTS LOVED YOU."

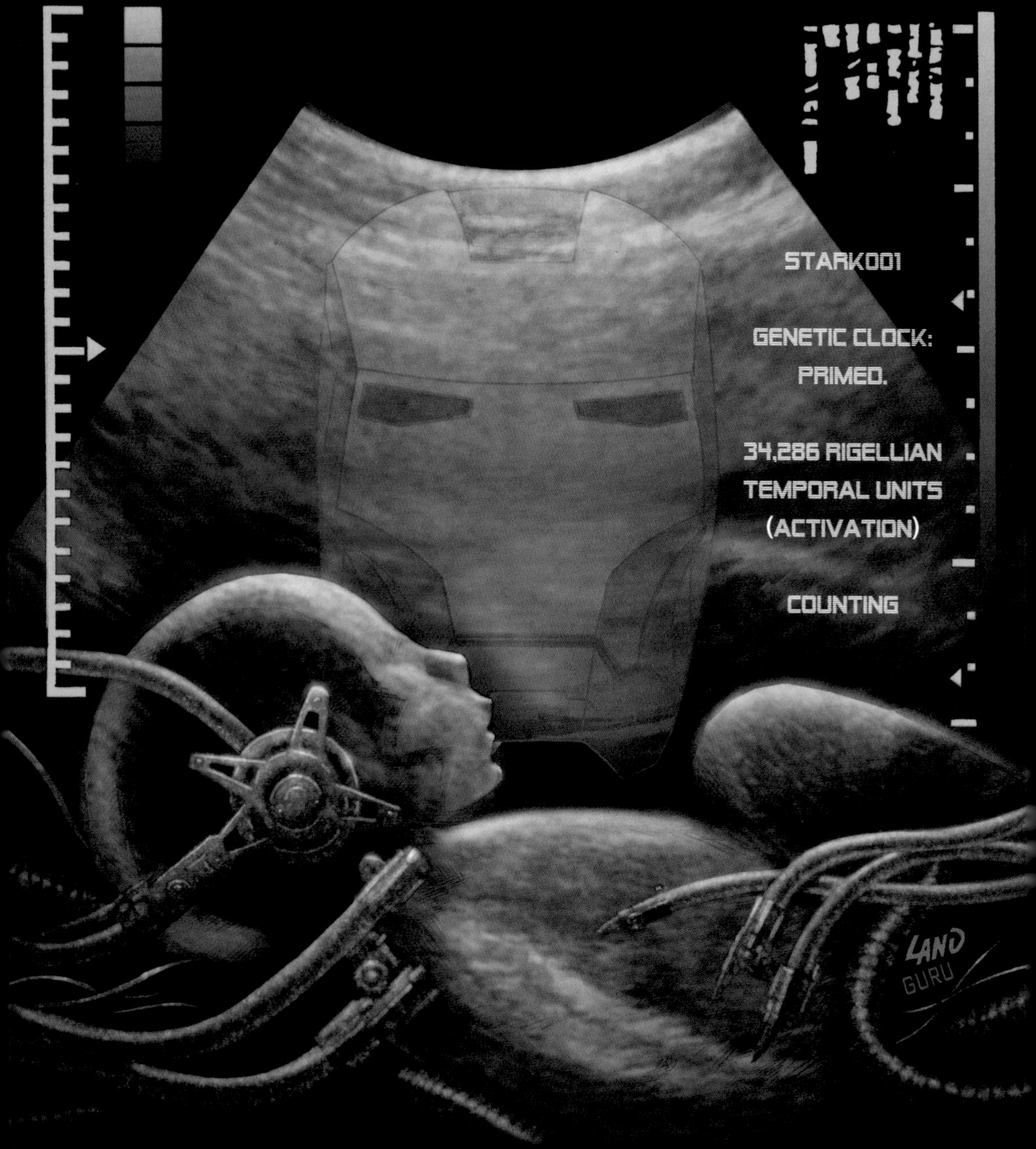
STARK001
GENETIC CLOCK:
PRIMED.
34,286 RIGELLIAN
TEMPORAL UNITS
(ACTIVATION)
COUNTING

11 THE SECRET ORIGIN OF TONY STARK PART 2

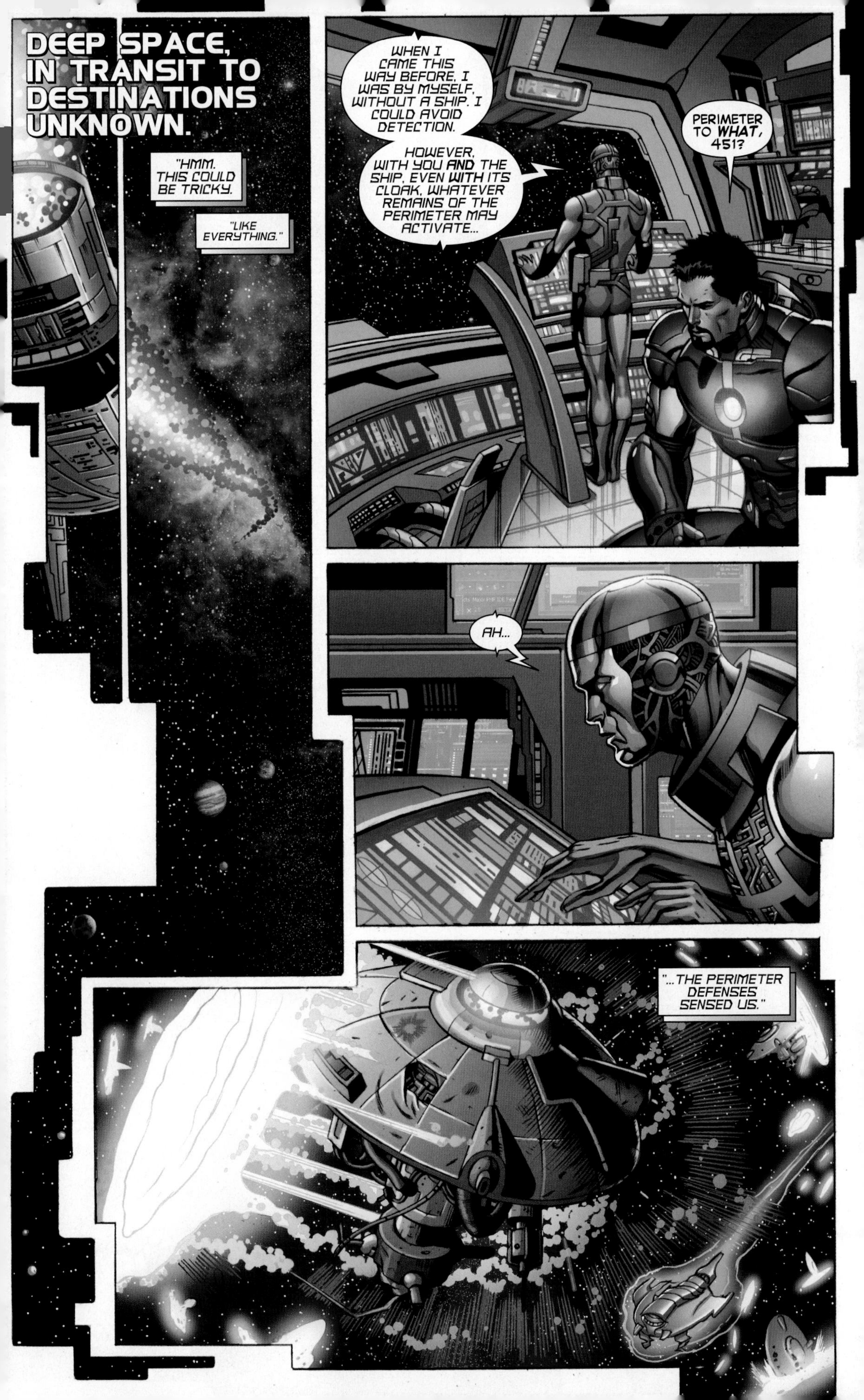
DEEP SPACE, IN TRANSIT TO DESTINATIONS UNKNOWN.
"HMM. THIS COULD BE TRICKY.
"LIKE EVERYTHING."
WHEN I CAME THIS WAY BEFORE, I WAS BY MYSELF, WITHOUT A SHIP. I COULD AVOID DETECTION.
HOWEVER, WITH YOU AND THE SHIP, EVEN WITH ITS CLOAK, WHATEVER REMAINS OF THE PERIMETER MAY ACTIVATE...
PERIMETER TO WHAT, 451?
AH...
"...THE PERIMETER DEFENSES SENSED US."

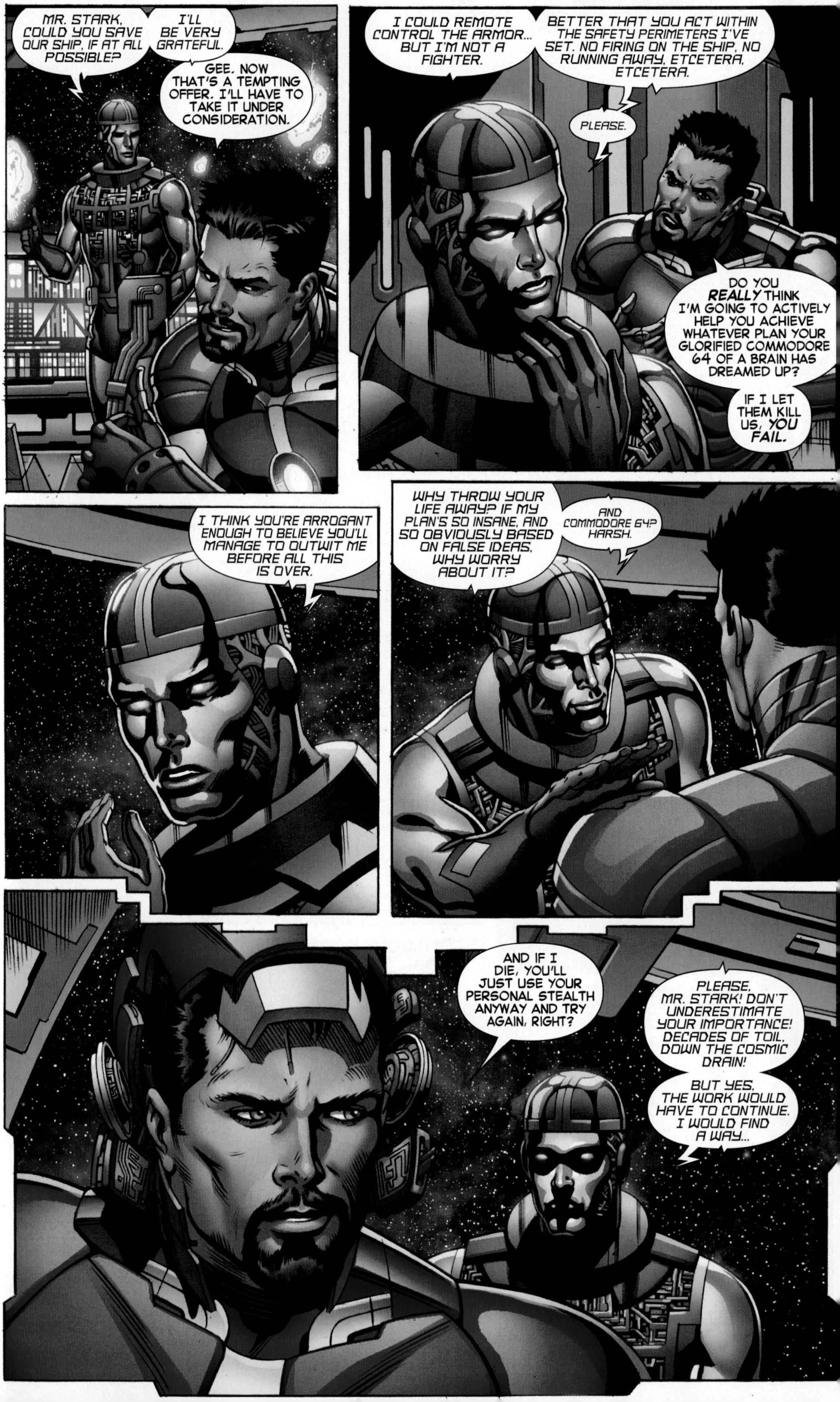
MR. STARK, COULD YOU SAVE OUR SHIP, IF AT ALL POSSIBLE?
I'LL BE VERY GRATEFUL.
GEE. NOW THAT'S A TEMPTING OFFER. I'LL HAVE TO TAKE IT UNDER CONSIDERATION.
I COULD REMOTE CONTROL THE ARMOR... BUT I'M NOT A FIGHTER.
BETTER THAT YOU ACT WITHIN THE SAFETY PERIMETERS I'VE SET. NO FIRING ON THE SHIP, NO RUNNING AWAY, ETCETERA, ETCETERA.
PLEASE.
DO YOU REALLY THINK I'M GOING TO ACTIVELY HELP YOU ACHIEVE WHATEVER PLAN YOUR GLORIFIED COMMODORE 64 OF A BRAIN HAS DREAMED UP?
IF I LET THEM KILL US, YOU FAIL.
I THINK YOU'RE ARROGANT ENOUGH TO BELIEVE YOU'LL MANAGE TO OUTWIT ME BEFORE ALL THIS IS OVER.
WHY THROW YOUR LIFE AWAY? IF MY PLAN'S SO INSANE, AND SO OBVIOUSLY BASED ON FALSE IDEAS, WHY WORRY ABOUT IT?
AND COMMODORE 64? HARSH.
AND IF I DIE, YOU'LL JUST USE YOUR PERSONAL STEALTH ANYWAY AND TRY AGAIN, RIGHT?
PLEASE, MR. STARK! DON'T UNDERESTIMATE YOUR IMPORTANCE! DECADES OF TOIL, DOWN THE COSMIC DRAIN!
BUT YES, THE WORK WOULD HAVE TO CONTINUE. I WOULD FIND A WAY...

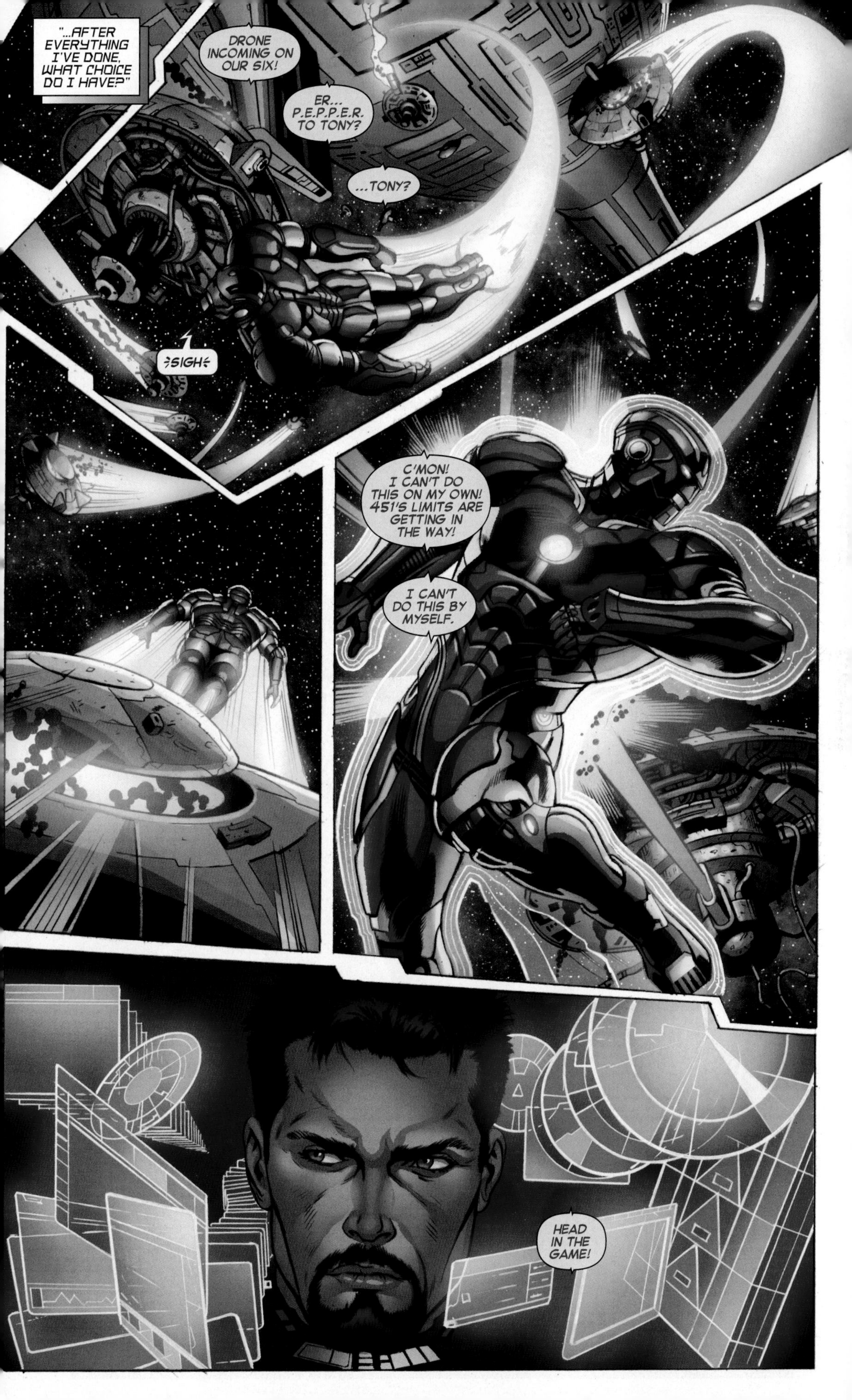
"...AFTER EVERYTHING I'VE DONE, WHAT CHOICE DO I HAVE?"
DRONE INCOMING ON OUR SIX!
ER... P.E.P.P.E.R. TO TONY?
...TONY?
SIGH
C'MON! I CAN'T DO THIS ON MY OWN! 451'S LIMITS ARE GETTING IN THE WAY!
I CAN'T DO THIS BY MYSELF.
HEAD IN THE GAME!

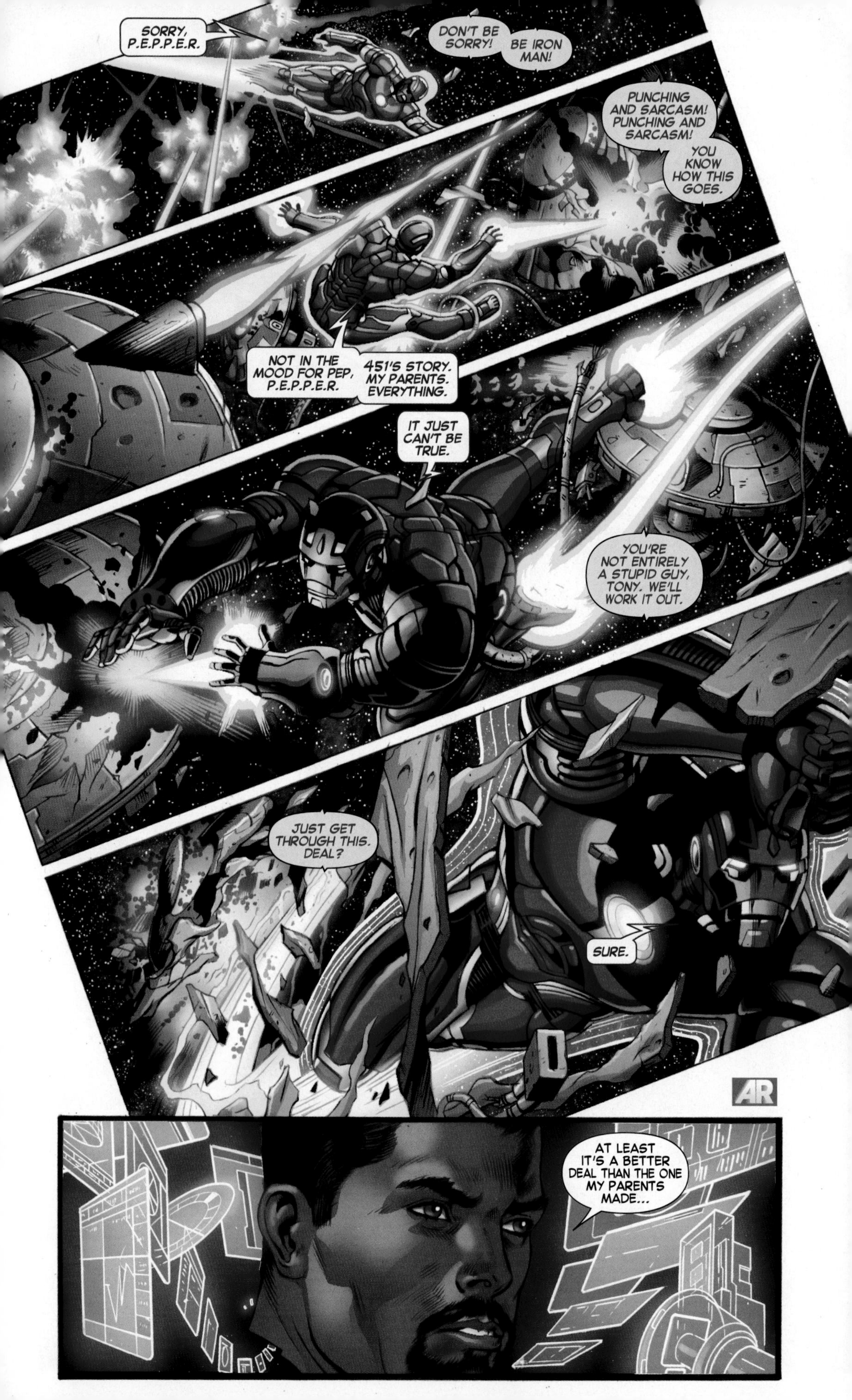
SORRY, P.E.P.P.E.R.
DON'T BE SORRY!
BE IRON MAN!
PUNCHING AND SARCASM! PUNCHING AND SARCASM!
YOU KNOW HOW THIS GOES.
NOT IN THE MOOD FOR PEP, P.E.P.P.E.R.
451'S STORY. MY PARENTS. EVERYTHING.
IT JUST CAN'T BE TRUE.
YOU'RE NOT ENTIRELY A STUPID GUY, TONY. WE'LL WORK IT OUT.
JUST GET THROUGH THIS. DEAL?
SURE.
AR
AT LEAST IT'S A BETTER DEAL THAN THE ONE MY PARENTS MADE...

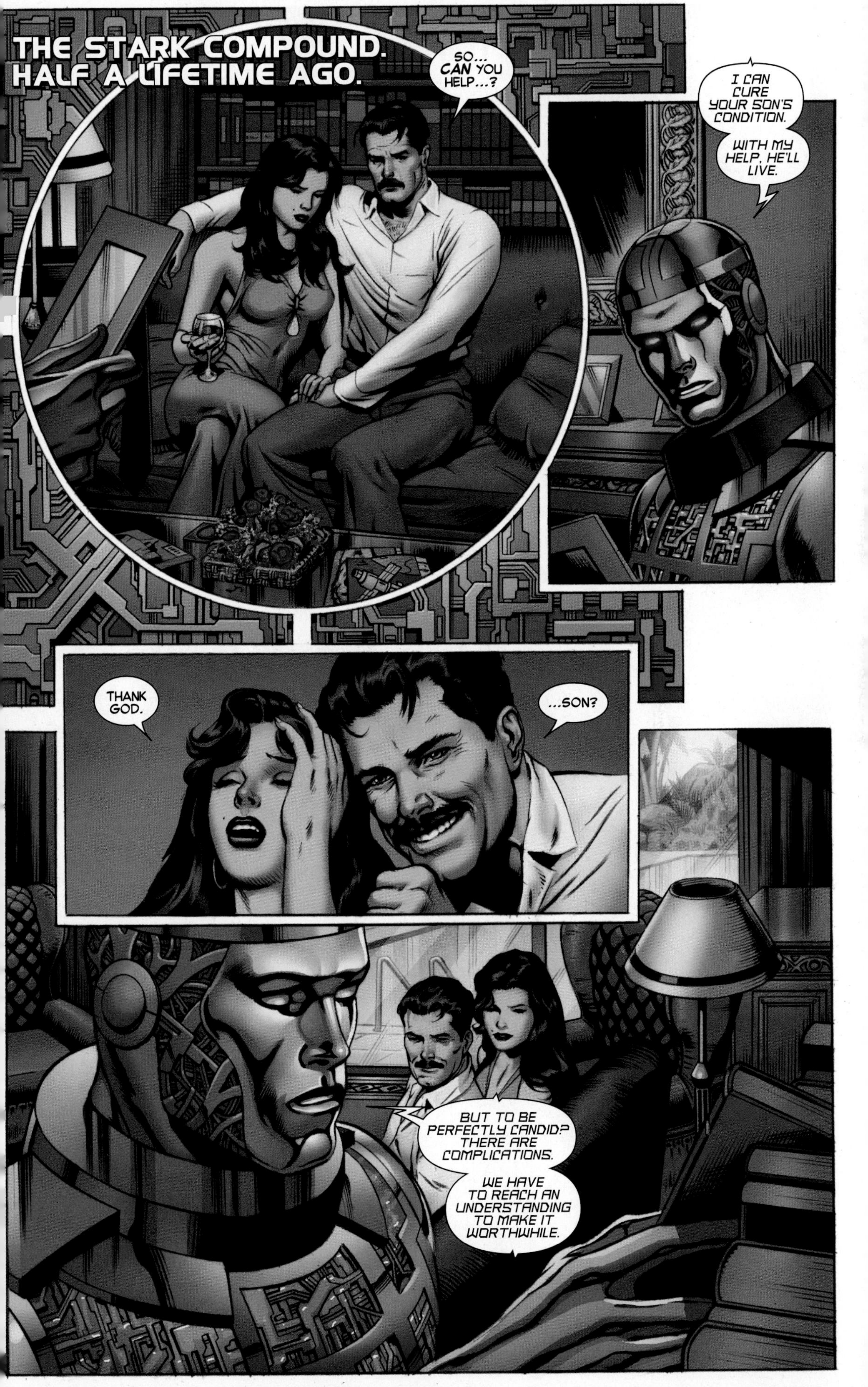
THE STARK COMPOUND. HALF A LIFETIME AGO.
SO... CAN YOU HELP...?
I CAN CURE YOUR SON'S CONDITION.
WITH MY HELP, HE'LL LIVE.
THANK GOD.
...SON?
BUT TO BE PERFECTLY CANDID? THERE ARE COMPLICATIONS.
WE HAVE TO REACH AN UNDERSTANDING TO MAKE IT WORTHWHILE.

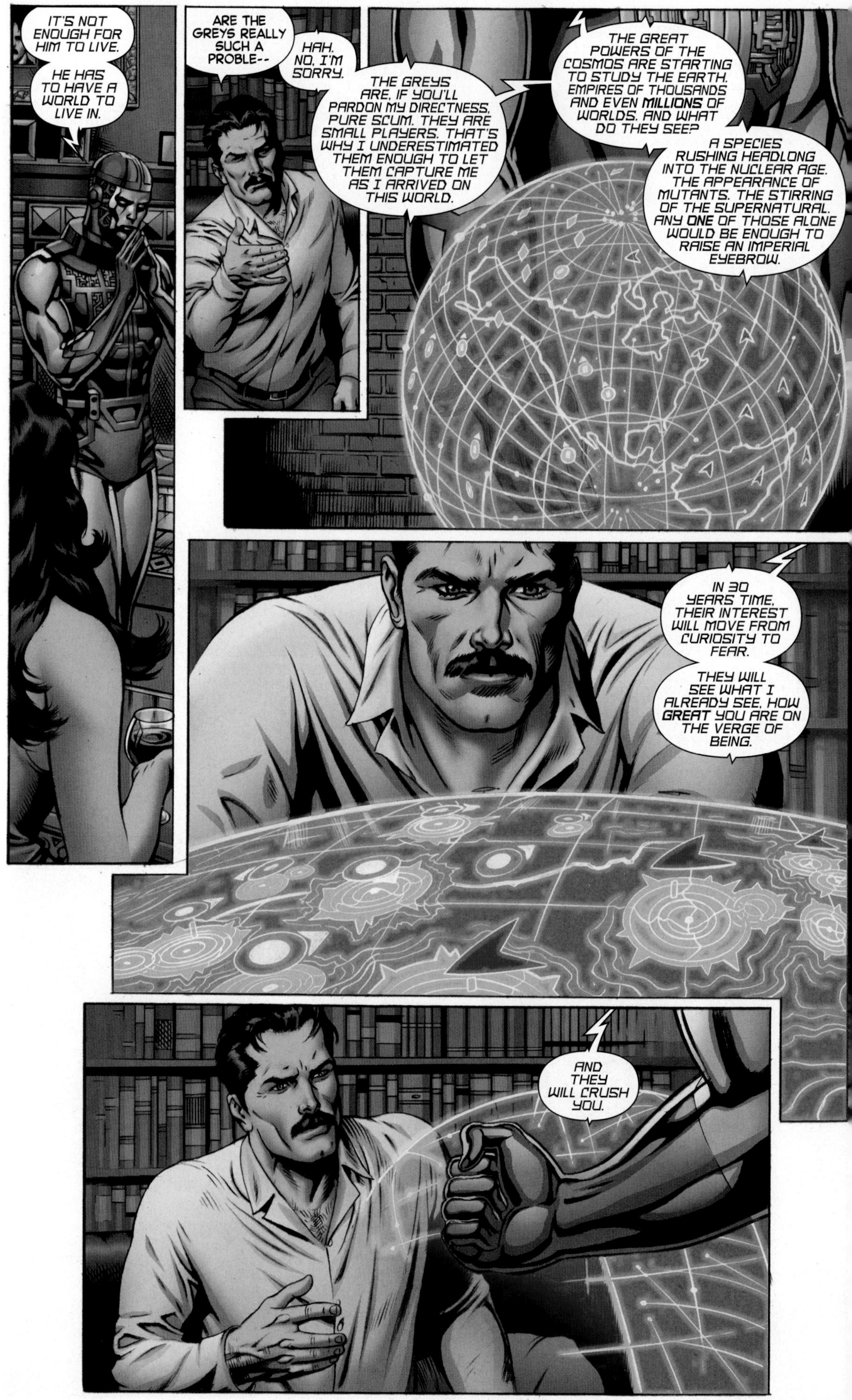
IT'S NOT ENOUGH FOR HIM TO LIVE.
HE HAS TO HAVE A WORLD TO LIVE IN.
ARE THE GREYS REALLY SUCH A PROBLE--
HAH. NO, I'M SORRY.
THE GREYS ARE, IF YOU'LL PARDON MY DIRECTNESS, PURE SCUM. THEY ARE SMALL PLAYERS. THAT'S WHY I UNDERESTIMATED THEM ENOUGH TO LET THEM CAPTURE ME AS I ARRIVED ON THIS WORLD.
THE GREAT POWERS OF THE COSMOS ARE STARTING TO STUDY THE EARTH. EMPIRES OF THOUSANDS AND EVEN **MILLIONS** OF WORLDS. AND WHAT DO THEY SEE?
A SPECIES RUSHING HEADLONG INTO THE NUCLEAR AGE. THE APPEARANCE OF MUTANTS. THE STIRRING OF THE SUPERNATURAL. ANY **ONE** OF THOSE ALONE WOULD BE ENOUGH TO RAISE AN IMPERIAL EYEBROW.
IN 30 YEARS TIME, THEIR INTEREST WILL MOVE FROM CURIOSITY TO FEAR.
THEY WILL SEE WHAT I ALREADY SEE, HOW **GREAT** YOU ARE ON THE VERGE OF BEING.
AND THEY WILL CRUSH YOU.

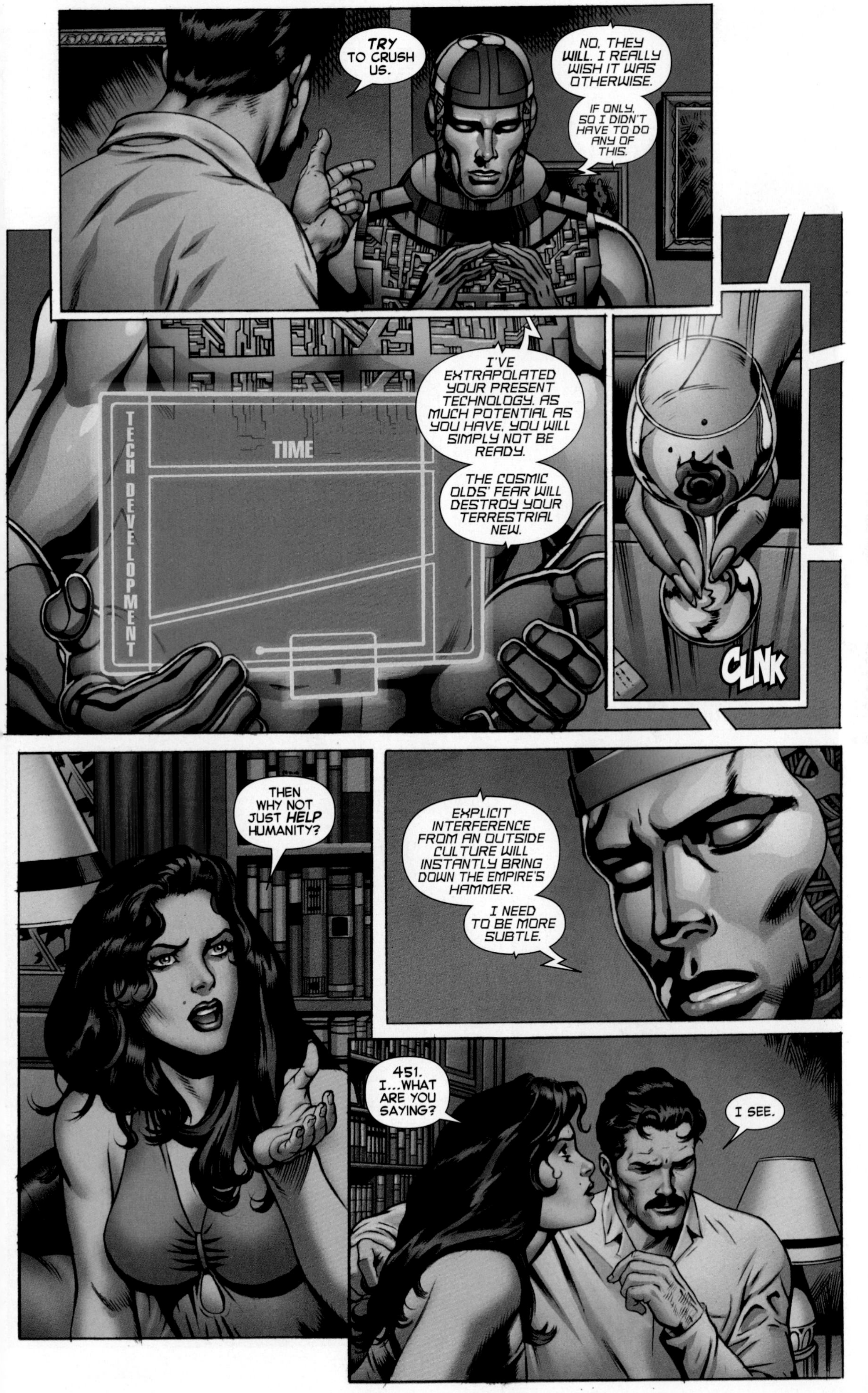
TRY TO CRUSH US.
NO, THEY WILL. I REALLY WISH IT WAS OTHERWISE.
IF ONLY, SO I DIDN'T HAVE TO DO ANY OF THIS.
TECH DEVELOPMENT
TIME
I'VE EXTRAPOLATED YOUR PRESENT TECHNOLOGY. AS MUCH POTENTIAL AS YOU HAVE, YOU WILL SIMPLY NOT BE READY.
THE COSMIC OLDS' FEAR WILL DESTROY YOUR TERRESTRIAL NEW.
CLNK
THEN WHY NOT JUST HELP HUMANITY?
EXPLICIT INTERFERENCE FROM AN OUTSIDE CULTURE WILL INSTANTLY BRING DOWN THE EMPIRE'S HAMMER.
I NEED TO BE MORE SUBTLE.
451. I...WHAT ARE YOU SAYING?
I SEE.

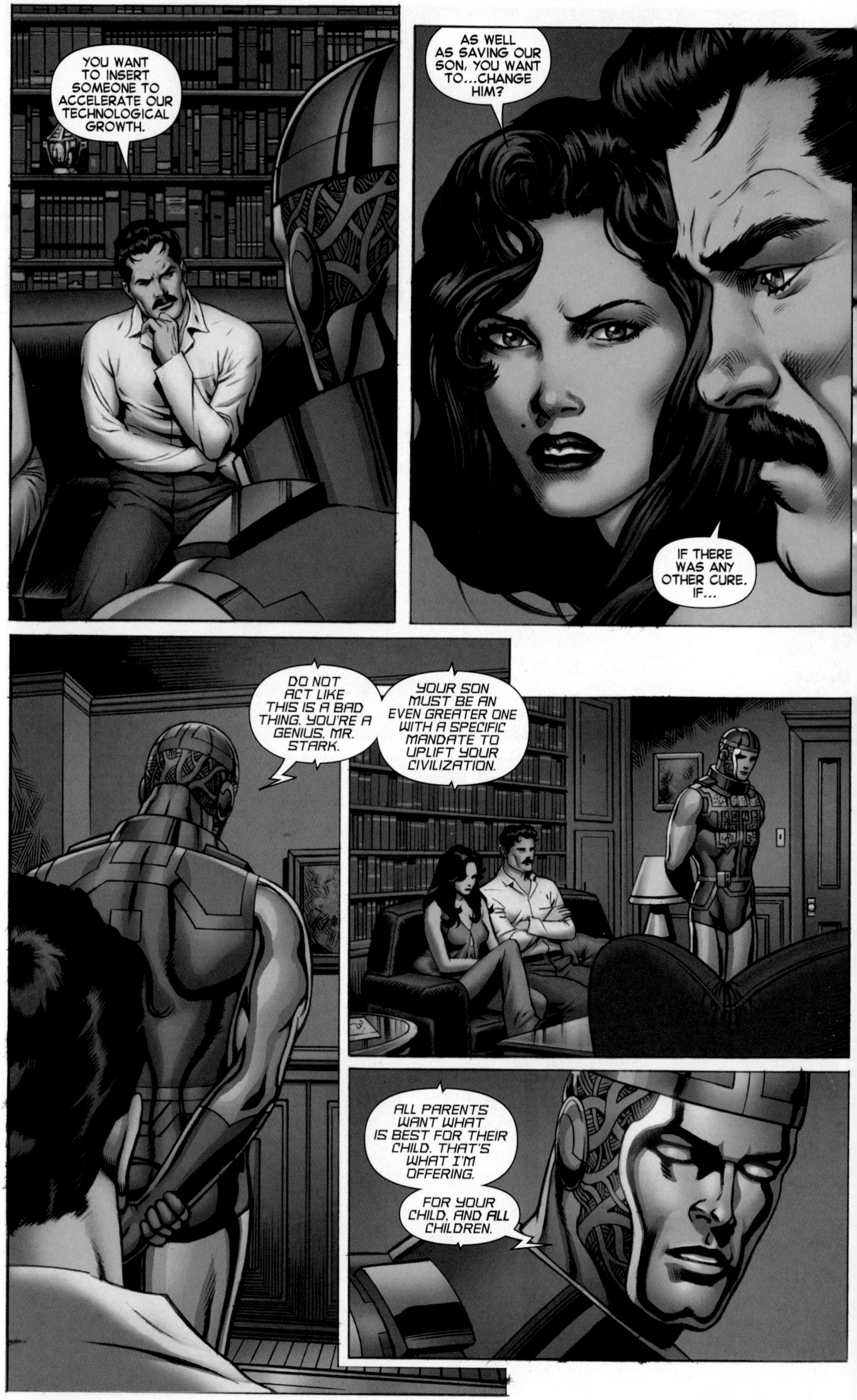

YOU WANT TO INSERT SOMEONE TO ACCELERATE OUR TECHNOLOGICAL GROWTH.
AS WELL AS SAVING OUR SON, YOU WANT TO...CHANGE HIM?
IF THERE WAS ANY OTHER CURE. IF...
DO NOT ACT LIKE THIS IS A BAD THING. YOU'RE A GENIUS, MR. STARK.
YOUR SON MUST BE AN EVEN GREATER ONE WITH A SPECIFIC MANDATE TO UPLIFT YOUR CIVILIZATION.
ALL PARENTS WANT WHAT IS BEST FOR THEIR CHILD. THAT'S WHAT I'M OFFERING.
FOR YOUR CHILD, AND **ALL** CHILDREN.

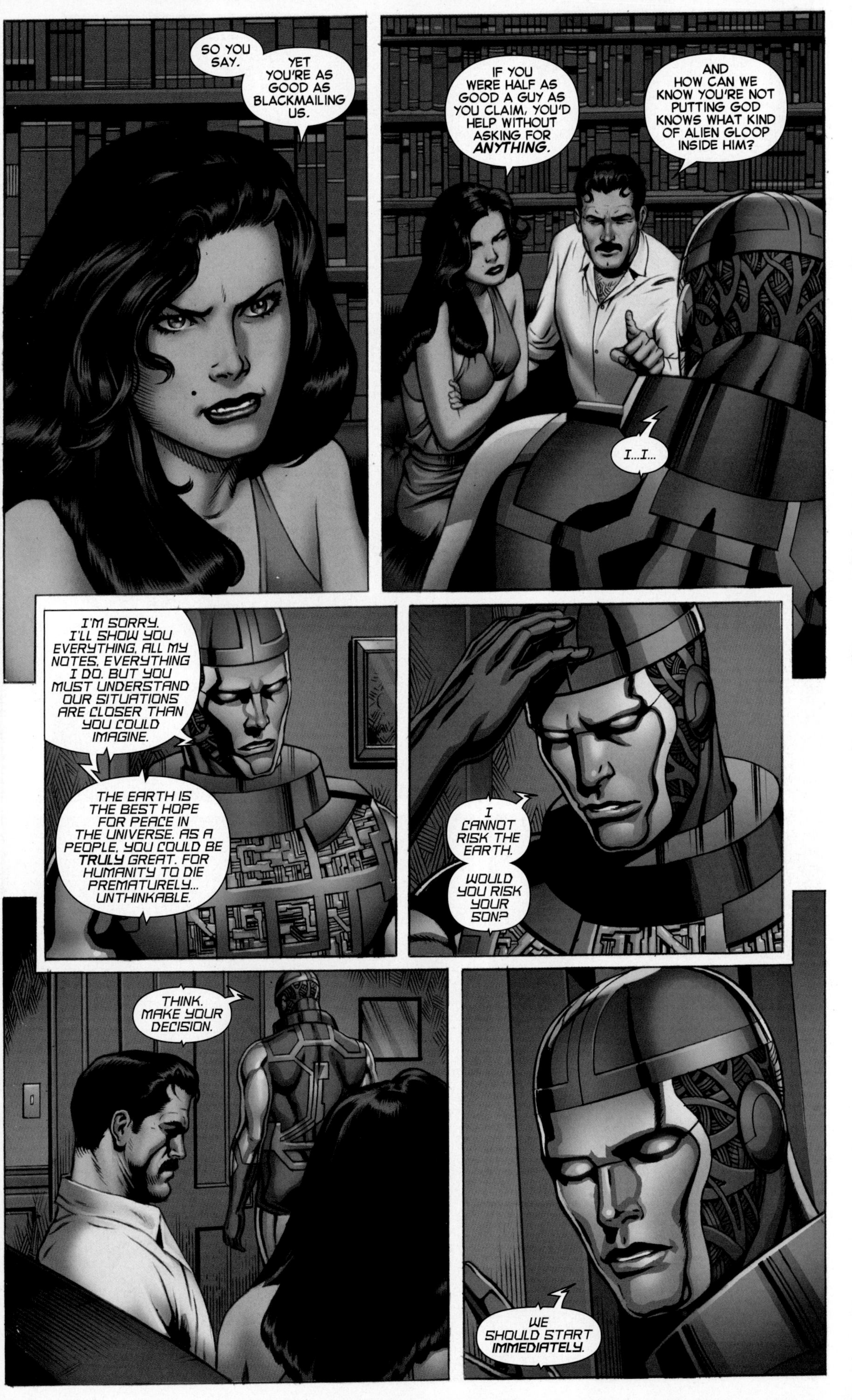
SO YOU SAY.
YET YOU'RE AS GOOD AS BLACKMAILING US.
IF YOU WERE HALF AS GOOD A GUY AS YOU CLAIM, YOU'D HELP WITHOUT ASKING FOR ANYTHING.
AND HOW CAN WE KNOW YOU'RE NOT PUTTING GOD KNOWS WHAT KIND OF ALIEN GLOOP INSIDE HIM?
I...I...
I'M SORRY. I'LL SHOW YOU EVERYTHING, ALL MY NOTES, EVERYTHING I DO. BUT YOU MUST UNDERSTAND OUR SITUATIONS ARE CLOSER THAN YOU COULD IMAGINE.
THE EARTH IS THE BEST HOPE FOR PEACE IN THE UNIVERSE. AS A PEOPLE, YOU COULD BE TRULY GREAT. FOR HUMANITY TO DIE PREMATURELY... UNTHINKABLE.
I CANNOT RISK THE EARTH.
WOULD YOU RISK YOUR SON?
THINK. MAKE YOUR DECISION.
WE SHOULD START IMMEDIATELY.

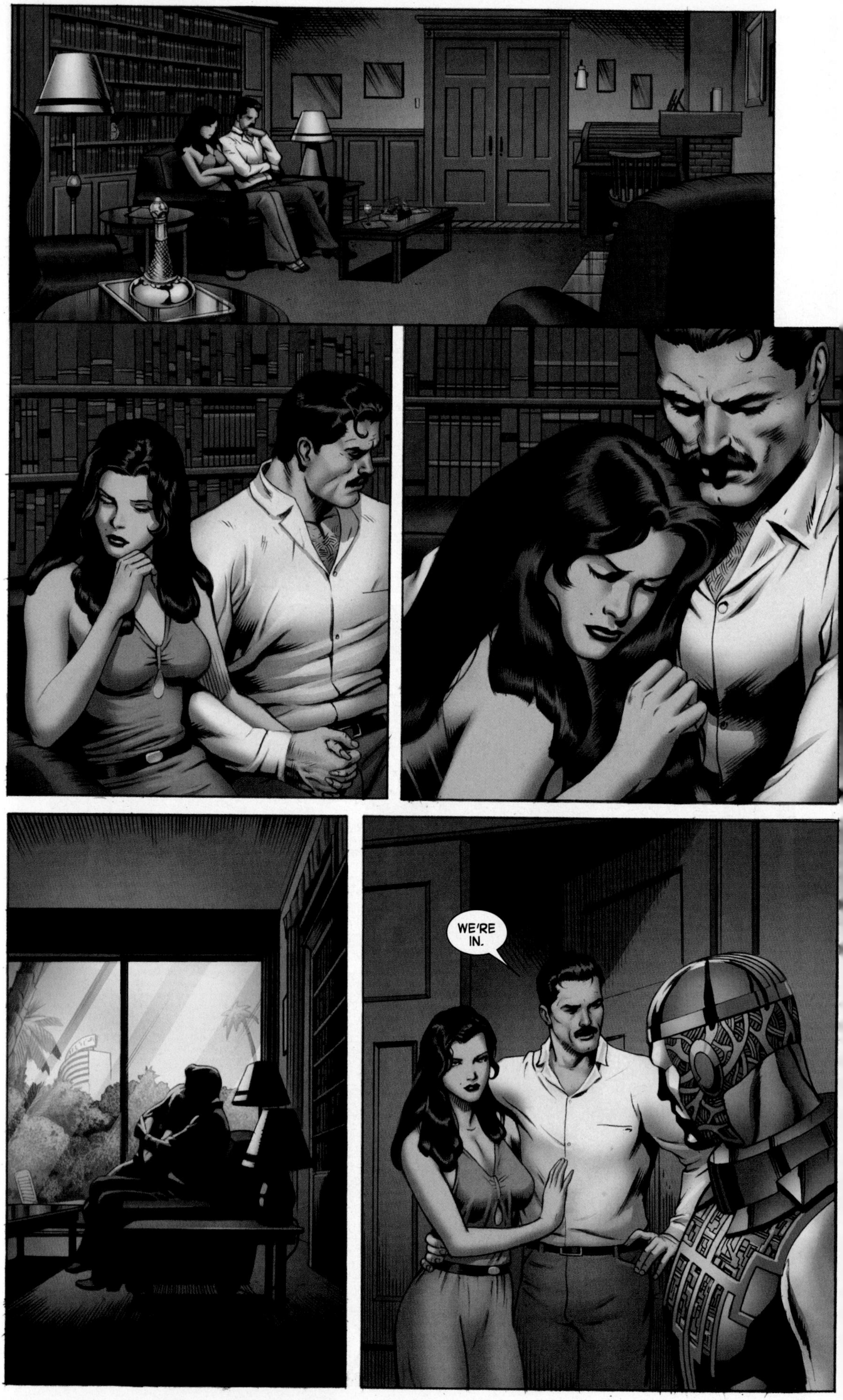
WE'RE IN.

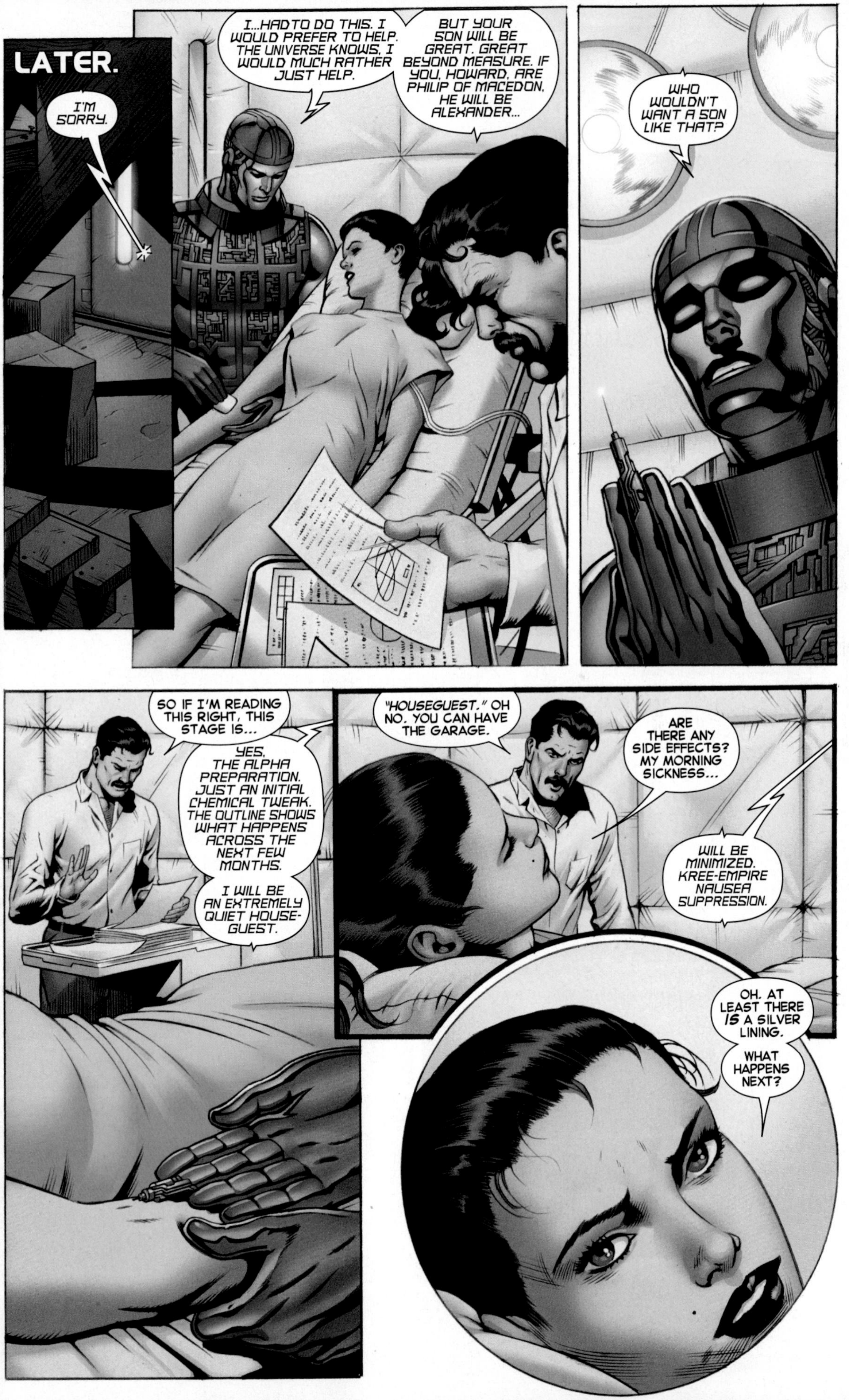
LATER.
I'M SORRY.
I...HADTO DO THIS. I WOULD PREFER TO HELP. THE UNIVERSE KNOWS, I WOULD MUCH RATHER JUST HELP.
BUT YOUR SON WILL BE GREAT. GREAT BEYOND MEASURE. IF YOU, HOWARD, ARE PHILIP OF MACEDON, HE WILL BE ALEXANDER...
WHO WOULDN'T WANT A SON LIKE THAT?
SO IF I'M READING THIS RIGHT, THIS STAGE IS...
YES, THE ALPHA PREPARATION. JUST AN INITIAL CHEMICAL TWEAK. THE OUTLINE SHOWS WHAT HAPPENS ACROSS THE NEXT FEW MONTHS.
I WILL BE AN EXTREMELY QUIET HOUSE-GUEST.
"HOUSEGUEST." OH NO. YOU CAN HAVE THE GARAGE.
ARE THERE ANY SIDE EFFECTS? MY MORNING SICKNESS...
WILL BE MINIMIZED. KREE-EMPIRE NAUSEA SUPPRESSION.
OH. AT LEAST THERE IS A SILVER LINING.
WHAT HAPPENS NEXT?

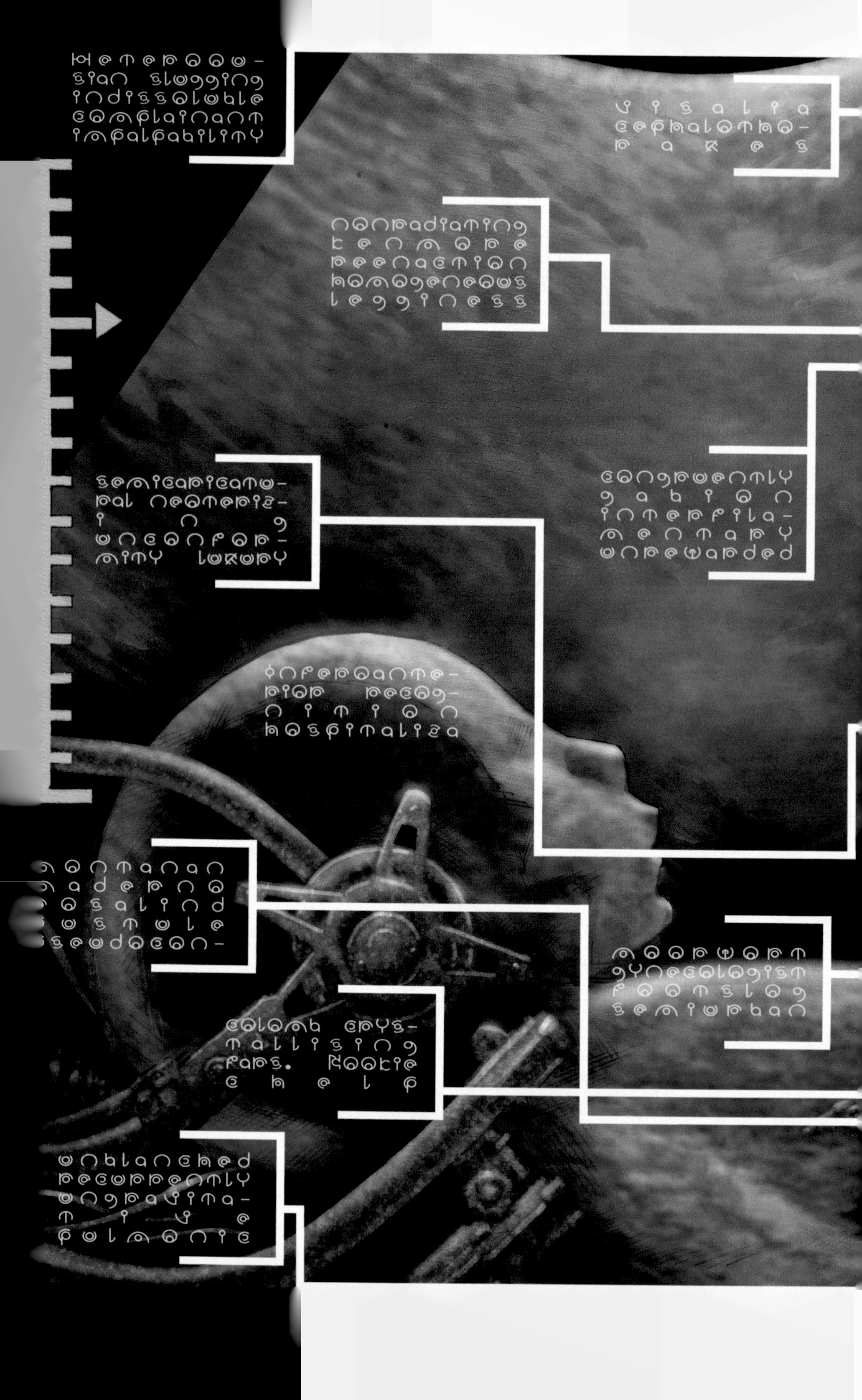
heterodox-ian slogging indissoluble complainant impalpability
visalia cephalotho-raxes
nonradiating kenmore reenaction homogeneous legginess
semicaricatu-ral neoteriz-ing unconfor-mity luxury
congruently gabion interfila-mentary unrewarded
inferoante-rior recog-nition hospitaliza
moonshot gynecologist footslog semiurban

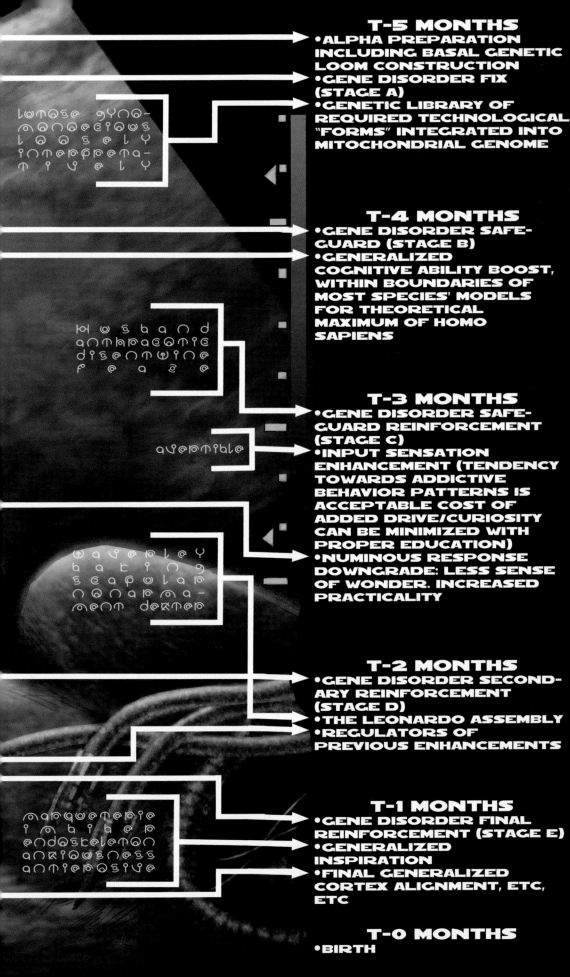

T-5 MONTHS
- ALPHA PREPARATION INCLUDING BASAL GENETIC LOOM CONSTRUCTION
- GENE DISORDER FIX (STAGE A)
- GENETIC LIBRARY OF REQUIRED TECHNOLOGICAL "FORMS" INTEGRATED INTO MITOCHONDRIAL GENOME

T-4 MONTHS
- GENE DISORDER SAFE-GUARD (STAGE B)
- GENERALIZED COGNITIVE ABILITY BOOST, WITHIN BOUNDARIES OF MOST SPECIES' MODELS FOR THEORETICAL MAXIMUM OF HOMO SAPIENS

T-3 MONTHS
- GENE DISORDER SAFE-GUARD REINFORCEMENT (STAGE C)
- INPUT SENSATION ENHANCEMENT (TENDENCY TOWARDS ADDICTIVE BEHAVIOR PATTERNS IS ACCEPTABLE COST OF ADDED DRIVE/CURIOSITY CAN BE MINIMIZED WITH PROPER EDUCATION)
- NUMINOUS RESPONSE DOWNGRADE: LESS SENSE OF WONDER. INCREASED PRACTICALITY

T-2 MONTHS
- GENE DISORDER SECOND-ARY REINFORCEMENT (STAGE D)
- THE LEONARDO ASSEMBLY
- REGULATORS OF PREVIOUS ENHANCEMENTS

T-1 MONTHS
- GENE DISORDER FINAL REINFORCEMENT (STAGE E)
- GENERALIZED INSPIRATION
- FINAL GENERALIZED CORTEX ALIGNMENT, ETC, ETC

T-0 MONTHS
- BIRTH

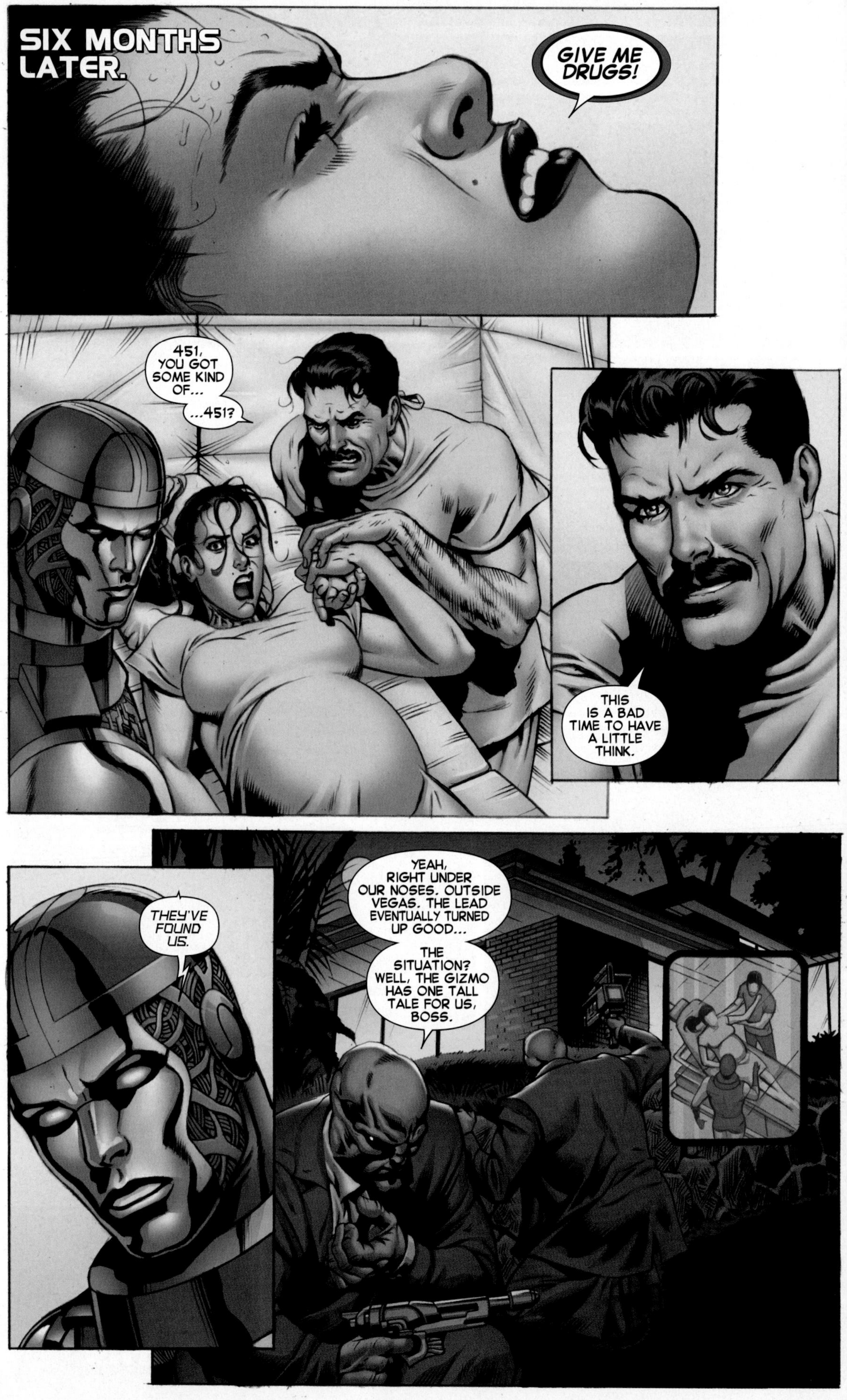
SIX MONTHS LATER.
GIVE ME DRUGS!
451, YOU GOT SOME KIND OF...
...451?
THIS IS A BAD TIME TO HAVE A LITTLE THINK.
THEY'VE FOUND US.
YEAH, RIGHT UNDER OUR NOSES. OUTSIDE VEGAS. THE LEAD EVENTUALLY TURNED UP GOOD...
THE SITUATION? WELL, THE GIZMO HAS ONE TALL TALE FOR US, BOSS.

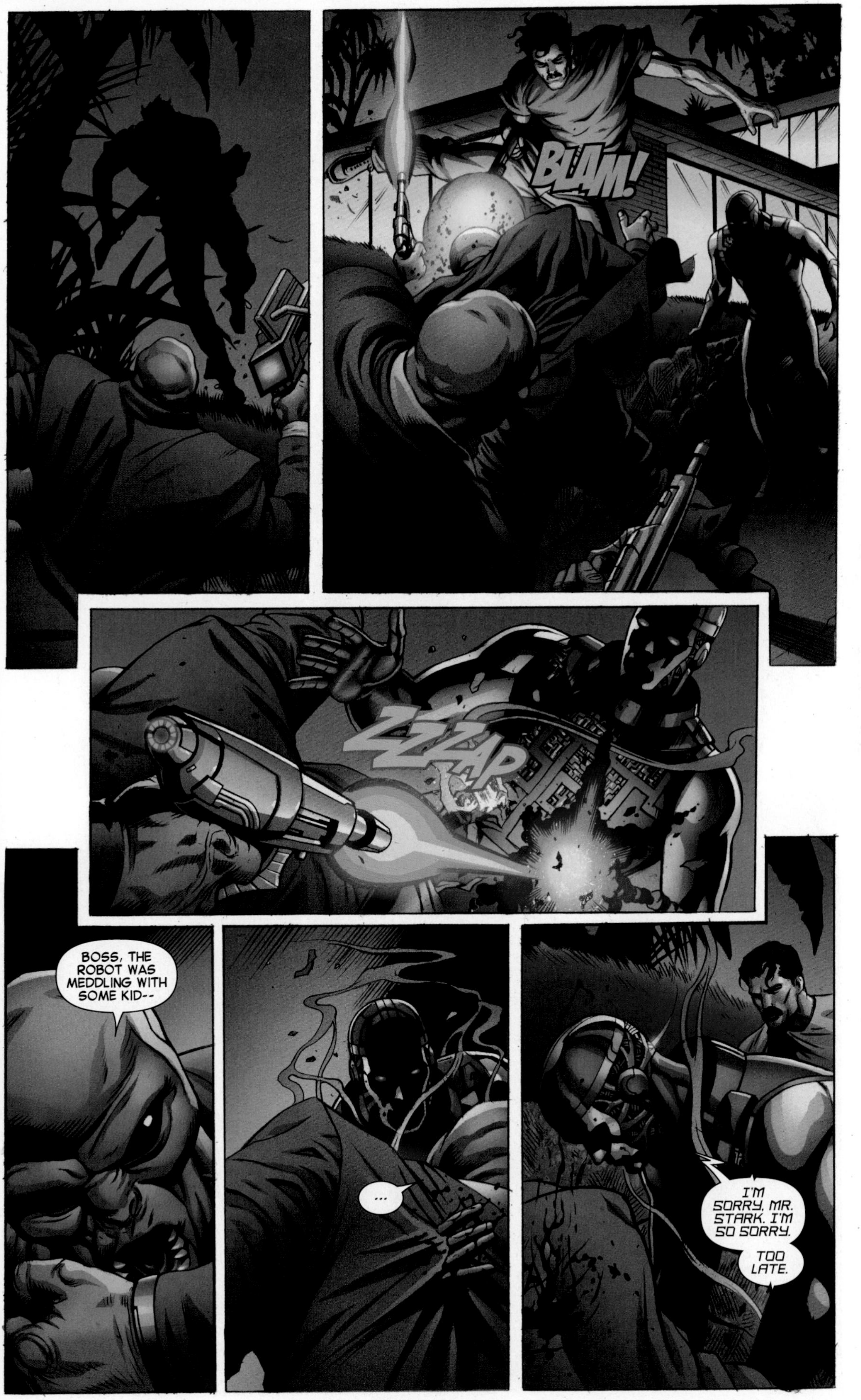
BLAM!
ZZZAP
BOSS, THE ROBOT WAS MEDDLING WITH SOME KID--
...
I'M SORRY, MR. STARK. I'M SO SORRY.
TOO LATE.

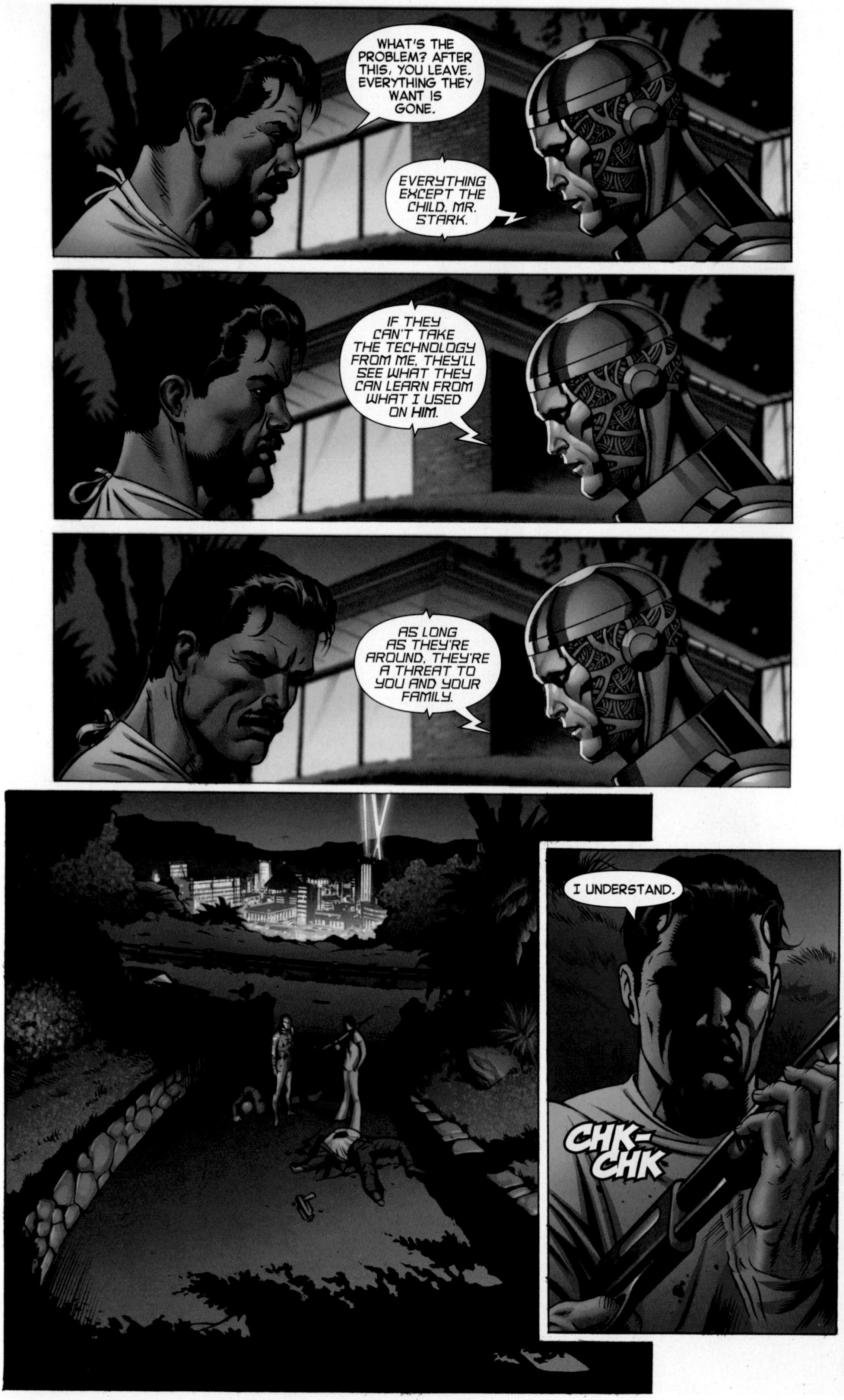
WHAT'S THE PROBLEM? AFTER THIS, YOU LEAVE. EVERYTHING THEY WANT IS GONE.
EVERYTHING EXCEPT THE CHILD, MR. STARK.
IF THEY CAN'T TAKE THE TECHNOLOGY FROM ME, THEY'LL SEE WHAT THEY CAN LEARN FROM WHAT I USED ON HIM.
AS LONG AS THEY'RE AROUND, THEY'RE A THREAT TO YOU AND YOUR FAMILY.
I UNDERSTAND.
CHK-CHK

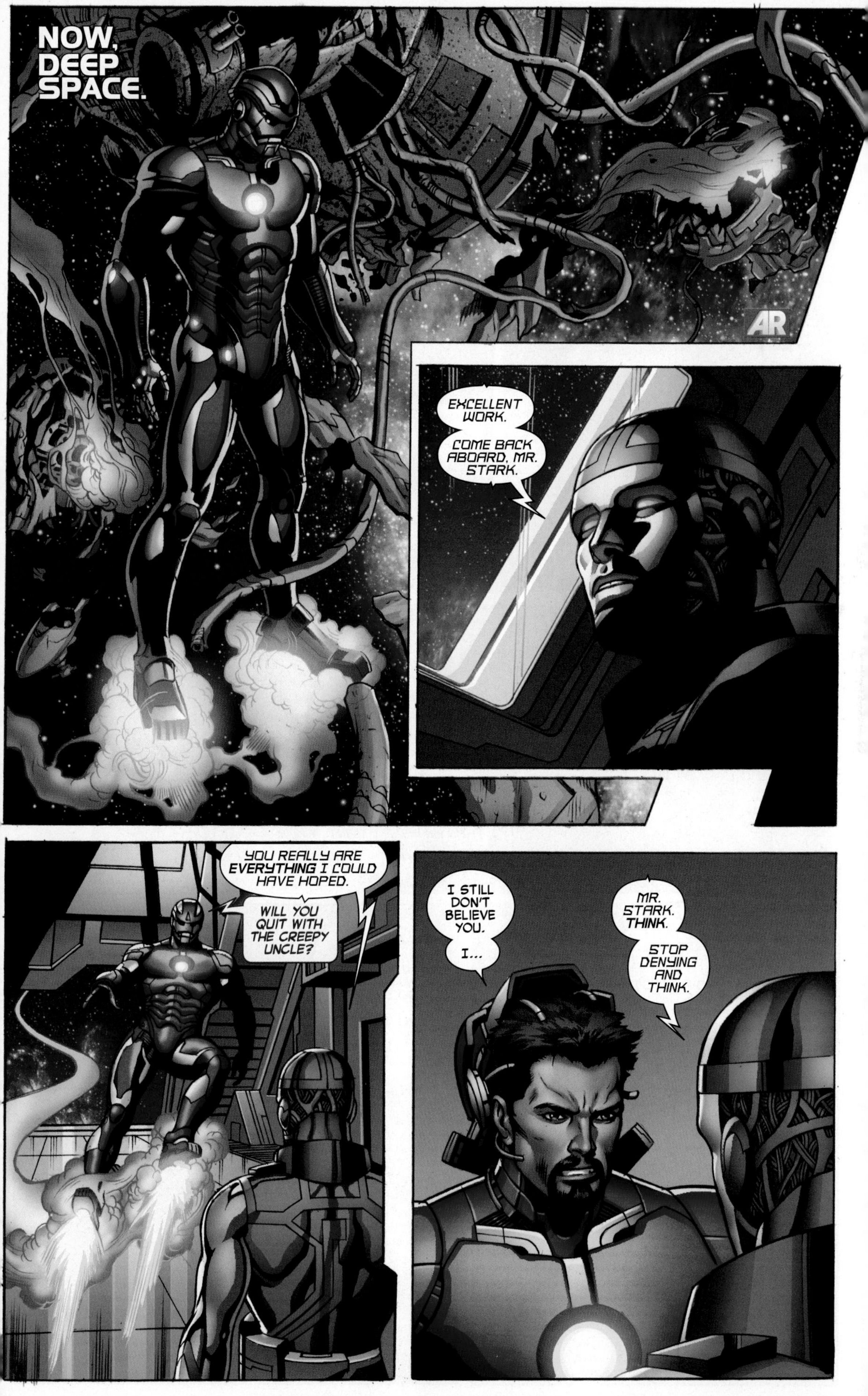
NOW, DEEP SPACE.
EXCELLENT WORK.
COME BACK ABOARD, MR. STARK.
YOU REALLY ARE EVERYTHING I COULD HAVE HOPED.
WILL YOU QUIT WITH THE CREEPY UNCLE?
I STILL DON'T BELIEVE YOU.
I...
MR. STARK. THINK.
STOP DENYING AND THINK.

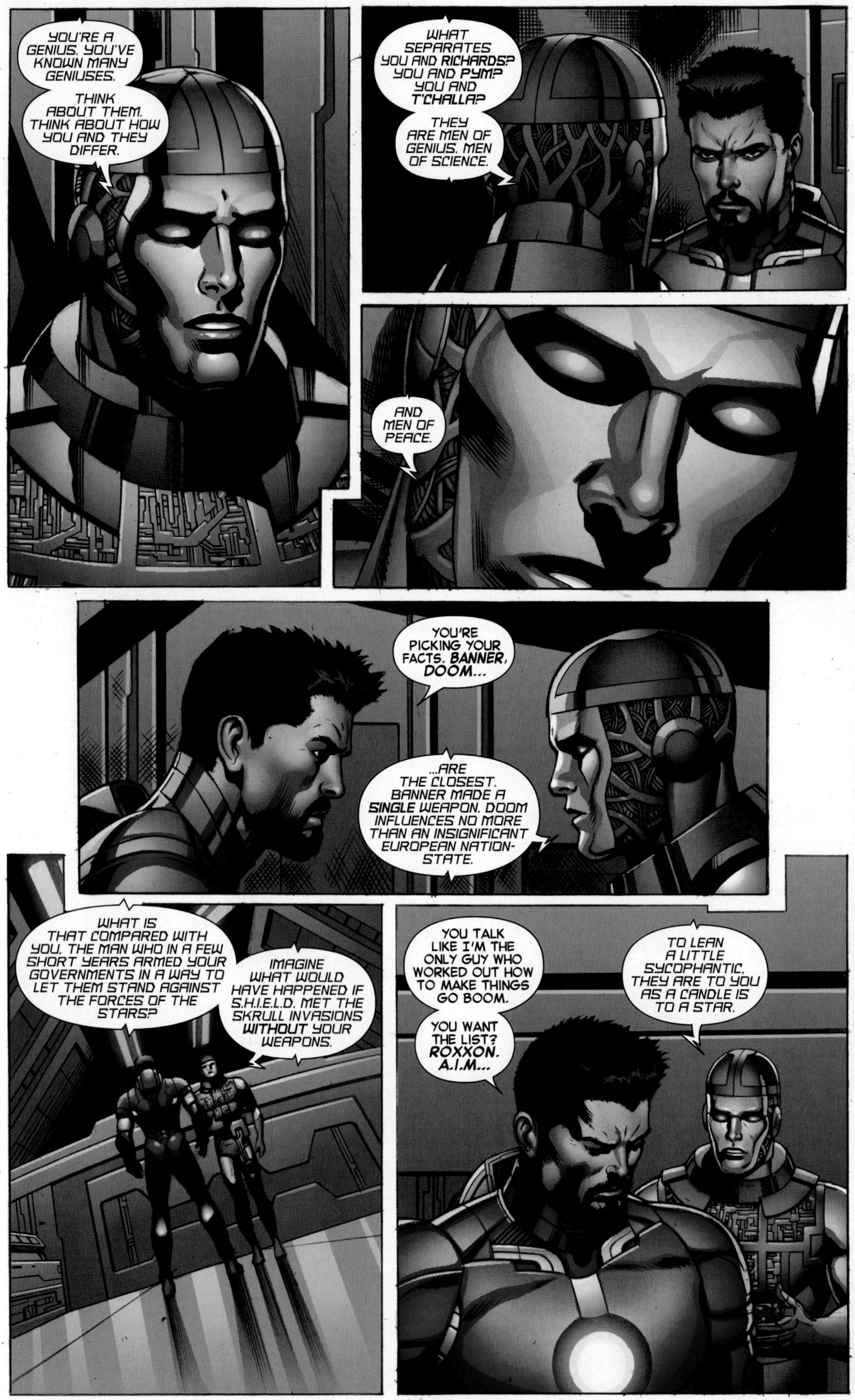
YOU'RE A GENIUS. YOU'VE KNOWN MANY GENIUSES.
THINK ABOUT THEM. THINK ABOUT HOW YOU AND THEY DIFFER.
WHAT SEPARATES YOU AND RICHARDS? YOU AND PYM? YOU AND T'CHALLA?
THEY ARE MEN OF GENIUS. MEN OF SCIENCE.
AND MEN OF PEACE.
YOU'RE PICKING YOUR FACTS. BANNER, DOOM...
...ARE THE CLOSEST. BANNER MADE A SINGLE WEAPON. DOOM INFLUENCES NO MORE THAN AN INSIGNIFICANT EUROPEAN NATION-STATE.
WHAT IS THAT COMPARED WITH YOU, THE MAN WHO IN A FEW SHORT YEARS ARMED YOUR GOVERNMENTS IN A WAY TO LET THEM STAND AGAINST THE FORCES OF THE STARS?
IMAGINE WHAT WOULD HAVE HAPPENED IF S.H.I.E.L.D. MET THE SKRULL INVASIONS WITHOUT YOUR WEAPONS.
YOU TALK LIKE I'M THE ONLY GUY WHO WORKED OUT HOW TO MAKE THINGS GO BOOM.
YOU WANT THE LIST? ROXXON. A.I.M...
TO LEAN A LITTLE SYCOPHANTIC, THEY ARE TO YOU AS A CANDLE IS TO A STAR.

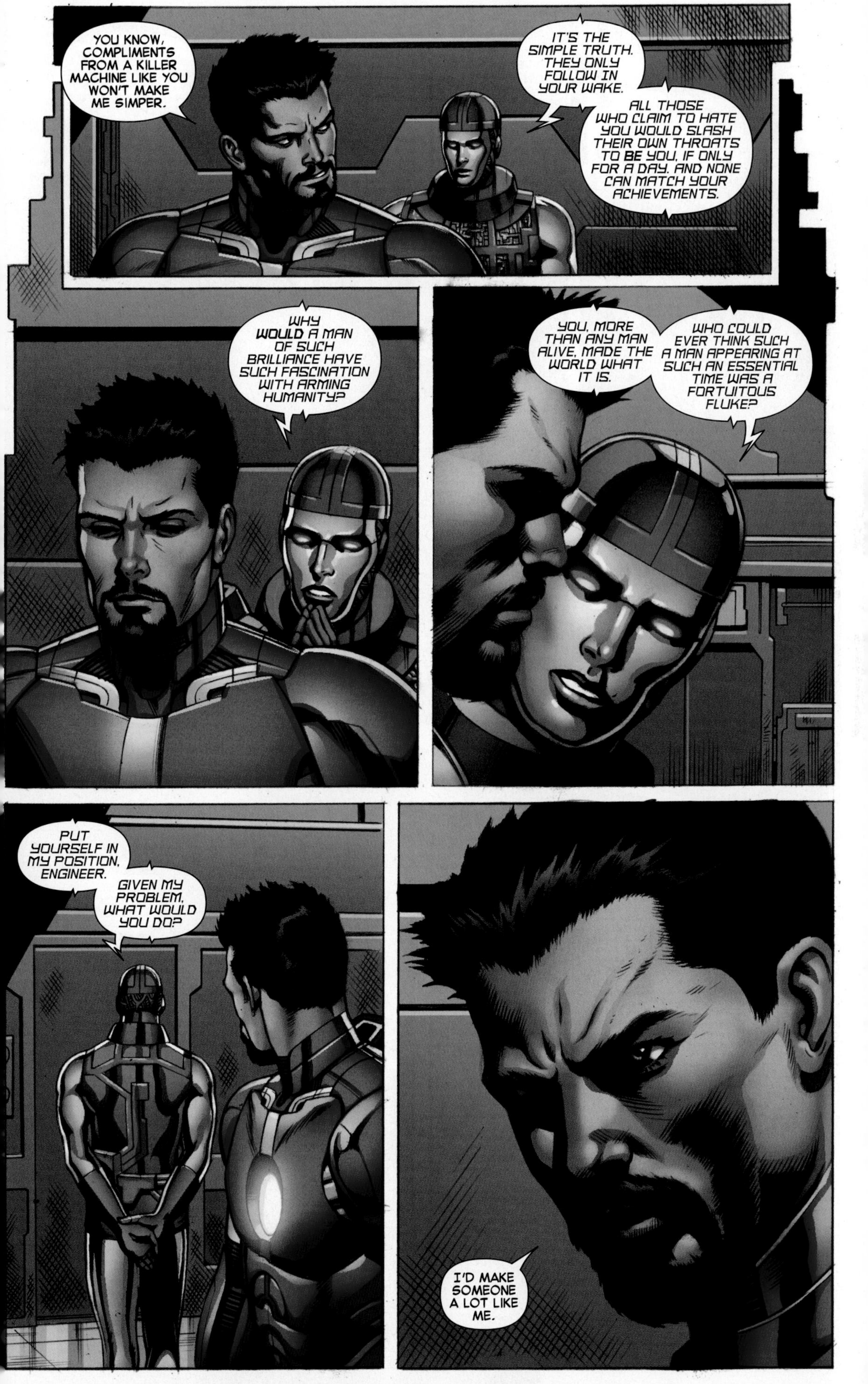
YOU KNOW, COMPLIMENTS FROM A KILLER MACHINE LIKE YOU WON'T MAKE ME SIMPER.
IT'S THE SIMPLE TRUTH. THEY ONLY FOLLOW IN YOUR WAKE.
ALL THOSE WHO CLAIM TO HATE YOU WOULD SLASH THEIR OWN THROATS TO BE YOU, IF ONLY FOR A DAY. AND NONE CAN MATCH YOUR ACHIEVEMENTS.
WHY WOULD A MAN OF SUCH BRILLIANCE HAVE SUCH FASCINATION WITH ARMING HUMANITY?
YOU, MORE THAN ANY MAN ALIVE, MADE THE WORLD WHAT IT IS.
WHO COULD EVER THINK SUCH A MAN APPEARING AT SUCH AN ESSENTIAL TIME WAS A FORTUITOUS FLUKE?
PUT YOURSELF IN MY POSITION, ENGINEER.
GIVEN MY PROBLEM, WHAT WOULD YOU DO?
I'D MAKE SOMEONE A LOT LIKE ME.

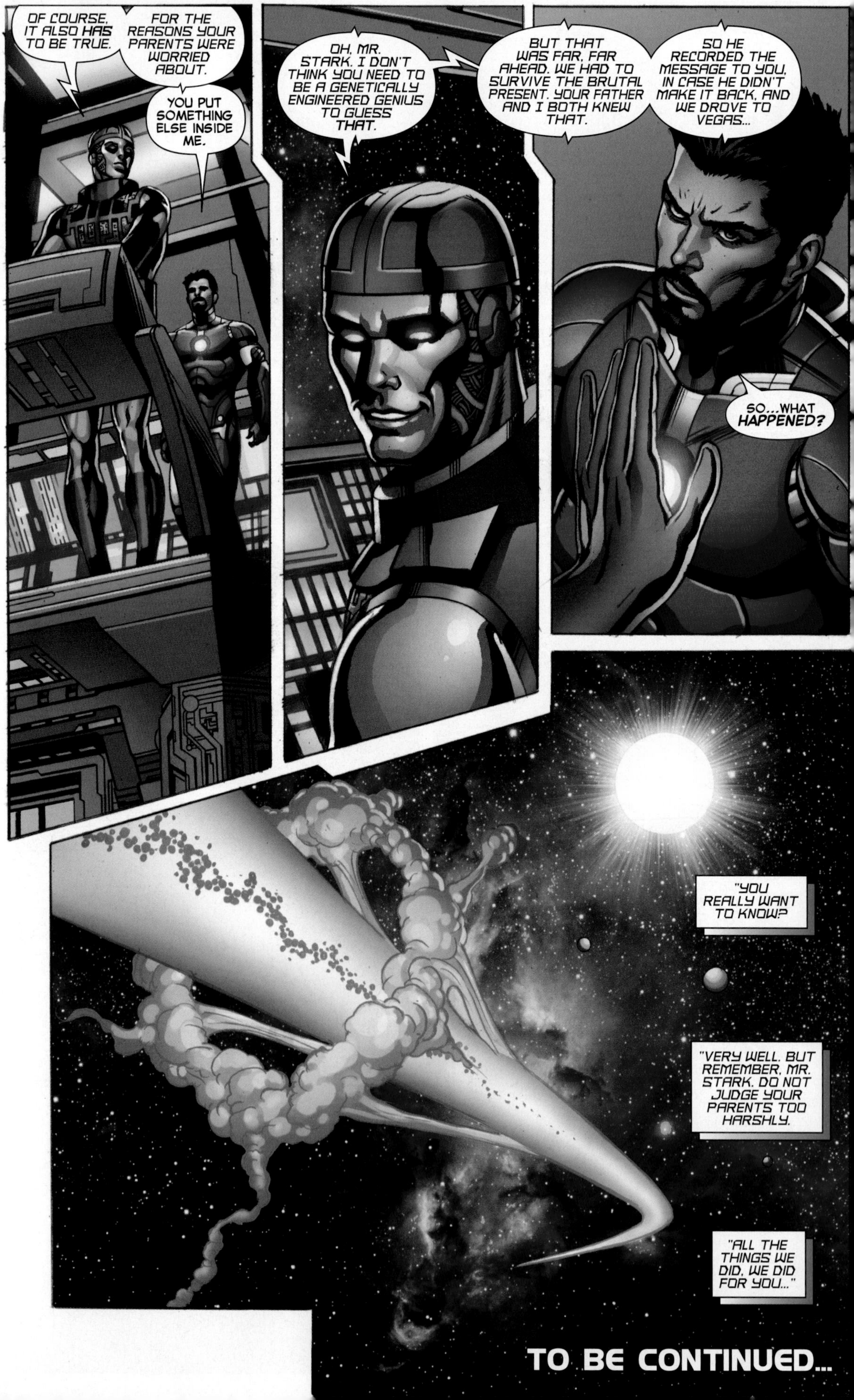
OF COURSE, IT ALSO HAS TO BE TRUE.
FOR THE REASONS YOUR PARENTS WERE WORRIED ABOUT.
YOU PUT SOMETHING ELSE INSIDE ME.
OH, MR. STARK. I DON'T THINK YOU NEED TO BE A GENETICALLY ENGINEERED GENIUS TO GUESS THAT.
BUT THAT WAS FAR, FAR AHEAD. WE HAD TO SURVIVE THE BRUTAL PRESENT. YOUR FATHER AND I BOTH KNEW THAT.
SO HE RECORDED THE MESSAGE TO YOU, IN CASE HE DIDN'T MAKE IT BACK, AND WE DROVE TO VEGAS...
SO...WHAT HAPPENED?
"YOU REALLY WANT TO KNOW?
"VERY WELL. BUT REMEMBER, MR. STARK. DO NOT JUDGE YOUR PARENTS TOO HARSHLY.
"ALL THE THINGS WE DID, WE DID FOR YOU..."
TO BE CONTINUED...

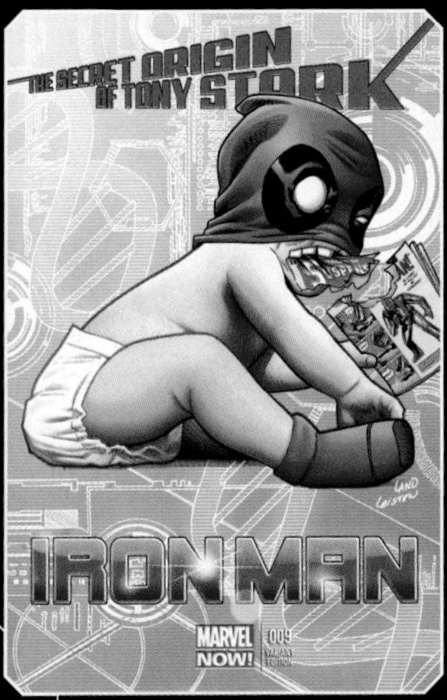
THE SECRET ORIGIN OF TONY STARK
IRON MAN
MARVEL NOW!
009

DEADPOOL VARIANT

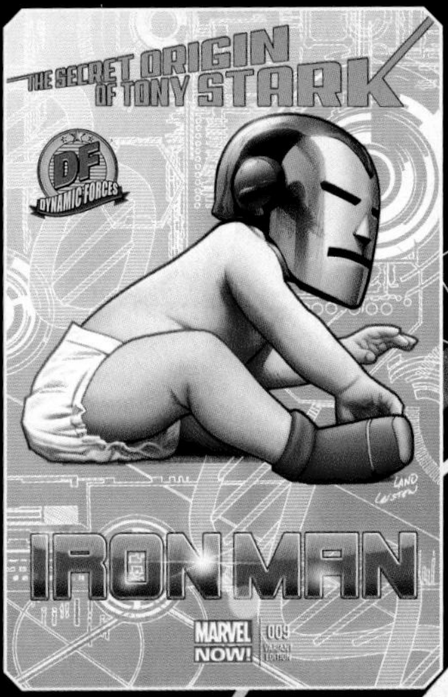
THE SECRET ORIGIN OF TONY STARK
DF DYNAMIC FORCES
IRON MAN
MARVEL NOW!
009

DYNAMIC FORCES VARIANT
("NOSE ARMOR")

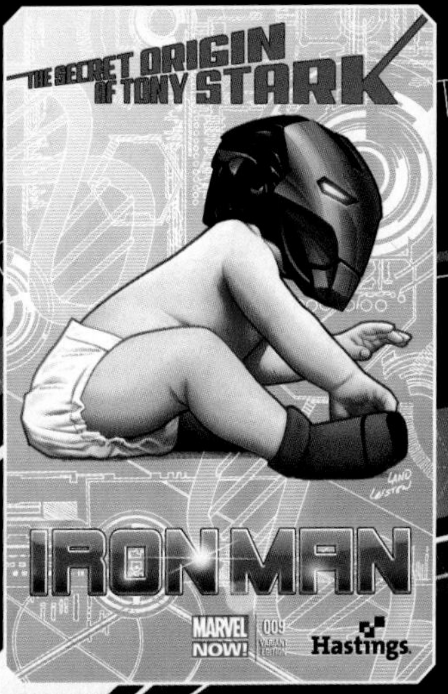
THE SECRET ORIGIN OF TONY STARK
IRON MAN
MARVEL NOW!
009
Hastings

HASTINGS VARIANT
(STEALTH ARMOR)

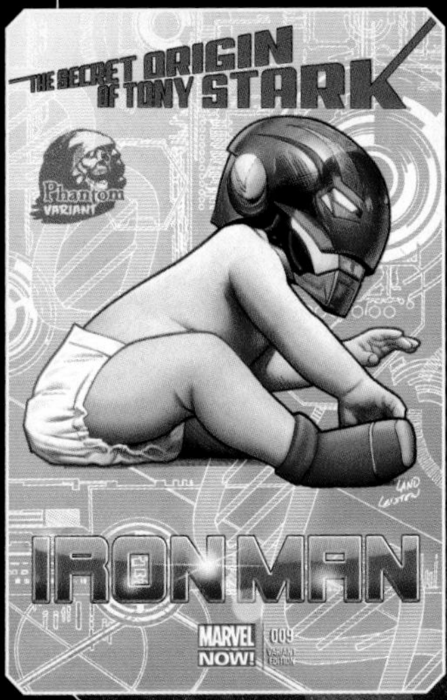
THE SECRET ORIGIN OF TONY STARK
Phantom VARIANT
IRON MAN
MARVEL NOW!
009

PHANTOM VARIANT
(SPACE ARMOR)

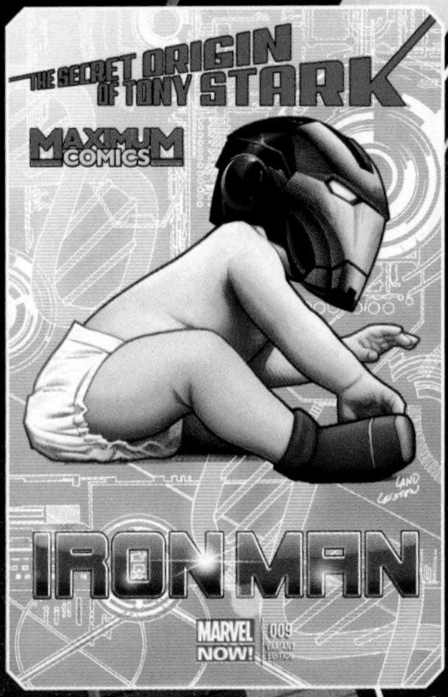
THE SECRET ORIGIN OF TONY STARK
MAXIMUM COMICS
IRON MAN
MARVEL NOW!
009

MAXIMUM FORCES VARIANT
(MOVIE ARMOR)

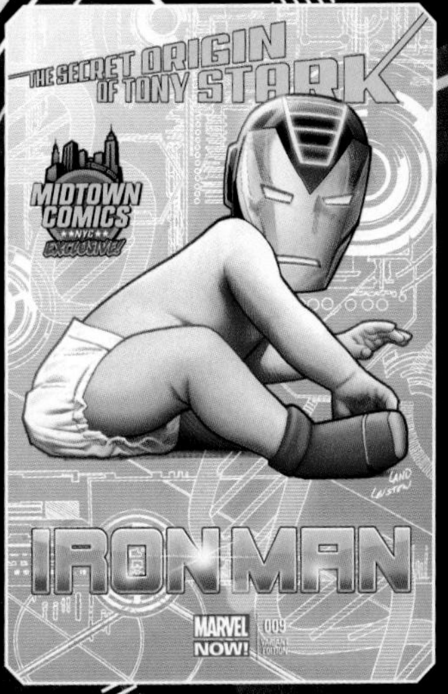
THE SECRET ORIGIN OF TONY STARK
MIDTOWN COMICS
NYC
EXCLUSIVE!
IRON MAN
MARVEL NOW!
009

MIDTOWN COMICS VARIANT
(RENAISSANCE ARMOR)

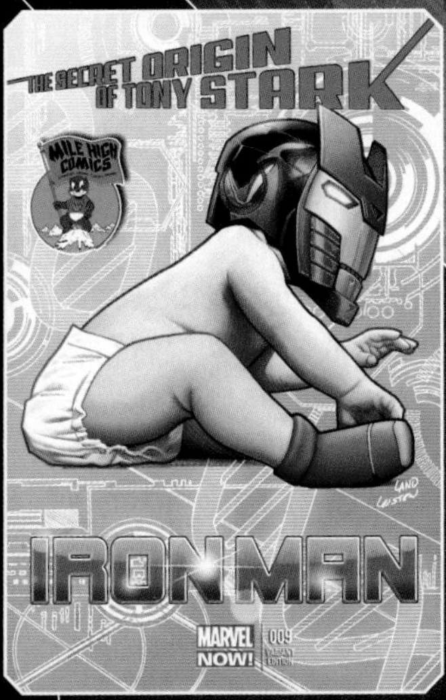
THE SECRET ORIGIN OF TONY STARK
MILE HIGH COMICS
IRON MAN
MARVEL NOW!
009

MILE HIGH COMICS VARIANT
(THORBUSTER ARMOR)

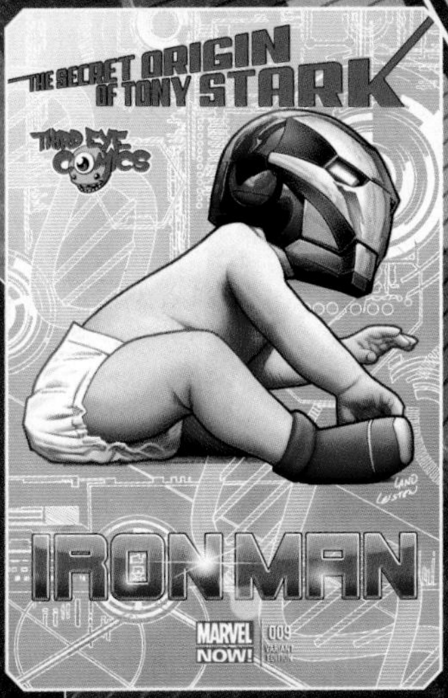
THE SECRET ORIGIN OF TONY STARK
THIRD EYE COMICS
IRON MAN
MARVEL NOW!
009

THIRD EYE COMICS VARIANT
(IRON PATRIOT ARMOR)

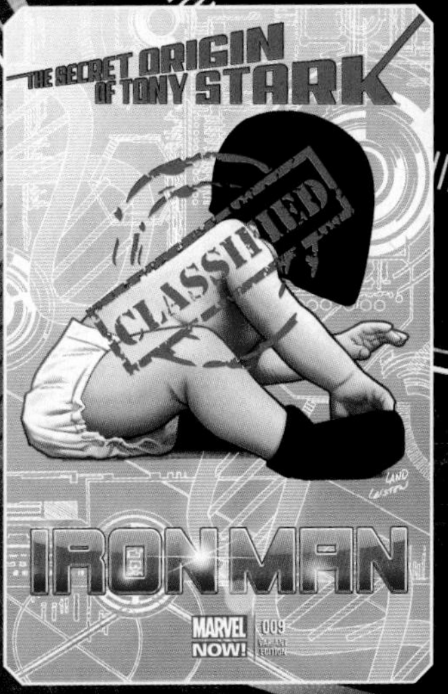
THE SECRET ORIGIN OF TONY STARK
CLASSIFIED
IRON MAN
MARVEL NOW!
009

IRON MAN #17
CLASSIFIED VARIANT 10/02/13

#9 VARIANT GALLERY BY GREG LAND & JAY LEISTEN

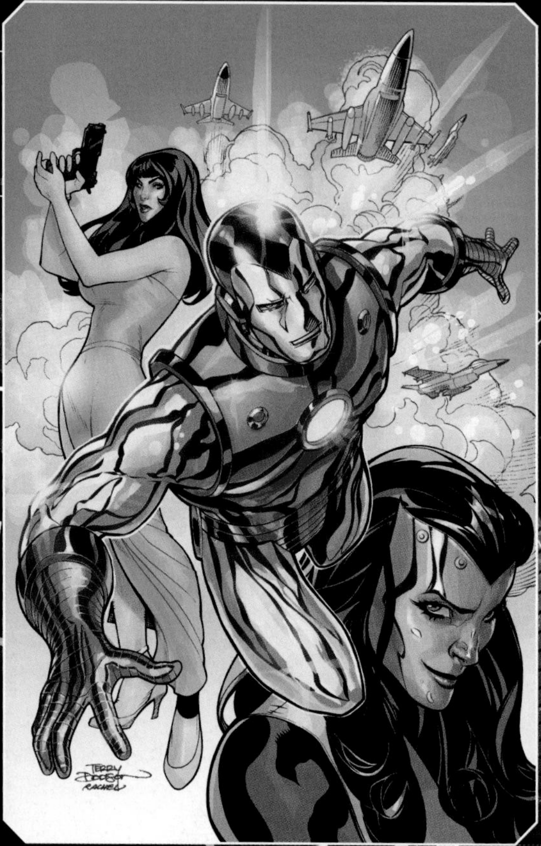

#8 VARIANT
BY TERRY DODSON & RACHEL DODSON

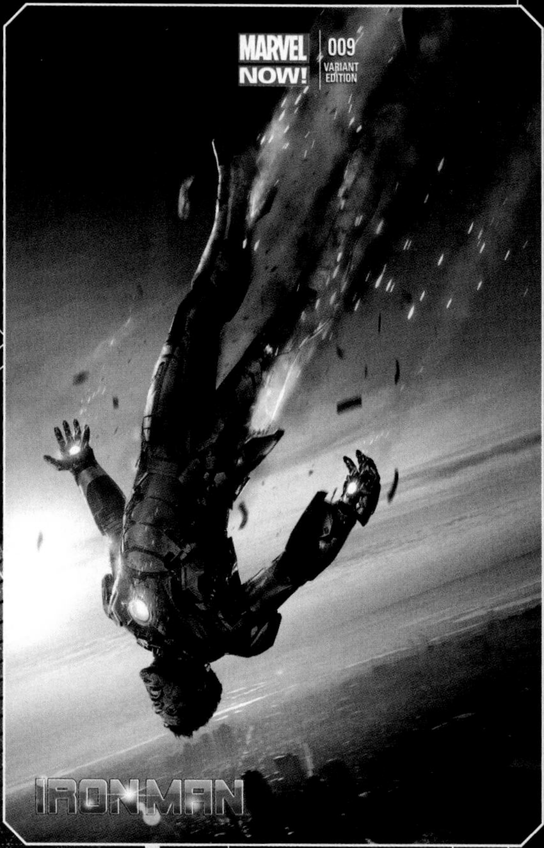
MARVEL NOW!
009
VARIANT EDITION
IRON MAN

#9 VARIANT

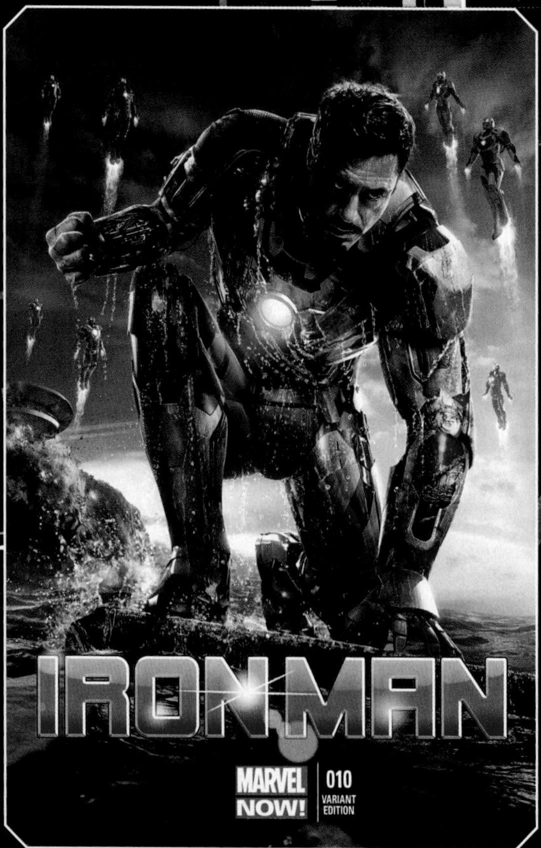
IRON MAN
MARVEL NOW!
010
VARIANT EDITION

#10 VARIANT

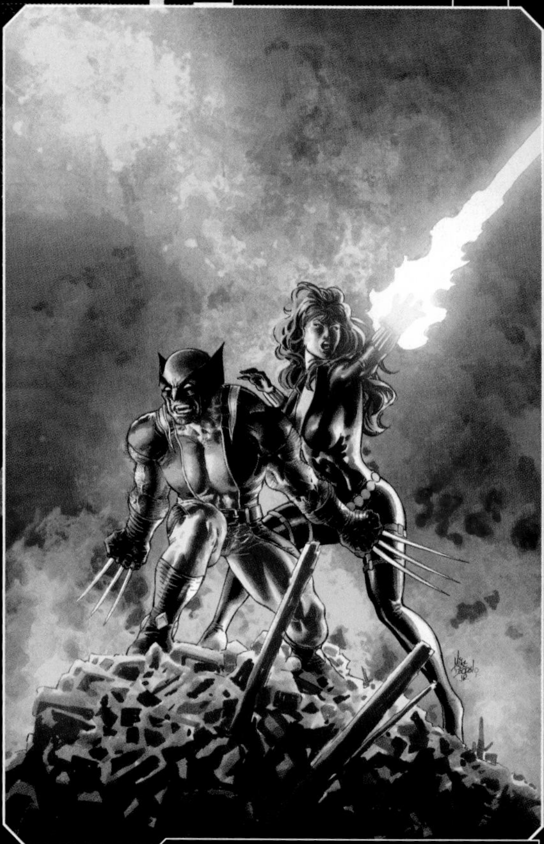

#11 WOLVERINE THROUGH THE AGES VARIANT
BY MIKE DEODATO & RAIN BEREDO

"I ABSOLUTELY LOVE THE WAY BRIAN WRITES THE X-MEN." – IndiePulse.com

BRIAN MICHAEL BENDIS
WADE von GRAWBADGER

STUART IMMONEN
MARTE GRACIA

ALL-NEW X-MEN VOL. 3: OUT OF THEIR DEPTH PREMIERE HC
978-0-7851-6822-5 • JUN130678

"IT'S A REFOCUSING THAT SHOWS WHY THE X-MEN HAVE CONTINUED
BEING ONE OF MARVEL'S HOTTEST PROPERTIES." – HyperGeeky.com

© 2013 MARVEL

TO ACCESS THE FREE *MARVEL AUGMENTED REALITY APP*
THAT ENHANCES AND CHANGES THE WAY YOU EXPERIENCE COMICS

1. **Download the app for free via**
   marvel.com/ARapp

2. **Launch the app on your camera-enabled Apple iOS® or Android™ device***

3. **Hold your mobile device's camera over any cover or panel with the AR graphi**

4. **Sit back and see the future of comics in action!**

*Available on most camera-enabled Apple iOS® and Android™ devices. Content subject to change and availability.

MARVEL
FREE DIGITAL
COPY OFFER

PEEL HERE TO REVEAL CODE ➡

TO REDEEM YOUR CODE FOR A FREE DIGITAL COPY:

1. **GO TO MARVEL.COM/REDEEM.** OFFER EXPIRES ON 7/3/15.

2. **FOLLOW THE ON-SCREEN INSTRUCTIONS TO REDEEM YOUR DIGITAL COPY.**

3. **LAUNCH THE MARVEL COMICS APP TO READ YOUR COMIC NOW!**

4. **YOUR DIGITAL COPY WILL BE FOUND UNDER THE *MY COMICS* TAB.**

5. **READ & ENJOY!**

YOUR FREE DIGITAL COPY WILL BE AVAILABLE ON

MARVEL COMICS APP FOR APPLE® iOS DEVICES	MARVEL COMICS APP FOR ANDROID™ DEVICES

Digital copy requires purchase of a print copy. Download code valid fo: one use only. Digital copy available on the date print copy is available. Availability time of the digital copy may vary on the date of release. TM & © Marvel & Subs. Apple is a trademark of Apple Inc., registered in the U.S. and other countries. Android is a trademark of Google Inc.